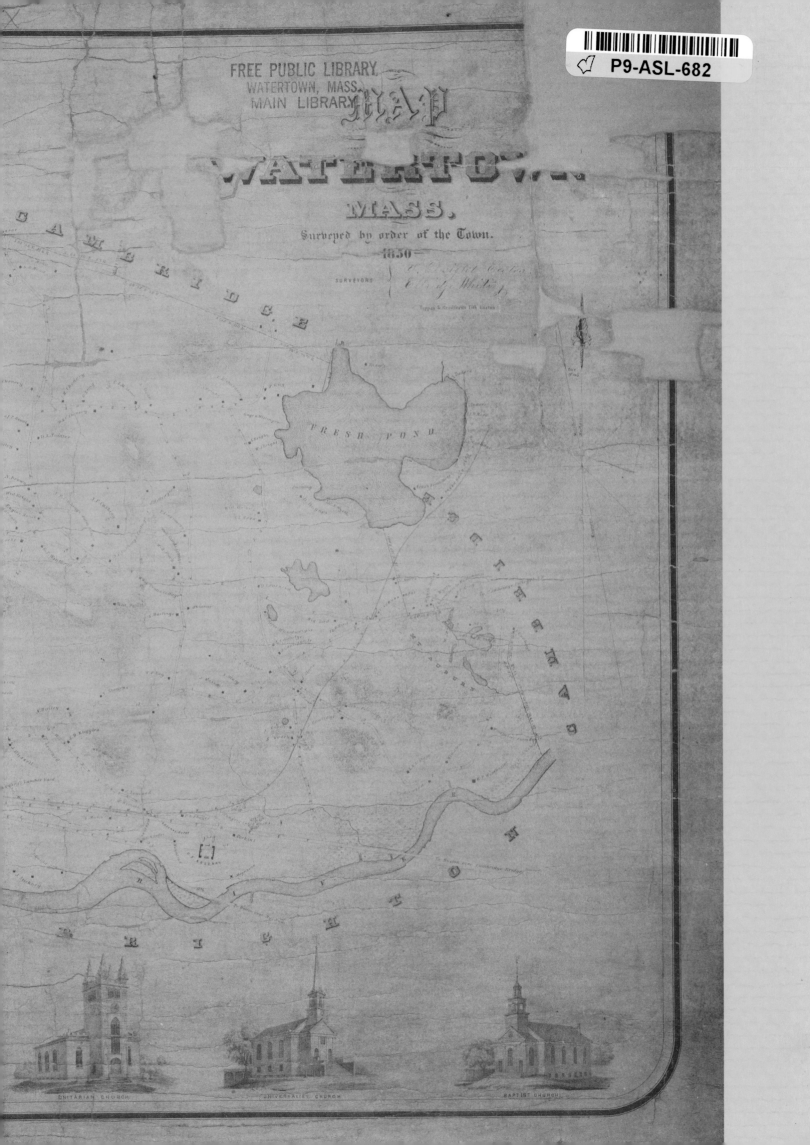

MAP

WATERTOWN

MASS.

Surveyed by order of the Town.

1850

SURVEYORS

FRESH POND

UNITARIAN CHURCH

UNIVERSALIST CHURCH

BAPTIST CHURCH

Crossroads
on the Charles

Crossroads on the Charles

A History of Watertown, Massachusetts

by

Maud deLeigh Hodges

Edited by Sigrid R. Reddy with an epilogue by Charles T. Burke

Published for the

WATERTOWN FREE PUBLIC LIBRARY

by

PHOENIX PUBLISHING

Canaan, New Hampshire

Hodges, Maud deLeigh,   1888-1972.
    Crossroads on the Charles.
    Based on the author's The story of our Watertown.
    Bibliography: p.
    Includes index.
    1. Watertown, Mass.—History. I. Reddy, Sigrid R.
II. Watertown, Mass. Free Public Library. III. Title.
F74.W33H76   1980   974.4'4   80-13753
ISBN 0-914016-68-7

Printed in the United States of America
by Courier Printing Company
Binding by New Hampshire Bindery
Design by A. L. Morris

Contents

Maud deLeigh Hodges

HIS BOOK, *Crossroads on the Charles,* is based on Maud Hodges' history, *The Story of our Watertown,* a manuscript used for many years in the Watertown Public Library. As the celebration of the 350th anniversary of the establishment of the town approached, the need for an up-to-date history led to the decision to prepare Miss Hodges' manuscript for publication.

Maud Hodges completed her history in 1956. Born in Melrose, Massachusetts, on July 29, 1888, Miss Hodges' family moved to Watertown when she was eleven years old. Her father was a foreman in the Walker & Pratt foundry. She attended Watertown schools and graduated from the high school with a record of high marks and perfect attendance. She earned her B.A. from Boston University in 1911 and from 1915 to 1919 taught in the Watertown schools. After World War I she worked briefly in a church headquarters office in Copley Square Boston, after which she was a reporter for the Watertown *Sun* and became interested in town affairs, serving as a town meeting member. Her home was at 22 Pequossette Street, near the Perkins School for the Blind, and her close association with the school led to her interest in the welfare of blind children. She supported herself by taking care of "boarder children."

Active in the Methodist Church, Miss Hodges' main interests became her church and the history of her town. She wrote a history of the Watertown High School and a short history, "My Town," in 1946. For ten years she did research in town records, town histories, and newspapers in the library's archives, finally producing *The Story of Our Watertown.* The book contains a wealth of detail, especially about the industrial life of Watertown. Miss Hodges generously gave her book to the library,

Foreword

where it has been used as a reference book by students, teachers, and researchers, as well as by the staff of the reference department. Copies were made and bound for use in the branches. The town owes a debt to Miss Hodges for her consuming interest in communicating to others, particularly to students, a knowledge and understanding of the town's history.

During preparations for the celebration of the Bicentennial of the American Revolution in 1975-1976, Mary McNally, assistant director of the library and head of the reference department, suggested that the publication of Miss Hodges' history would be an asset to the town. The trustees of the library supported the project and the library obtained from Miss Hodges' heirs the rights to publish the manuscript. At about this time Galen LaRose of the Barry Wright Company became interested in helping the library publish the manuscript as a Bicentennial gift to the town. His company, accordingly, offered to match by an equal amount the $3,000 we thought at that time would be half the amount needed. The executive board of the Chamber of Commerce supported the publication and recommended that the book be hardbound and illustrated. We approached Phoenix Publishing of Canaan, New Hampshire, which had had considerable experience in publishing town histories, and decided to embark on a more ambitious publication.

Several attempts to raise the requisite $31,000 which was needed to publish a well-illustrated and edited work resulted in frustration. Finally, in the fall of 1979, a group of persons interested in local history met with members of the library staff to discuss the project with A.L. Morris and A.A. Paradis of Phoenix Publishing. The group consisted of Ann Bromer of Bromer Booksellers;

Frank Jackson of BayBank Union Market; Charles Burke, trustee of the library; David Choate, executive secretary of the Watertown Chamber of Commerce; James Fahey, town clerk; and James Sullivan, retired town engineer. Stephen Bayle, Assistant Director; Jane Eastman, Supervisor of Adult Services; and Helene Tuchman, reference librarian, represented the staff of the library. The group decided to request the needed amount at a special town meeting which was to convene on November 26. A petition was drafted and the requisite signatures were obtained.

James Sullivan presented the article requesting funds for the publication of Maud Hodges' history to the town meeting, and was successful in gaining approval for the expenditure. Work was started at once on the manuscript so that it could be ready for the celebration of the town's 350th birthday in 1980. Charles Burke, an expert in Watertown history and a student of Miss Hodges', agreed to write a final chapter to cover the events of the last twenty-five years. The book required extensive editing and many chapters have been rewritten in the light of recent events. We decided that much of Miss Hodges' material which seemed relevant in 1956 could be omitted from this edition and replaced with more current information, and changes could be made to make the book appealing to a current readership. Charles Burke and James Sullivan read the manuscript and recommended certain changes in emphasis. In doing the research for certain periods I discovered interesting material which it appeared would add to the book's value, and so I have included a good deal of supplemental material. Several portions were deleted or shortened. The early part of the book is based entirely on Miss Hodges' research, but the responsibility for the following sections is mine: the expansion of the sections on Benjamin Curtis and the Dred Scott case; the Fowles; Ellen Robbins; Theodore Parker; Sterling Elliott; the Stanley Brothers; Charles Brigham; the banks; the library; the Underwood Company; the secession of Belmont; Sarsfield Cunniff; the Boston Elevated Railway; the textile industries; Lewandos; Lewis-Shepard; Underwood; United Soda Fountain, and Celia Thaxter. A number of new sections were added, including Lucy Stone and the Stone Family, the Adams Express Company, the "Haunted House," Rosamond Coolidge, and the Perkins School. The sections on the Hood Rubber Company and the Arsenal were entirely rewritten.

During her tenure at the library, Mary McNally corrected errors in the manuscript as they surfaced. Diane Pascuzzi prepared an index to the contents. Mr. Burke compiled footnotes to elucidate certain portions of the text. Helene Tuchman, reference librarian, was in charge of research, compiled most of the documentation, the bibliography, and the index, and helped reorganize the latter part of the book into new chapters. The reference staff, consisting of Jeanne White, Ellen Wendruff, Dorothy DelRose, and Carole Jansky, under the supervision of Jane Eastman, conducted many searches for information and compiled lists of data for the book. Eileen Waldron typed the first part of the revised manuscript. The major part of the book, however, was enthusiastically typed by Gayle Roberts-Cullen as each section was completed.

Illustrative material has been collected from many sources: the library's picture collections, from photographs given to us by individuals and companies, and from museums and archives. Forrest Mack of the library's technical services department saw to the restoration of many old photographs and printed materials which would otherwise have been unusable.

I am greatly indebted to the following persons who furnished information and helpful advice: Louis Andrew and Patrick Ford for the section on the Hood Rubber Company; Jim Sullivan for recollections of recent events and interesting personalities in Watertown; Charles W. Chamberlain, Jr. of the Watertown Savings Bank on the history of the banks, and Quinton Jones, Assistant Town Clerk.

The sections on the newcomers to Watertown were generously contributed by the following persons: The Reverend Dajad Davidian wrote The Armenians; Michael McDermott, The Irish; Jack Zollo, The Italians; Charles Avery, The Greeks; Joseph Delaney, The Canadians; and Emma Neiberg Taylor, The Jews. Mary Barry and the Reverend A.J. Metaxas also contributed information. Michael O'Connor wrote the history of the Watertown *Sun* and Robert Ford the history of the *Press* for the chapter on the newspapers. Watertown businesses and employers were asked to contribute histories of their companies; those that responded have their stories included in the section entitled "Business in Watertown in 1980." Mr. Burke, as promised, wrote the Epilogue.

We wish to thank the many townspeople who supported the publication project, and the staff of the library who helped. Thanks are especially due to Charles Burke, whose unsentimental view of local history contributed to our objectivity, and to Mary McNally who conceived the idea. We hope Miss Hodges would be pleased with what we have done with her book.

Sigrid R. Reddy

February 20, 1980

Crossroads on the Charles

The Early Years

1628/1750

"The Arbella in mid-ocean," from an early steel engraving.

1

Passage From England

ATERTOWN, Massachusetts, was founded in the year 1630 and was the first inland settlement in Massachusetts. It began as a Puritan settlement and became a hub for trade and commerce; during the Revolutionary War period it was a center for organizing resistance against the British; and in the nineteenth century it became an important industrial town. Waves of migration brought to Watertown Puritans escaping from English religious persecution; Irish fleeing starvation and want; and Italians, Armenians, Greeks, Jews and Canadians seeking new opportunities. Today the town is a mix of cultural, racial, educational, and economic diversity.

THE PURITANS

The English Puritans began the migration to the New World in significant numbers in 1630. At this time, Charles I was king of England; he and his bishops controlled the Church of England. A great number of people desired to be free from this absolute authority over their lives and worship. All England was torn with disputes over religion; some objectors left the church and were called separatists. Such were the Pilgrims. Other objectors kept their membership but worked for reform. In mockery they were called Puritans because they undertook to purify the church of its evils and at long last, they too became separatists.

As these Puritans met in groups for discussion, each group was called a congregation. In their meetings they discussed the Bible under the leadership of preachers, many of whom had studied at Cambridge University. In fact, Cambridge was the hotbed of this mass uprising, with other strong centers among London merchants and along the south coast. Spies and officers of the bishops and the king pursued and persecuted these independent thinkers. Many were jailed, but although King Charles's father had said, "I will make them conform, or I will harry them out of the land," punishment did not force them to conform. Thus an obdurate king drove out thousands of worthy men with their families. Those who remained eventually became strong enough to set up the Puritan Commonwealth.

For those who could flee from their country, fortunately a new land awaited. From New Plymouth and Virginia and the West Indies came favorable reports from traders who crossed the Atlantic for fish and furs. There were roving scouts like Capt. John Smith, the map maker. To the New World the Puritans would escape and build homes and worship in their own way. They believed that

3

The South part of New-England, as it is Planted this yeare, 1634.

The above very ancient Map is an exact copy of the first that was made after Massachusetts was settled. It was taken from a Rare Book by William Wood, entitled, NEW ENGLAND'S PROSPECT

Wood says, These be all the towns that were begun when I left for England, which was the 15 of August, 1633, viz.

Boston	Medford, Mistick	Marvill.head
Roxberry	Newtowne, Cambridge.	Saugus, Lynn.
Dorchester	Watertowne	Agawam Ioswich.
Wessagustus Weymouth	Winnisimmit. Chelsea	Merrimac, Newbury.
Charlestowne	Salem.	Nahant.

The original Map was engraved in London where the Book was printed.

*Entered according to Act of Congress.
In the year 1846 by Wm B. Fowle. Clerk's Office of the District Court of Massachusetts.*

God was leading them to a promised land as he had the Hebrews of old.

There was discontent, not only about church affairs, but also about high taxes. A great number of non-Puritans joined the migration, drawn by the hope of making a living from free land and trade. This movement to New England constituted about one-third of the emigrants from different parts of Europe to different parts of America in the early 1600s.

In the year 1628 plans were laid to sail. Many conversations were held among Puritan gentlemen in Lincolnshire, and letters were exchanged with merchant friends in London and on the south coast. They formed the Massachusetts Bay Company in advance of their departure.

In the spring of 1628 they bought from some merchants, called the Western Adventurers, a grant of land situated between the Charles and Merrimack rivers and including three miles on the farther banks. Profits from this land would repay investors whether they stayed or sailed. The company found Capt. John Endicott of the Puritan faith who would lead an advance party of fifty persons the following summer. He was to establish a settlement that came to be known as Salem and he served as its temporary governor. Unfortunately, five years earlier the merchants had given a permit for the same tract of land to another party, with the approval of the previous king. However, plans went forward in buying supplies for the voyage. In 1629 the company shipped two hundred more persons, including servants, to Salem with a cargo of cattle. The servants soon had to be set free to find their food because of its scarcity.

King Charles gave his royal seal to a charter which stated the rights of this company. Concerning the charter, a meeting of the company Court was called at Cambridge, England. There an important agreement was signed with names which would take their place in American history: Saltonstall, Winthrop, Johnson, Dudley, and others. By their compact, the signers

would embark with their families for the plantation in New England by the first of March next, to inhabit and continue there, provided that before the last of September the whole government together with patent for plantation be first by order of the Court legally transferred . . . to remain with them and others who shall inhabit upon said plantation.

This was a bold step, standing alone in the history of English colonization. Although the king had intended that the new colony would be governed from England as had the Plymouth settlement, these signers insisted on carrying their charter with them. The first of these was Sir Richard Saltonstall, later a founder of Watertown. Sir Richard stipulated that he and his family would leave to live in New England only on condition that the company's

4

Court meet on the new soil, not in faraway England. Moreover, Sir Richard was the first member of a committee which soon prevailed on the Court to permit transfer of the charter to the new land. It was held best to be secret about any religious motive lest word leak out to the king. The Court granted the request, and its importance escaped the king's notice.

The company held an election. Mr. Matthew Cradock, an investor, resigned as first governor, because he was to stay in England. The new governor was John Winthrop, with Thomas Dudley as his deputy. A governor's council was composed of eight to eighteen assistants, one of them being Sir Richard. Court opened with prayer, as is still the custom in the Massachusetts General Court. On departing, they swore an oath of loyalty to the king and received a license to leave.

THE VOYAGE

In the spring of 1630 preparation went forward among the ships of Winthrop's fleet on the south coast of England. Seventeen vessels were to sail during the year with about two thousand colonists. Immediately after Easter, four ships of the fleet, with a thousand aboard, were ready to start, but contrary winds and heavy rain caused a week's delay. On a day of prayer they wrote a farewell to the English church. In it were these words:"We leave our dear Mother, the Church of England, blessing God as members, and shall always rejoice in her good." The flagship of this convoy was renamed *Arbella* in honor of Lady Arbella, wife of the richest settler, Isaac Johnson. Both she and her husband were on that ship. Other passengers were Sir Richard Saltonstall with five or six of his motherless children, Rev. George Phillips, Governor Winthrop, and Deputy Governor Dudley. Phillips was a freethinker who joined this Puritan colony. "We have much cause to bless God for him," wrote the governor.

This vessel was not built with a deep keel, and her hull was rounded, so that she rolled on the swell of the ocean. She had three masts rigged with square sails and twenty-eight cannon were mounted on her deck to be used for signaling and salutes as well as for defense if she met unfriendly seacraft. She carried a cargo of 240 cattle and 60 horses.

While the Arbella was still at her mooring, Grace, Saltonstall's little daughter, narrowly escaped death when a carpenter's helper collided with her at a grating. Had he not nimbly caught her, she would have fallen to her death in the hold.

During the first week a high wind swept away a tub of fish which was needed for food. On the second Sunday the sky cleared, and in a few days the sails were unfurled. On the third Lord's Day two of the ships collided, coming off with a torn sail and a broken anchor. Pastor Phillips was not feeling well, so there was no preaching on that day. The high winds made many passengers seasick, so on Monday a rope was strung from stern to midship; the seasick ones, facing each other along this rope

Charles I, as King, from the painting by Daniel Mytens.

5

and taking hold of it, raised and lowered it. This exercise warmed them, and soon they were feeling well again.

Governor Winthrop's diary is the source of much information about this trip. He mentions his two small sons who slept with him, contentedly wrapped in a rug. Their mother and other children of the family remained in England and were to cross later. "We have many young gentlemen in our ship," wrote the governor, "who behave themselves well." During most of the voyage there was rain and more wind than was needed to fill the sails. A case

of measles broke out. Three babies were born. As the supply of fresh fruit and vegetables gave out, some of the passengers fell ill with scurvy from lack of vitamins.

Finally early on a June morning, the twelfth, the *Arbella* cast anchor off Salem. The other three ships came to harbor in a few days. Although they had barely enough food for themselves, the people of Salem prepared a good dinner of venison. "In the meantime," we read in Winthrop's diary, "most of our people went ashore and gathered [a] store of fine strawberries."

2

Founding of Watertown

AN EARLY PLAN of the Massachusetts Bay Colony included a settlement with Salem as its center. Since half of its settlers had sickened and died, the newcomers could find temporary room there.

But "Salem pleased us not," wrote the governor. Some of the settlers were sent to the Boston Harbor to explore tributaries for a convenient place to settle. "We found a place that liked us better, three leagues up Charles River and there-upon shipped our goods into other vessels and brought them in July to Charlestown," wrote Dudley. "Many of our people—brought with us, being sick of fevers and the scurvy—dispersed." The settlers needed plentiful spring water, timber, and space for the planting of vegetable gardens.

TRADER JOHN OLDHAM

Another reason for the dispersal of Winthrop's colonists was that they had run into competition. John Oldham, a clever trader with a quick temper, lived at Nantasket, doing business with the Indians and English merchant vessels. Oldham was in England while the Bay colonists were preparing to emigrate. There he had an opportunity to purchase an inheritance to a stretch of land along the Charles River, granted by a previous king, which would entitle him to the area now known as Watertown, Cambridge, Belmont, Arlington, Somerville, and Charlestown. In trying to raise money to claim this land, his tall stories about profits to be made in cattle raising and in trading fish and furs in this most desirable locality piqued the interest of those who heard him boast—he claimed that they could triple their money.

Oldham's energy had captured the heart of the daughter of the former postmaster of Scrooby, England, Elder Brewster of New Plymouth. The Oldham family (eight, including servants) disembarked in 1623 from the ship *Anne* at Plymouth. Oldham was sent from England by the Plymouth Company to find out why the Pilgrims were sending back good reports but no profits. His interest in church affairs offended them to the extent that they expelled him from their town. He left his family at Plymouth and went to the Nantasket trading post.

A secret message "to take possession of the chief part thereof" was sent in 1629 by a swift ship to John Endicott in Salem. A copy of the message went out two weeks later with the two hundred additional Salem colonists. At once, Governor Endicott sent his surveying engineer to lay out

Bronze bas relief by Henry Kitson depicting the landing of Roger Clap in 1630 was unveiled in 1931 to commemorate the founding of Watertown.

Charlestown. Fifty of the Salemites went there to live in tents and wigwams, on the strip of land between the mouths of the Charles and Mystic rivers, but by now King Charles had granted John Oldham's claim to the Massachusetts Bay Company. The race was on between the colonists and Oldham.

Also in the spring of 1630 another ship brought a new congregation bound for Charlestown. The "Dorchester men" (after Dorchester, England) had been actively planning the migration for some time. Twenty-year-old Roger Clap describes the betrayal of their trust: "When we came to Nantasket, Capt. Squeb, who was captain of that great ship of 400 tons, would not bring us into Charles River, as he was bound to do, but put us ashore and our goods on Nantasket Point, and left us to shift for ourselves in a forlorn place." It was May 30. Here stood the hut where John Oldham lived and did his coastwise trading. Oldham, it appears, had returned from England.

On a June day, even as the Winthrop convoy was nearing Salem, ten of the Dorchester men borrowed a boat at Nantasket, perhaps from Mr. Oldham, and rowed with the tide up the Charles River. Roger Clap was among them and wrote the story:

We stopped at Charlestown, where we found some wigwams and one house; and in the house there was a man which had a boiled bass but no bread that we see. But we did eat of his bass. We went up Charles River until the river grew narrow and shallow and there we landed our goods with much labour and toil. The bank being steep and night coming on, we were informed that there we had by us 300 Indians. One Englishman (an old planter) that could speak the Indian language went to them and advised them not to come near us in the night; and they hearkened to his counsel and came not. I myself was one of the sentinels that first night. In the morning, some of the Indians came and stood at a distance off, looking at us, but came not near us. But when they had been awhile in view, some of them came and held out a great bass towards us; so we sent a man with a biscuit, and changed the cake for the bass. Afterwards

8

they supplied us with bass, exchanging a bass for a biscuit, and were very friendly unto us—We had not been there many days (although by our diligence we had got up a kind of shelter to save our goods in), but we had an order to come away from that place, which was about Watertown, unto a place now called Dorchester, because there was a neck of land fit to keep our cattle on.

This historic event was recorded by the architect Charles Brigham on the town seal.

The place with a steep bank is the present site of Perkins School for the Blind. Clap's men perhaps chose high land for safety. Indian relics have been dug from its soil, and the Indians may have used this high land for a stockade. John Oldham, who claimed this territory, may have been the guide; he was friendly with the Indians and could speak their language.

The order to move to another location soon came from Governor Winthrop. His training in law, his energy, and his keen mind fitted him for dealing with such problems. When he arrived in Charlestown he must have learned about the doings of the Clap men and advised them of a good place to locate south of the river. The governor had outwitted Oldham.

ESTABLISHMENT OF WATERTOWN

Many passengers of the *Arbella* convoy moved from Salem to Charlestown, but they failed to find any springs save one of bitter water. They were forced to spread out along the waterways and thus founded Medford, Roxbury, and Lynn. Those who chose to follow Sir Richard Saltonstall and his minister, George Phillips, became the founders of Watertown. Summer days were fast slipping by, and work had to be done before cold weather set in. Leaving their families in Charlestown, a group of men set out to row up the Charles River. The Clap men had departed, leaving their shelter behind. The Saltonstall planters stopped short of Clap's Landing. They had followed the winding river which Indians called the "Big Eel" to the area later named Gerry's Landing. On that July day the water spread out wide and shallow. Just west of the present location of the Mt. Auburn Hospital a marker reads: "Sir Richard's Landing. Here at the river's edge, the settlers of Watertown, led by Sir Richard Saltonstall, landed in July 1630." There, four miles upriver from Charlestown, they established the settlement which would become Watertown.

Land for a dwelling, a well for water, and a barn were granted free to each planter, at first by the Court, later by the town. As far as possible each man chose the place he wanted for his homestead. These first homes were built close together for protection against wolves and Indians. Drainage was planned, and shelters were provided for the animals. Trees were felled for constructing houses, barns, and fences.

One hundred families were ready to move over, and for the time being, they called their village Saltonstall Plantation. Some who built their homes between the river and the Fresh Pond area were named Wellington, Captains Beers and Jennison, Keyes, Taylor, Bond, Bright, Stearns, Warren, Page, Freeman, and Deacons Child and Firman. Bas-reliefs on the Founders Monument near Watertown Square record this event.

To the settlers all this open land looked as attractive as a nobleman's park in England. The Indians had burned over the ground, clearing away the underbrush and leaving only large trees.

THE INDIANS

Indians belonged to the Pequossette Tribe who, like the Nonantums along the south bank, were a subtribe of the Massachusetts Indians. They called the open land Pequog. They planted their fields of corn near the river from which they took fish for fertilizer. At spring planting time the tidal river provided thousands of herring which the Indians netted at the river falls. After having dug holes in the rich soil with their stone hoes, they planted five corn kernels with a fish for fertilizer in each.

Indian implements have been unearthed near the Charles River and in Belmont west of Fresh Pond. In the nineteenth century when earth was being removed on the Hill farm on Pleasant Street

9

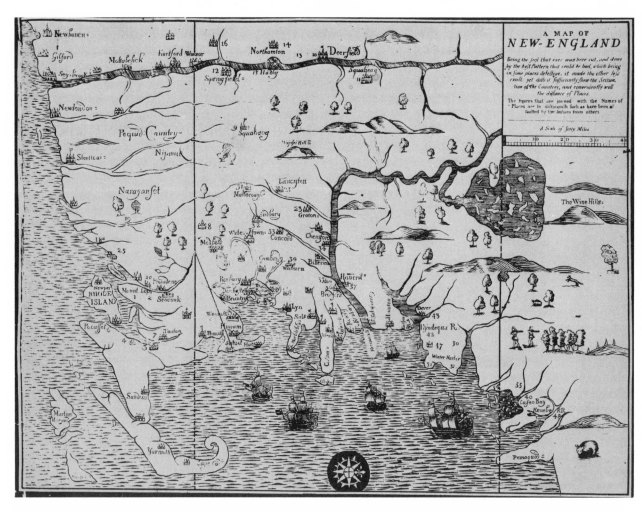

Exact copy of the first map engraved in this country and published in 1677.

in Belmont, an Indian skeleton was discovered seated in a bowl surrounded by his weapons. Later the Hill barn caught fire, and this rare find was irretrievably lost. Indian tribes had lived here for thousands of years, perhaps having traveled from Russia across the land bridge to Alaska and Canada. Their first contact with white men occurred about 1000 A.D. when Viking explorers from Norway built their city called Norumbega in a region they called Vineland. Eben Norton Horsford of Harvard University believed that the Norsemen settled on Watertown soil, led by Leif Ericson. The settlement was abandoned, but traces of it have survived to the present time.*

From the beginning, the Massachusetts Indians

*Horsford's identification is now discredited.

were friendly toward the early settlers. Some years earlier a sickness the natives probably caught from traders had killed a majority of this tribe. Their name meant "Great Hill" and referred to Blue Hill in Milton. About three hundred of the tribe occupied the land near the harbor. They moved inland in summer, trapping otter and beaver and bringing their skins down to the coast to trade during the winter months. They set up their wigwams near the ocean where they could depend on saltwater fishing for food. The Bay Company officials advised the settlers to deal fairly with the natives and to try to convert them to Christianity. When an Indian brought a claim for a tract of land, he had to be paid for it. Trade of implements and clothing was encouraged, but transfer of weapons to the Indians was forbidden.

In Charlestown there was increasing anxiety about the sick and undernourished because the ocean voyage had weakened many. Of nearly two hundred who died, one was Mrs. Phillips, the minister's wife, who left a small son. An only child, she had left the safety of home and family to accompany her husband to America. She was buried in Salem near the grave of Lady Arbella. A sister of the young Earl of Lincoln, in whose family Deputy Governor Dudley had been a steward, the Lady Arbella was much loved for her sweet disposition. In the space of a few weeks her sorrowing husband, Isaac Johnson, also died. Some colonists were discouraged by these adversities and returned to England. Even Governor Winthrop's family was not immune. His son Henry, a youth of twenty, had missed the sailing of the *Arbella* but sailed on a later ship. On the day after landing in Salem, he was drowned while swimming in a stream. "O my son, my son Henry, the poor child," lamented the governor to his wife.

Because of this sickness and grief, a day of prayer and humility was set for Friday, July 30, in Salem and Charlestown. A letter from Salem was sent to notify the Pilgrims in Plymouth and referred to their sorrow as "the hand of God upon" the colonists. At the end of their prayer service, they would enter into solemn agreement, and "since they [the new settlers] are so disposed of in their outward estates as to live in three distinct places, each having men of ability amongst them, there [they would] observe the day and become three distinct bodies." The three groups were the Saltonstall Plantation in Watertown; the church headed by Governor Winthrop's minister, in Boston; and the third comprised the Dorchester men, who at that time were staying in Charlestown waiting to move across the river to their new homes.

It is not known whether the Saltonstall men signed their covenant in Charlestown or at their newly chosen site in Watertown. Roger Clap said of those days in Charlestown, "their meeting place being under a tree, I have heard Mr. Wilson and Mr. Phillips preach many a good sermon."

The Saltonstall men gathered in a group of forty to sign a paper in which they promised to band together as a church town, subject only to God. They remembered the "long voyage to New England

Model for Henry Kitson's nine-foot bronze statue of Sir Richard Saltonstall erected in 1931.

in America to serve Him without fear" and hoped for a better future for "even them that are yet unborn." Their pledge avoided narrow rules and beliefs.

Thus was established the second church on New England soil, the first having been at Salem. On that July 30 a covenant for the Boston church received only four signatures, those of the church's leaders. The Dorchester men had already signed their covenant in England. Having signed the covenant for his new congregation, the Reverend George Phillips now called them together for church and town business. A copy of the pledge and the forty signatures hangs in First Parish Church. Bond's *Genealogies of Watertown* records copies of the leaders' signatures and their family trees.

No portrait of Pastor Phillips exists; thus, the bas-relief of him on the Founders Monument is imaginary. The figure of Sir Richard Saltonstall, however, is a true likeness. Henry Hudson Kitson, the sculptor, shows Sir Richard in cape and

11

square-toed riding boots. With plumed hat in hand and sword hanging from his shoulder, he looks like the king's cavalier that he was. In his hand he holds the charter of the Massachusetts Bay Company, a partly open scroll hung with royal seals. His success in securing approval for the company's charter earned him the appellation of "that good knight." Considered the best statesman among the Bay settlers, he became first assistant in the governor's council. Perhaps because he was not a rigorous enough Puritan, he was never elected governor.

Pastor Phillips was an ancestor of many notables, including the first mayor of Boston and Phillips Brooks, pastor of Trinity Church and author of the well-known Christmas carol, "O Little Town of Bethlehem."

Other descendants founded Phillips Andover and Phillips Exeter academies. In Watertown the Phillips School, the Phillips Church, and Phillips Street endure as reminders of the first pastor. Both Saltonstall and Phillips were liberal in their theology and respected the opinions of others, in contrast to many of the early settlers.

JOHN MASTERS' LETTER

Mention of the first small meetinghouse appears in a letter to Lady Barrington of England dated March 14, 1631, at "Watertown neere Charles River, New England." It was written by John Masters, manager of Sir Richard's household and property. Masters' letter is the only original document from Watertown's first year, after the founding covenant, and is preserved in the British Museum. After greeting his "right worshipful" friends of the Barrington family, Masters continued:

because I could not write before I had some experience of the country, I thought it fitte to deferre it until now. The country is very good, and fitt to receive lords and ladies if there were more good houses, both for good land and good water, and for good creatures to hunt and to hawke, and for fowling and fishing, and more also, our natures to refresh in. And if you or any of yours will come here, I knowe you might have good cheere. But because the right worthy Sir Richard Saltonstall hath putt mee in place to oversee his great family, with his worthy sonne, and that his business being so great as it is, I cannot write so large as I would. For besides his great family, he hath many cattle and kyne, and horse and swine, and some goats and poultry, hee hath also much building at his owne house, and fenceing, ploweing and planteing, and also to helpe build the new citty, and first for a house for God to dwell in. These things will require my best dilligence, because that Sir Richard will be long absent and therefore seeing that hee is now come over, to advise with the wise, to advance the glory of God in planteing the Gospell here, and to helpe forward those that intend the good of this country, therefore I pray you, to conferre with him of the same.

THE FIRST HOMES

Work now went forward on the homes of this first inland settlement. A commodious house was built near the water's edge, the first on a road which would lead from the wooden landing, on land now owned by Mt. Auburn Hospital. In it would live Sir Richard; his son, also Richard; and his younger children, Henry, Robert, Samuel, Grace, and Rosamund, with their servants. There was ample room for shelter for the many cattle on their sixteen acres. Farther along this road was the pastor's house. Overhanging second stories were the style of the day, as were heavy beams, hewn with hand tools that supported low ceilings locked into the outer wall framework with tongue and groove, sparing the supply of nails. The rich brought glass with them from England to make diamond-shaped panel windows, but light had to pass through oiled paper in the windows of humbler cabins.

Huts with rounded roofs were quickly fashioned for shelter. The Indians showed the settlers how to bend young trees to form the framework for a dwelling which sufficed for summer but was neither warm nor fireproof. Few bricks were available and chimneys were constructed mainly of wood covered with clay, which overheated easily. Fires were frequent and many huts burned. In the first year the cabins of Goodmen Benjamin, Firmen, and Finch burned to the ground, and all the belongings of the Finch family were destroyed.

Chairs and chests came fron England while household furnishings were packed in large trunks covered with cowhide. Home life was primitive at best. Meals were eaten from wooden or pewter plates with iron knives and spoons; forks were not used. Water for food and washing had to be carried, usually by the children, who were always kept busy and were expected to obey quickly. If a child awoke in the morning and found the fire dead, he would snatch a fire scoop and run to a neighbor's for live coals. Cooking utensils were made with legs to stand in the coals, and meat was roasted by being turned slowly on a spit in an open fireplace. There were no bricks for constructing ovens for baking bread.

In September, Boston and Dorchester received their names from cities in England, and the new town of Watertown (or "Waterton") received its name from the council of assistants, of which Sir Richard was a member. Sir Richard's grandfather, Gilbert, had lived in the village of Waterton in the West Riding of Yorkshire, and its spelling was perpetuated in the early records. Watertown was an appropriate name for a town well watered by streams from both above and below ground. Soon, they hoped, the river would turn millwheels to grind corn and other grains.

Capt. John Smith explored the New England coast and called the river the "Massachusetts" after the Indian tribe. Prince Charles (later King Charles I) later changed the river's name to his own; this event is recorded on the Galen Street Bridge.

The neighborhood of The Landing grew in size and importance and was referred to as "the Town." As a center, however, it was soon left behind, and no part of the original land which was settled falls within the present boundaries of Watertown. The townsmen moved their farms and homes westward, and the town's center came to be nearer the rapids upriver. Captain Johnson, a passenger on the *Arbella* who settled in Charlestown, wrote in his history that Watertown was the center town and metropolis of the colony, and indeed for many years its population was greater than Boston's.

The Town Seal, designed by
Charles Brigham, architect.

3

Settling the Land
and Governing Themselves

THE GENERAL COURT

HILE WATERTOWN men wanted to be left alone to conduct their own affairs, they carried their share of responsibility in the general business of the colony. In October 1630 they and the other settlements submitted to the government a list of planters who might become freemen, propertied Puritans who had the right to vote. They elected the governor, his deputy, and a council of assistants. In 1634 forty-five deputies, chosen by freemen, were elected to sit with the Council, forming the General Court. In voting for office or for a proposition, a kernel of corn was cast to mean yea and a bean represented a nay.

Although the landowners of a settlement could attend town meeting and were permitted to speak, most of them were not voters. Only freemen could vote in town meeting or in the Court, and they had to be members of a Puritan church society. Robert Feake, son-in-law of Governor Winthrop, came to Watertown from England in 1630 and was admitted as a freeman in 1631.

In order to maintain unity the new government could force out any person who threatened it. It called to arms, taxed, and sat in judgment of disputes. For the first two years no freeman was in-

John Winthrop, from the 1834 painting by Charles Osgood.

14

vited to sit with the Council. When the Council held sessions, it met in the Watertown meetinghouse or in any other town as the need arose. The Council, with governor and deputy, formed the Court.

In its first spring the Court voted on the names which had been submitted to be freemen. Twenty-five planters were then appointed to represent Watertown, being a large proportion of the total membership of one hundred. On the list were the pastor, the elder, and two military officers. John Oldham was an exception, for although he owned property he was not yet a Puritan church member. Oldham lost no time in becoming a part of the plantation, since his name was submitted three months after its founding. Business prospects locally must have appealed to his shrewdness, and he

seemed to fit the community's independent spirit. His wealth, friendly personality, and keen judgment were welcome to the practical Puritans.

On a voyage to Virginia he was shipwrecked off Cape Cod but managed to reach his destination. In Virginia he was taken sick, and possibly this experience softened his quick temper, for on his return he was readmitted to the Plymouth Colony, where he is presumed to have made his peace. Finally he came to live in Watertown, having established business interests in the town. The Court of Assistants granted Oldham the rights to a farm at Clap's Landing, where he is thought to have lived in the little house built by the Dorchester men until it burned in 1632.

THE BROWNE CASE

On the Lord's Day, early in 1631, Elder Richard Browne preached the afternoon sermon. (An elder was a church member who was authorized to preach.) In his sermon Elder Browne asserted that "the churches of Rome are true churches," meaning that the Roman church, in the Christian line of successors, could baptize people and appoint ministers. Pastor Phillips agreed, but the narrow Puritans of Boston, Rev. John Wilson, Deputy Governor Dudley, and even Governor Winthrop, were affronted. The two Watertown preachers were called to give account of themselves, and later the Boston and Watertown congregations met at Watertown to discuss the Browne case. A letter was sent to Watertown asking if Browne was fit to be an elder. The Watertown pastor and his elder replied that they would seek to make matters right if they were told what the opposition claimed to be untrue. The Phillips flock was badly split over the dispute, and both factions took their views to the governor. Again the governor and his friends came to Water-

town, at which time Pastor Phillips, showing his dislike of interference, suggested that they should act only as visitors, not as judging magistrates. The Watertown meeting ended quietly, a day of prayer was set, and the pastor gave thanks. Pastor Phillips, a remarkable man of liberal views, retained the respect of everyone in this controversy as well as in later disagreements. However, feelings continued to run high for two years, ending only when Richard Browne was removed from his position as church elder.

Although no longer an elder, Browne was permitted to carry on a ferry service from his house near the Landing, taking travelers across the river for a fee. Since there was no bridge, the settlers crossed by ferry to reach the new towns of Roxbury, Dorchester, Quincy, Muddy River (Brookline), and Boston. At low tide those who wished could cross the river on foot or by horseback at shallow places.

SETTLING THE TOWN

Other occupations were necessary for the economic life of the plantation. Fishing, farming, animal husbandry, and blacksmithing were typical occupations. A tanner, Nathaniel Biscoe, processed cowhides for leather. Christopher Grant, a glazier living near Fresh Pond, kept the meetinghouse

windows repaired at a cost of three to four dollars a year. Candles were supplied by a chandler, but because candles were scarce at first, pine knots and oil lamps were often used for light. The schooling of boys was the task of the minister's assistant, and girls learned spinning, weaving, and household

15

chores. Housewives planted vegetable gardens and raised herbs for flavoring food and for making medicine.

To maintain public order, two constables and officers drilled a monthly train band. The captains were named Jennison and Patrick. In his *Journal* Governor Winthrop wrote:

At a training at Watertown . . . a man of John Oldham's having a musket which had been long charged with pistol bullets, not knowing it, gave fire and shot three men, but it was so far off as the shot entered the skin and stayed there, and they all recovered.

This incident demonstrated that muskets were notoriously inaccurate and resulted in the passing of a law against carrying loaded guns. Although training was not required of servants, ministers, and magistrates, all other able-bodied men between the ages of sixteen and sixty were required to serve. The General Court passed a law forbidding shooting a musket in the dead of night.

Great pains were taken to be friends with the Indians. Punishment was imposed on anyone caught giving them any weapons or powder or doing them any injustice. John Hopkins learned this in an unpleasant experience when he sold muskets and powder to Indians and made merry with their squaws. His offense was thought to deserve death, but he was whipped and had his cheek branded instead. Presumably reformed, he settled in Watertown and became a respected citizen. One James Woodward, a Saltonstall servant, and another man slept one night in empty wigwams. Not having extinguished their fires, they were awakened to find the wigwam in flames. The Indian owner, John Sagamore, complained to the Court, and while it was sitting at the time (on the plain benches of the little Watertown meeting-house), it ordered Sir Richard, Woodward's master, to pay damages of seven yards of cloth.

SIR RICHARD SALTONSTALL RETURNS HOME

In March 1631 Sir Richard left his new settlement to return to England. A man of clear vision and with a strong belief in personal freedom, he had invested his wealth and energy in the venture of establishing the Watertown colony. He had promised to settle there permanently if the company was granted a charter. He, as its leader, his friends, and the Reverend Phillips were entitled to choose the best locations for their farms. However, Sir Richard was fined several times for small offenses. In the first November, the record shows that "Sir Richard was fined five pounds for whipping two several persons without the presence of another assistant, contrary to an act of Court formerly made." Previously he had been "fined four bushels of malt for his absence from this Court." Sir Richard had sold his estate in Yorkshire but had not yet received a return on his investments, so he refused to pay these two fines, and many years later they were excused. Affronted by the constant attack on private rights by the governor's group, Winthrop's first assistant avoided a confrontation by returning to London with his daughters and one of his sons; there he served the colony as its representative and used his influence against the

enemies of the Bay Colony. Eventually, he also served as agent for the Connecticut colony. Sir Richard was evidently too independent to accept the strictures imposed by the Watertown colony, but his leadership had left its stamp on the settlement. Captain Johnson of Charlestown wrote a poem about Sir Richard, including these lines:

Thou worthy knight, Saltonstall hight
Why wilt thou back, and leave us wreck
*   this worthy work begun?*
Art thou back-sore, Christ will send more
*   and raise instead thy son.*

Richard Saltonstall, the younger, was on the first list of Watertown freemen, and his brother Samuel also remained in Watertown, while Robert Saltonstall moved to Boston. These three sons carried on their father's business in New England. The Court granted the family a large number of farming acres in the western part of Watertown near the present location of the Gore estate. Saltonstall's daughters made their homes with relatives in England. Sir Richard remarried and became ambassador to Holland where he had his portrait painted

Sir Richard Saltonstall, from H. W. Smith's engraving of Rembrandt's portrait.

by Rembrandt. The painting, in the possession of the Saltonstall family in America, was copied by the Watertown artist Rosamond Coolidge and can be seen in the First Parish Church.

In response to the news of their rigidity and the intolerance of Governor Winthrop's government, Sir Richard wrote to the pastors, Wilson and Cotton:

Reverend and deare friends, whom I love and respect; It doth not a little grieve my spirit to heare what sadd things are reported daily of your tyranny and persecutions in New England, as that you fynne, whip, and imprison men for their consciences.

4

Here the American Idea Was Born

URROUNDED by sickness and death and with their number diminishing quickly, the settlers in Watertown, Roxbury, Dorchester, and Charlestown worked hard to establish permanent communities. The traders built their houses close together in compact villages near the harbor. The Watertown farmers, however, requiring land for crops, soon complained of crowding near the Landing. In January 1632, led by Governor Winthrop, a scouting trip was organized to open new farmlands to the west of the river falls. To his map he added the names of Beaver Brook, Masters Brook, and Mt. Feake (near the present location of Waltham cemetery). With him were

John Masters, manager of the Saltonstall interests and a church opponent of Elder Browne, and Robert Feake, a Watertown farmer who, having married Henry Winthrop's widow, was now a member of the governor's family.

The colonists also needed to find a location for their government, a city which could be fortified against invaders. The deputy governor, Dudley, chose Cambridge, near the clustered homesteads which Watertown men called "the Town," for his own home. Governor Winthrop, however, moved his home to Boston, convinced that it was a better location. The Court palisaded Cambridge for a place of refuge; the colonists feared hostile Indians as well as the French.

NO TAX WITHOUT A VOTE

The Court decided some matters without consulting the towns, since traveling to a meeting place was not easy during the winter. Having no representative in the Court after Sir Richard's departure, when the vote to tax the settlements for the palisade was taken in the General Court, Watertown's share was forty dollars, as much as that levied on Boston.

Disturbed by this injustice, Watertown's leaders called for a town meeting at the meetinghouse on May 16, 1632, to discuss what to do. Pastor Phillips

did not question the need for public money to build defenses for Cambridge, but he did question the tax's imposition without representation from the town, saying, "It is not safe to pay moneys after this sort lest we bring ourselves and our posterity into bondage." Elder Browne, who had become the colony's leading citizen in the absence of Sir Richard Saltonstall, supported his pastor.

In voting not to pay the tax, the men on the Charles sought to check the power of the General Court. Other colonists supported this stand in

18

favor of voluntary taxation. "No tax without a vote in it" became the cry during the American Revolution, which later opposed the domination of the British King. The English colony on the island of Barbados, West Indies, had also protested taxation without representation but had not refused to pay taxes.

Warrants were served on the voters, and the pastor and elder were summoned to the Court in Boston to state their case. According to the Governor's *Journal,* they submitted and were excused. The result of Watertown's resistance was that in June, the very next month, two deputies were appointed to represent each of eight settlements to advise the Court on matters of public money, al-though they had no vote. Heading this list of deputies was John Oldham, with John Masters as his associate; thus, the Massachusetts General Court was forced to be more responsive to the people.

Watertown's no-tax vote had a lasting effect and was felt whenever the General Court attempted to enforce its will against the colonists. It was felt when the colonists, protesting the tax on tea, dumped the tea into Boston Harbor. Later the Declaration of Independence protested to King George "for imposing taxes on us without our consent." For this reason the American Constitution declared that "the Congress shall have power to lay and collect taxes" and "all bills for raising revenue shall originate in the House of Representatives."

IMPORTANCE OF FISH

Soon after the furor over taxation the citizens of Watertown turned their attention to fish. Particularly at spawning time, great quantities of bass, salmon, and herring were borne upstream on the tides, many of them pushing their way over the rapids to quiet waters. As many as a hundred thousand fish could be netted in a day, so easily that young boys would wade into the stream and fill a bucket with fish.

The tide flooded the channel and overflowed into the marshes. The town asked the General Court for a permit to build a weir as preparation for the spring catch, which would provide both food for the people and fertilizer for the crops. Governor Winthrop, sure that the Court would favor it, gave his approval in advance. In spite of criticism from Dudley, who disapproved his taking such authority upon himself, the permit was approved by the Court.

To construct the fish weir, stakes were driven in a row from the shore out into the riverbed. Branches woven into a network were attached to the stakes, and when the tide receded the fish were caught by the weir. Weirs had traditionally been built by Indians living south of the river. Above and below the weir (probably located downstream from the present bridge), and along the river's south bank, stretched a tract of two hundred by sixty rods known as "weirland." Here the fish was distributed for fertilizer, laid out to dry, or salted in barrels for shipment to England. A cooper prepared barrels, and salt was brought for preserving the fish. Scows were loaded with barrels of fish and floated downstream to the Boston wharves for export. The weir was first town-owned, later became private property, and was eventually purchased by the town and leased to individual bidders. The fishing industry continued to be regulated by the Court.

"Exploration of the Charles," from an early wood engraving.

Bronze bas relief by Henry Kitson depicting Reverend George Phillips leading the freeman in protest against taxes levied without consent, a companion
piece to the bronze on page 8.

Not far from his first shelter, which burned, John Oldham was granted a farm opposite the weirland, and when he sold this farm it included the weir. No trace of his family survives. Oldham traded for furs with the Indians; he sailed along the coast and traveled fearlessly inland where he met an Indian chief who invited him to the lower valley of the Connecticut River. A Mohegan chief, he feared his warlike neighbors, the Pequots, who in-habited Block Island and the shore nearby. In the autumn of 1633, with three companions, Oldham made a journey of 160 miles, mostly through wooded wastelands. The small group spent the nights in Indian villages. The Indians gave Oldham black lead, beaverskins, and hemp. He also received gifts of five hundred bushels of corn and an island measuring six by two miles in Narragansett Bay.

WATERTOWN: "THE MOTHER TOWN"

At this time the Indians of the Connecticut Valley looked to the English settlers for protection against their common enemy, the Pequots. After Oldham returned from his expedition, several Watertown families went to colonize Pequog, a meadow claim on the Connecticut River. They first named this place "Watertown" after their home; it was later changed to Wethersfield, its name today.

Among these families were the Finches (who had lost their wigwam and belongings to fire); the Abbotts; and Robert Seeley, captain of the vessel *Arbella*. Before leaving Watertown Captain Seeley, a surveyor, had worked with Abraham Browne, Richard Browne's nephew, laying out roads. A descendant of Oldham's, who bore his name, lived in Wethersfield until recently.

Oldham could be described as the pioneer of the westward movement, and other settlers from Watertown followed his example. Wethersfield was the first town to organize in Connecticut. Watertown men acted in their usual independent manner and established the town without obtaining the consent of the colonial government. For this reason many families throughout the country trace their origins to Watertown, which is why it is called the "mother town." On Oldham's return from Connecticut the town took another step toward self-government. Two years had passed since Oldham had headed the list of deputies to advise the Court about the expenditure of public funds. In the spring of 1634 deputies from the various plantations held a meeting. On reading the colony's charter they discovered that it gave them the right to a vote in the General Court. Thereupon at the following annual Court they asserted the right "to make laws, to raise moneys and taxes, dispose of lands, and deal in all other affairs of the commonwealth" except the election of magistrates and other officers, "wherein every freeman is to give his own voice." Up to this time such authority had been assumed by the governor and his assistants. In May 1634 the Court ordered that deputies be elected by their freemen, the voters of the town; previously they had been appointed by the governor. Oldham was elected as one of three representatives from Watertown, the other two being Robert Feake and Richard Browne.

Oldham stayed in Watertown long enough to be entrusted with two other duties: he took charge of

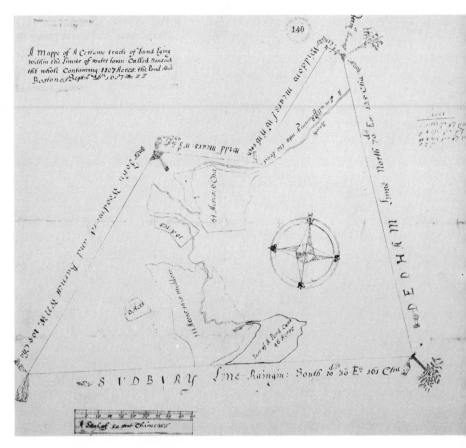

1687 plan of 1107 acres in the southwestern part of Watertown.

the gunpowder supply in Watertown and Medford, and he was one of the men who "followed the bounds of the towns," assuming the responsibility of the yearly inspection of the town boundaries.

MAYHEW'S MILL

By 1634 the town employed Thomas Mayhew to build a water-driven corn mill at the river falls. Mayhew was agent for former Governor Cradock's shipyard on the Mystic River. Windmills were impractical in this valley because they failed to take the harvest west winds. One windmill, which had proved useless, was disassembled and moved to Boston's Copp's Hill. From Medford Mr. Mayhew sent by messenger a letter dated June 1634 asking for a two-day loan of the governor's "teeme" to cart timber for the new mill and for help from a Mr. Doomer who was to provide carpenters.

Mayhew built the mill behind the later location of Lewando's Dye Works near the falls. Later it was

moved to the present "delta." A stone dam was built at the rapids to hold back the flow of water for the mill. An arc-shaped canal bore water from above the dam, and at the head of the canal a gate was raised and lowered to control the flow of water. In later alterations of Watertown Square the canal was filled in. Until modern times, Mill Creek, as it was called, was the oldest millrace in America in continuous use.

Governor Winthrop's Journal records that one day "a five-year-old son of a man named Smith fell into the race-way near the mill-gate and was carried by stream under the revolving wheel. One of the paddles of the wheel had fallen off, and it seems (by

Early print of Indian fish weir, similar to that built on the Charles by the Watertown planters.

special Providence) he was carried through under that gap for otherwise if an eel pass through, it is cut asunder. The miller noticed the sudden checking of his wheel, and looking out found the child unhurt sitting up to the waist in the shallow water below the mill."

The new mill provided the means for farmers from surrounding towns to grind their grain, and while waiting there they exhanged news and opinions. Inevitably the mill town became the marketplace, replacing the old Landing as a town center while more and more townspeople moved westward to new farms.

Thomas Mayhew became owner and manager of the mill, and the Mayhew family built their own house on a site from which they could see the mill. Mayhew purchased the interest of Thomas Cradock and Elder How and became prominent in the affairs of the settlement.

The construction of the mill indicated that the population was growing and that the harvests were increasing. Wheat and rye as well as corn were brought to be milled into flour. A road led east to the Saltonstall home, following an Indian trail for a distance of about two miles. It was first called Mill Road and was later renamed Mt. Auburn Street. Along it mules, laden with sacks of grain or flour in panniers or saddlebags, went to and from the mill.

GRANTING THE LAND

North of the mill a tract of two hundred acres westward to Warren Street was set apart as a town property. Further west Beaver Brook Plowlands were granted to the Saltonstall and Phillips families and to several other inhabitants. Divided by the brook, these plowlands were called Little or Hither Plains and Great or Further Plains. A tract of five hundred acres, opposite the present location of the former Waltham Watch factory, was granted to John Oldham by the Court.

North and west of the plowlands were four equal rectangles called the Great Divides, Dividends, or Squadrons. All four measured the same distance and were separated by stone walls. Each divide was surveyed to be 160 rods wide. Portions of each were given out as timberland with thatch supply; as pasturage, according to the number of cattle owned; and for planting. Between the small lots and the divides ran a driftway (a common road for cattle), which is now Gore Street. These assignments of land can be found listed in the first printed volume of town records.

To be thus divided the land required much surveying. All the lots were grants to homeowners, and the titles were legal only when approved by the Court. Any land left over was sold. The land granted to settlers was purchased by order of the Court from the Pequossette Indians for the sum of thirteen pounds, seven shillings, sixpence. But the colonists still felt crowded. A clerk recorded:

Letter of Thomas Mayhew to Governor Winthrop dated June, 1634.

Agreed, by consent of the freemen (in consideration that there be too many inhabitants in the Town, and the Town is thereby in danger of being ruinated) that no foreigner coming into the Town shall have any benefit of commonage or land undivided, but what they shall purchase.

23

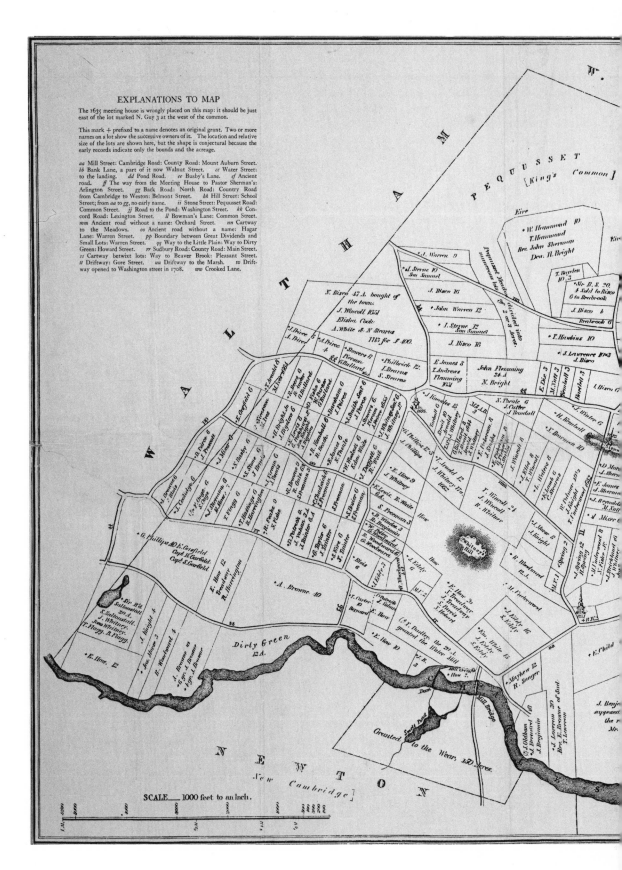

EXPLANATIONS TO MAP

The 1635 meeting house is wrongly placed on this map: it should be just east of the lot marked N. Guy 3 at the west of the common.

This mark + prefixed to a name denotes an original grant. Two or more names on a lot show the successive owners of it. The location and relative size of the lots are shown here, but the shape is conjectural because the early records indicate only the bounds and the acreage.

aa Mill Street: Cambridge Road: County Road: Mount Auburn Street. *bb* Bank Lane, a part of it now Walnut Street. *cc* Water Street: to the landing. *dd* Pond Road. *ee* Busby's Lane. *ff* Ancient road. *ff* The way from the Meeting House to Pastor Sherman's: Arlington Street. *gg* Back Road: North Road: Country Road from Cambridge to Weston: Belmont Street. *hh* Hill Street: School Street; from *aa* to *gg*, no early name. *ii* Stone Street: Pequusset Road: Common Street. *jj* Road to the Pond: Washington Street. *kk* Concord Road: Lexington Street. *ll* Bowman's Lane: Common Street. *mm* Ancient road without a name: Orchard Street. *nn* Cartway to the Meadows. *oo* Ancient road without a name: Hagar Lane: Warren Street. *pp* Boundary between Great Dividends and Small Lots: Warren Street. *qq* Way to the Little Plain: Way to Dirty Green: Howard Street. *rr* Sudbury Road: County Road: Main Street. *ss* Cartway betwixt lots: Way to Beaver Brook: Pleasant Street. *tt* Driftway: Gore Street. *uu* Driftway to the Marsh. *vv* Driftway opened to Washington street in 1708. *ww* Crooked Lane.

SCALE ____ 1000 feet to an Inch.

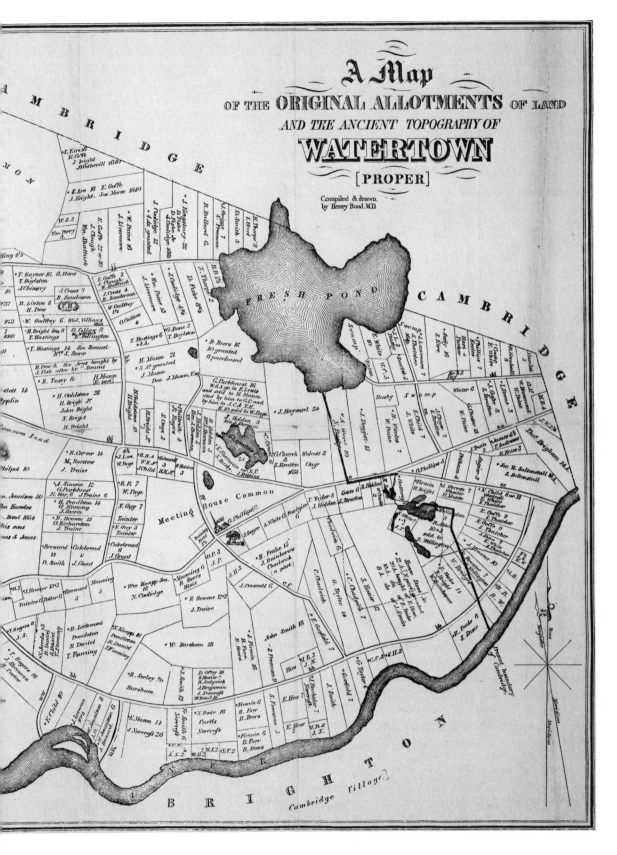

A Map OF THE **ORIGINAL ALLOTMENTS** OF LAND *AND THE ANCIENT TOPOGRAPHY OF* **WATERTOWN** [PROPER]

Compiled & drawn by Henry Bond, M.D.

"John Gallup's Exploit," from an early steel engraving.

WATERTOWN'S SYSTEM OF GOVERNMENT

At this time there were about one hundred families on the plantation, not including laborers who wandered from place to place picking up work or servants who hired themselves out. About half of the adult men voted in town meeting. Since the numbers were cumbersome for handling all the business, the Watertown meeting chose three selectmen, the first settlement to do so, although other towns soon followed suit. The colony's charter had failed to provide for local government, and thus the settlers devised a system of government still in use today in many towns. Notice of the Watertown action is recorded in these words:

Agreed by the consent of the freemen, that there shall be chosen three persons to be the ordering of the civil affairs of the Town. One of them to serve as Town clerk, and shall keep the records of the Town. The three chosen are William Jennison, Brian Pembleton, John Eddie.

At other times there were as many as seven selectmen. Beginning in 1634, the town clerk kept the record of town meetings. These town books, in the clerk's handwriting, were consulted by Convers Francis and Henry Bond for their histories of Watertown.

Richard Browne, already mentioned, once more had occasion to irk Governor Winthrop. No longer an elder of the church, he protested to the Governor's council about an impulsive act in Salem at which Capt. John Endicott had caused the red cross to be slashed from the center of the Union Jack. To Endicott the red stripes suggested superstition, but, said Mr. Browne, this cutting of the flag could

26

insult the king. In England a struggle was going on between king and Puritans, but the leaders in New England were seeking to avoid controversy and to avoid trouble. They wrote a halfhearted apology and punished Captain Endicott.

THE MURDER OF OLDHAM

Because of the persecutions of the Puritans, immigration to the New World increased. Two thousand settlers came with Winthrop's fleet in 1630; by 1633 their number had increased to three thousand. As the pressure for land increased, the Indians became alarmed, and the Pequots decided to do something to repel the intruders while there was still time. Word of their plan to kill every Englishman came to the ears of Jonathan Brewster, brother of Mrs. Oldham. Brewster, who was now in Wethersfield, received the information from the friendly Mohegans, who feared the Pequots. Brewster tried to get word to his brother-in-law, but Oldham was away on a fur-trading journey to the Pequots of Block Island.

A seaman, John Gallop, was sailing near Oldham's party. He and his companion recognized the Oldham pinnace and perceived that Indians were in possession of the boat. Pouring gunshot over its deck, he forced the savages, who had captured the ship, to jump into the sea. When they boarded the vessel they found Oldham brutally murdered, his head cut from his body, which was covered with a net and still warm. Suspicion was fixed on the Narragansetts, two of whom had accompanied Oldham. Their tribe, displeased because he had opened peace talks and attempted to trade with their Pequot enemies, had probably laid this trap for him. The murder of Oldham caused alarm among the colonists, who were dismayed by this treachery to one who had been friendly with the Indians.

At the time of his death Oldham was a church member, although he did not display the religious zeal of his Puritan friends. He was not an educated man, but his sharp wits and courage won him a place in history. Oldham's contribution was that of a trader and an explorer; certainly he was not a success as a farmer.

THE STRUGGLE AGAINST AUTOCRACY

The climate was hard; the fields were full of stones; and the Pilgrims lived in constant fear of wolves and Indians. Added to their difficulties was their distance from the government in England. The Puritans, however, were strong in their faith and in devotion to their families, and they placed great hope in their charter. Although not all the colonists were Puritans, the Puritan element was strong enough in the state church to dominate the lives of all the Massachusetts colonists, exercising constant control over both civil and religious life. Opposing this was the developing sense of New England independence and resistance to authority wherever it was manifested.

A stray pig dramatized the struggle of the colonists against autocracy. Mrs. Sherman charged an eminent gentleman with killing her pig. Hearings took several weeks and the Court decided in the lady's favor. The gentleman appealed, and the

Sketch of the old Watertown Grist Mill.

27

Mayhew House, built by Thomas Mayhew in the 1630s.

majority of the Governor's Council (the upper house of the General Court) reversed the decision, voting in his favor. An uproar broke out among the people, backing their freemen in the Court, so that the Council was obliged to grant to the deputies the right of veto. Thereafter the two bodies sat separately, each acting as a check on the other as in the present legislature. John Winthrop complained that the colony was in danger of becoming "a mere democracy."

The Court met in various towns in March, August, and December to handle its business. An attempt was made to cut the number of deputies from three to two per town, since more and more towns were being settled and the Court feared the strength of the people's vote. An appeal for the laws to be codified was resisted by the clergy on the grounds that it was not called for in the charter. A grand jury was called into being to try one hundred cases, including complaints against magistrates. Between Court sessions emergency decisions were made by the governor's council. Every May a new General Court was elected by the freemen, who were the only eligible voters. Because the freemen were often absent from their homes trading or defending their towns against Indians, a new plan was devised for voters in remote towns (such as Salem) to send their votes in by proxy. After the vote was taken, deputies took the written, sealed ballots, along with a list of the voting freemen, to the Court.

The Council now moved to perpetuate some of the members in office for life. The magistrates elected for life terms were Governor John Winthrop and Deputy Thomas Dudley. Their life terms, however, were changed to three-year terms, opposition coming from young Richard Saltonstall, among others. Although Richard held office as an assistant, he shared his father's sympathy for the people.

The right of all men to enter into discussion of matters affecting their lives provided the basis for growth in individual freedom and perhaps helped save the Puritan adventure. Watertown's settlers made an important contribution to the right of the individual to speak out and to vote. Watertown's significance lay both in her development of the democratic process and in her contribution to the beginnings of the westward movement.

5

Mapping the Town

HE FIRST small meetinghouse near Sir Richard's Landing was used for five years, but was soon outgrown and left behind as the farmers moved into their new allotments of land in the western part of the town. Most settlers had no close neighbors and lived far from any assembly hall, which served as the spiritual, civic, and social center for the community. The second site was more centrally located.* It was situated on the Meeting-House Common, which lay in a forty-acre triangle between Mt. Auburn and Belmont streets, and reached west to what is now Winsor Avenue. The new building stood "on a rising ground" where the Coolidge School now stands.

Although better located, the new meetinghouse was still a long distance from many farmers. For example, the Whitney** family lived several miles away on the present location of Lexington Street near the north fire station.

BEFORE THE FIRST SETTLERS

Meeting-House Common was at the northwest corner of the present intersection of Arlington and Mt. Auburn streets at one end of a long hill, now situated between Mt. Auburn and Belmont streets, being partly used by the Country Club's golf links. Its highest point, called Strawberry Hill, or Meeting-House Hill, was 250 feet above sea level and reached out in a spur along present Spruce Street. West of it and nearer the plantation center was Whitney Hill, two hundred feet high.

These heights in the settlement proper, as well as Ridgelawn along Main Street near the present Browne School, were drumlins. They were smooth gravel deposits, and around their bases a flattened circle could be drawn. They were formed millions of years ago when a melting glacier moved slowly southward. It scoured out Boston Basin and left a rim of hard-rock hills on the north (at Arlington Heights) with the Blue Hills closing the other side of the basin. Watertown was situated in the center of this basin. Beacon and Bunker hills are also drumlins. A mound 125 feet high later took the name "Mt. Auburn," from whose tower can be seen the Charles River valley. The highest point in early Watertown was Prospect Hill, nearly four hundred feet high, which could be seen by sailors at sea.

*The location of the Second Meeting House has been disputed, and the Coolidge School location doubted. A committee of the Historical Society in 1906 examined the records and came to the conclusion that the Second Meeting House was at the Hillside Road site identified by a marker.

**Eli Whitney, inventor of the cotton gin, was descended from this family, from which Whitney Hill gets its name.

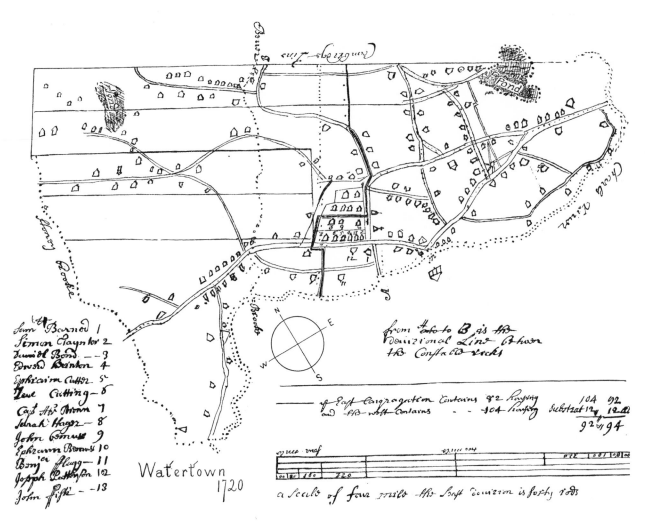

Watertown
1720

1720 map of Watertown showing streets and residences.

Near it, and almost as high, was Bear Mount in the present city of Waltham. The average height of Waltham was two hundred feet higher than that of Watertown, and settlers built their farms and homes on all these slopes and also on the bluffs across the river.

Chunks of ice from melting glaciers created "kettle holes" as in Fresh Pond, leaving sandy banks. Other ponds within the original bounds of the town were called Walden and Nonesuch. In its scraping the icesheet exposed "pudding stone" and slate; one old slate quarry existed at Templeton Parkway. Watertown soil held its moisture under a

protective stratum of clay, and many underground streams flowed along this stratum. Down from the hills came abundant surface brooks, emptying into the Charles River. The largest brooks were Stony and Beaver in Waltham; to the south was Smelt Brook; and in the center Treadaway Brook (a family name), spreading throughout the town.

The Charles and Mystic rivers had originally been one large stream but changed their courses after the glacier receded. The Charles rose twenty-five miles away in Hopkinton, but its winding course was over one hundred miles long. At Watertown its flow tumbled in a series of rapids, and this was used as the base for the dam. The river attracted settlers because of its beauty, its wealth of fish, and as a means of transport. Its rapids later provided waterpower for gristmills while the plains rolling between hills and the river were partly shorn of trees and quite ready for plowing.

THE EARLY YEARS

Watertown in those early years was a much larger town in area compared with its present size of about one by three miles. It then sprawled out over meadows and hillsides and included what is now Weston, Waltham, and large sections of Lincoln, Belmont, and Cambridge. It was referred to as "the old hive," from which swarms of settlers moved to establish the towns of Dedham, Concord, Lancaster, and Groton.

The Court granted a petition from the chief inhabitants requesting that, because they were crowded for meadows, they be allowed to move and settle a plantation on the Sudbury River. This new town was called Sudbury.

Sudbury Road (Main Street), Country or Boston Road (partly Galen Street), and Mill or Cambridge Road (Mt. Auburn Street) were the principal highways leading into Watertown. Beginning at Sudbury Road, Lexington Road crossed northward to Back Way or North Road (now Belmont Street). Common Street led from Mill Road to a great public pasturage known as Pequossette or King's Common, now part of Belmont and including Waverley. There cattle were tended by a herdsman who was paid twenty-five pounds a year in corn. At the sound of the alarm he herded the cows into a pen at the east end of the common, where there was also a refuge for the cattle against attacks by wolves, and for settlers against Indian attack. Cow's milk was used to supply butter and cheese, and beef cattle were driven to pastures in Sudbury for grass feeding from spring through autumn.

Abraham Browne, nephew of Richard, surveyed and laid out roads about one hundred feet wide to allow for driving the cattle. These were built and repaired by the farmers, who contributed their labor in lieu of taxes. In 1637 the town voted to set aside eight days for road repair. Every man was to appear with a wheelbarrow, a shovel, and a mattock. A fine time was enjoyed by all for the town furnished the men with wine and rum. The town taxed each family about five dollars a year, and part of it was paid to the Massachusetts Bay Colony.

Travelers from Boston westward passed through Watertown whether they took the north or south bank of the river. Some ferried across from Boston to Charlestown and traveled by way of the Cambridge Road. Others rode along Boston Neck, then through Roxbury and by Boston Road to the shallows at Watertown. Even before the bridge was built Galen Street, then part of the Boston Road, brought the traveler to the river crossing. From this point travelers turned west via Sudbury Road.

Among the thousands of colonists who arrived in the first years there were numerous ministers, most of whom were not long out of Cambridge University and retained memories of Cambridge on the Cam, Deputy-Governor Dudley's "dreamtown." In order to provide for the education of ministers and other young men who did not wish to travel back to England to attend Oxford or Cambridge universities, a college was founded in Cambridge in 1636. After the college received John Harvard's legacy and his library, it took the name of Harvard. A separate building was set aside for the use of the Indians, but only one native took advantage of this opportunity. Sir Richard Saltonstall made a bequest to the college, and Watertown voted money for its support. Watertown men complained that the college ferry, which carried students between Cambridge and Boston, interfered with the town's trade on the river. The operators of river barges who used the river to ship goods or float logs downstream to Boston did not welcome more traffic on the Charles.

Indians lurked on tree-covered bluffs on the river's southern edge. For self-protection the settlers did not establish homesteads in this vicinity at first. A thirty-acre lot, which Pastor Phillips is believed to have owned in the present location of Brighton, was offered to a dissatisfied congregation led by the Reverend Thomas Hooker. This lot, together with Boston's offer of adjoining land, could make a township for the Hooker flock. When they declined a committee of the General Court changed the proposed boundary line, so that Watertown lost the Phillips land to Cambridge. This disdain for the Watertown plantation may be found expressed in the words

31

that it was not "a place for much trade, no shipping port, only reached by small vessels, and no resort for official men and capitalists."

Mill owner Thomas Mayhew thought the wooded highland across the river looked inviting. On the north bank next to Mayhew's house he bought the Oldham farm that included the weir.

Next he secured by Court grant a tract of five hundred acres along the south bank from the Brighton boundary west, including present-day Newtonville, with such buildings as had already been erected on it. Galen Street, known then as Old Country Road, was part of the road from Boston.

THE HOOKER MIGRATION

The Hooker Company had decided to become independent of the Boston leaders, and with their permission they left Massachusetts and settled on the Connecticut River. Ever since the Mohegan chief had invited John Oldham to trade there, many towns had sprung up in the Connecticut Valley. Pastor Phillips had had friendly arguments with Hooker's son-in-law, a Cambridge preacher, and so it was that the group was welcome to camp in Watertown after its first day's journey. When they left, they were joined by a few adventurous inhabitants of Watertown.

Dame Hooker refused to be left behind, even though she was fat and sick and had to ride in a curtained horse litter. The company traveled for about two weeks before arriving at the new town of Hartford. Their progress was slow, for they drove before them a herd of a hundred cows for milk. Their leader, Thomas Hooker, who had pioneered

in the establishment of the new colony of Connecticut, was called "the light of the western churches."

At the mouth of the Connecticut River, Saybrook was built as a fort to protect the colonists against both Indians and the Dutch of New York. New Haven, the nearby settlement, was supported by Sir Richard Saltonstall, who sent a ship from England—a ship which was mysteriously lost. John Winthrop, Governor Winthrop's son, was a leader of the New Haven settlement.

The royal commissioners responsible for the colonies heard reports of the success of the Massachusetts Colony but did not trust its leaders. They became suspicious because of the complaints of dissatisfied settlers that Winthrop, Dudley, and others had tyrannized the settlers. Repeated demands came from England to turn in the charter, but the colonists' leaders replied that more time was needed.

INDIAN PROBLEMS AGAIN

These thousands of settlers escaping from the rule of King Charles I and pushing into Indian country alarmed the Pequots. Immediately after the Indians had murdered John Oldham. John Endicott, captain of a seaborne band of unpaid volunteers, set upon and butchered as many of the tribe as could be found near Block Island. This massacre drove the Indians to attack the settlements, kidnapping and scalping many. Capt. William Jennison of Watertown was active in organizing attacks against the Pequots, being responsible for raising and supplying recruits. The volunteers were placed under the command of Captains Mason of Connecticut and Underhill of Massachusetts. They surprised and set fire to the enemy stockade at Stonington on the Connecticut shore, and the next day a company of Watertown men under Captain Patrick arrived at the fort.

George Munnings, a volunteer from Watertown, lost an eye in the campaign. Another expedition wiped out the remnants of that brave Indian tribe. The other tribes, terror-stricken by the colonists' attacks, were afraid to resist, and during the next forty years the settlers breathed easily.

The next year, 1638, saw three thousand new settlers arrive in twenty ships. During the decade of the 1630s about twenty thousand settlers landed in New England. A New England Confederacy was formed by the four colonies—the Massachusetts Bay, the New Haven, the Connecticut, and the Plymouth. Although only a loosely knit union was formed for military protection, it met with disfavor from the king. The Bay colonists had also constructed fortifications on Castle Island in Boston Harbor for defense against hostile vessels.

32

EDUCATING THE YOUNG

The colonists busied themselves with clearing land for farms, establishing trade, and educating the young. Children were often taught lessons at home, and the fortunate were sent to dame schools conducted by women in their homes. Higher studies were now possible at Harvard College, and in Cambridge in 1638, Stephen Daye established the first printing press in America. The British authorities, fearing the publication of seditious ideas, were not pleased with this development.

A teaching assistant was often employed by the pastor to prepare older boys for Harvard. Because many New England families wished at least one son to study for the ministry, John Knowles was invited to Watertown in 1639. No notice was sent to the government, and without their consent or the presence of church leaders, the Watertown congregation ordained him to the ministry and named him as their associate pastor. This independent action was unprecedented, and by it the Watertown church became self-sufficient. It was the first independent church society in America.

THE SAGA OF PASTOR PHILLIPS

According to tradition, Pastor Phillips lived at the corner of Arlington Street. In one direction was the meetinghouse, and nearby was a drill field on which were held two annual fairs on the first Fridays of April and July.

Across Mill Road from the parsonage was the burying ground, enclosed with a five-foot fence. The oldest grave bears the date 1642. Bodies were buried with their feet pointing toward the east. Graves at Mt. Auburn and Belmont streets, perhaps of those who died before 1642, were apparently dug deep and filled with stones to discourage hungry wolves.

Pastor Phillips was granted by the Court $150 a year, or thirty pounds in English money, augmented by various household supplies. His salary was paid by the town, although this met with objections from some inhabitants who were not church members.

Mr. Phillips suffered from attacks of "indigestion," and he died in 1644 from one of these attacks. The location of his grave is unknown. A good man, he was mourned by all. The scholarly minister had read the entire Bible six times a year, searching earnestly for guidance, and each time finding something new. He left his widow, Elizabeth, and several children, and the town paid to educate his son, Samuel, who inherited his father's books, eventually becoming a minister.

Only one of Phillips's writings has endured to the present day, and in it he expressed his controversial ideas on infant baptism. These views he recorded for Nathaniel Biscoe, who disapproved of them. Biscoe, a rich tanner, sent the paper to England where it was printed together with opposing arguments. When he received a copy Pastor Phillips wrote a reply to the opposing arguments, which was published after his death by his Cambridge friend, the Reverend John Shepherd. Mr. Biscoe was fined for his part in the affair. Pastor Phillips's preaching did not prevent dissension among his own flock, but they apparently confined their arguments to their own church. His ideas about infant baptism caused the dismissal of President Dunster of Harvard College.

ANNE HUTCHINSON AND GOVERNOR WINTHROP

While the Watertown church debated infant baptism and who was eligible for church membership, a seething Boston public turned on a woman who called herself a prophetess. Anne Hutchinson was attractive, excitable, and ambitious. Her house stood opposite that of Governor Winthrop, and she was a friend of the Reverend John Cotton. Cotton and Wilson, both ministers in Boston, took opposite sides in this controversy. Governor Winthrop lost three consecutive elections because of his opposition to Anne Hutchinson's teaching, which asserted that divine love in the heart was law enough

33

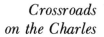

to keep a person good, rather than the laws and power of the clergy. Finally they drove her out of the colony, and she and nearly all of her fourteen children were massacred by Indians in Pelham Bay, New York. At an annual May meeting of the General Court during the Antinomian controversy involving Mrs. Hutchinson, the members nearly came to blows. When the freemen restored John Winthrop to the governorship, they failed to reelect young Richard Saltonstall as assistant because of his liberal views. After this bitter dispute, and until the Quaker and witch trials, comparative peace prevailed.

Pastor George Phillips was a tolerant man and did not favor persecution. His basic objective was to win the hearts of his people. Captain Johnson, author of many ditties, sang of Phillips, "Though thou thy days hast ended on this earth, yet still thou livest in name and fame always." Shortly before the death of Phillips the Puritan migration was slowing, since the Puritans in England had gained sufficient power in their war against the royalists.

6

The Pastors

URING the pastorate of Knowles in Watertown, John Eliot, a Roxbury preacher, was doing missionary work among the Nonantum Indians. Their camp was on Nonantum Hill, located in the present area between Newton Corner and the Newton-Brighton line. Theirs was the first settlement of Christian or "praying" Indians in the British colonies. Nonantum meant "rejoicing" in the Indians' language. Eliot translated the Bible into their language, and the city of Newton has honored John Eliot with a stone terrace on Eliot Memorial Drive. The inscription reads:

Here on Monday October 28, 1646 in Waban's wigwam near this spot, John Eliot began to preach the gospel to the Indians. Here he founded the first Christian community of Indians within the English colonies.

Eventually the Mayhew family sold their interests in the area and took advantage of a royal grant of Martha's Vineyard and the Elizabeth Islands over which he became governor. He and his son, a minister, gathered the two hundred Indians inhabiting the island into a church society; when the son was shipwrecked, two grandsons carried on the work of preaching. The elder Mayhew died, white haired, at ninety-two. The family is honored by a stone at the lower end of Riverside Street.

Mayhew had constructed a simple bridge across the stream, perhaps as a private convenience so

"Eliot preaching to the Indians," from an early engraving.

that he could reach his 150 acres on the south shore. If the Mayhews had stayed in Watertown until 1643 they would have seen the construction of the first public bridge to span the Charles. Wide enough only for a horse or a single person on foot, it crossed the river a short distance downstream from the mill. Nathaniel Biscoe and Isaac Stearns oversaw its construction.

The townspeople who needed timber for houses and wood for four-rail fences to enclose their lots as well as for firewood, made the town fathers anxious over the shortage of trees. They fined anyone found cutting down a tree on the public highways or on the town common. Biscoe and Sherman were ordered to mark such trees with a "W."

During Pastor Knowles' lifetime the settlers of New England petitioned the court to allow non-Puritans to become freemen with the right to vote. One of the signers, Sam Maverick, a rich "old planter," lived with his wife on Noddles Island in Boston Harbor. He had abandoned the Church of England in his youth and refused to become a Puritan. Ordinarily only freemen were voters, but they could attain that status by passing an examination in the Puritan creed. The nonvoting majority of colonists longed for greater liberty, seeking a form of government which would allow each person to live according to his own beliefs while at the same time respecting the rights of others. Governor Winthrop, having opened secret letters, declared the petition Maverick had signed a plot, and it was suppressed. The rule of the clergy was sustained, and the people's rights had to wait for more propitious times.

Governor Winthrop died shortly thereafter. His task of building a Puritan state was a hard one, and he was faithful to the Puritans' precepts regarding the relationship between church and state. On his deathbed he turned away from Thomas Dudley, who was pressing him to sign a writ of persecution. "Of that work," he said, "I have done too much already." When the "father of Massachusetts," as he became known, died, Thomas Dudley and John Endicott in turn proved harsher governors than John Winthrop had been. Back in England, Charles I was beheaded, and the Puritans came to power under Oliver Cromwell and set up the first Puritan Commonwealth.

THE FIRST SCHOOLHOUSE

During the 1650s we find the first mention of a schoolhouse in Watertown. The town was ordered by the General Court to provide schooling, lest their children grow up unable to read the Bible. The record of a town meeting in November 1650 states that:

it was voted and agreed that Mr. Richard Norcross was chosen school master for the teaching of children to read and write and so much of Latin, according to an order of Court, as also if any of the said town have any maidens that have a desire to learn to write, that the said Richard should attend them for the learning of them; as also that he teach such as desire to cast account, and that the town did promise to allow the said Richard for his employment 30 pounds for this year.

The schoolhouse was built on Strawberry Hill, which became Schoolhouse Hill, and later Common Street Hill. Its proximity to Belmont Street made it convenient to the population center. John Sherman was engaged as carpenter. A busy man who had assumed many public duties, he took more than a year to complete the job. The building contained one room of twenty-two by fourteen feet and had a turret on the roof. Long seats were made from logs sawn in half, and shelves were fastened to the walls to serve as desks. A master's desk stood in the center of the room.

The first master was Richard Norcross, ancestor of the present-day Norcross family. Richard Norcross taught for thirty years until the age of seventy-nine. He was allowed to augment his salary of thirty pounds by giving private lessons, but broken schoolhouse windows were his responsibility. While waiting for the completion of the schoolhouse, Norcross taught in the meetinghouse or in private homes. Watertown's schoolmaster was good enough to attract pupils from outside the town; twice his salary was increased to pay for the extra pupils.

School was in session from 7:00 A.M. to 5:00 P.M. during the summer, but for only four hours in the winter. The pupils furnished the firewood, and if a boy failed to do his share he would be punished by being seated farthest from the fireplace.

On entering, pupils greeted the master. School opened with the reading of the Bible and with prayer, and on Monday the master questioned the pupils about the content of Sunday's sermon. Much time was devoted to learning to spell from a hornbook. First the students were taught reading, then writing and arithmetic. A few of the older boys progressed far enough to learn Latin, which was required for entrance into Harvard College. Only boys attended classes; the girls were taught at home or learned their letters and sewing in dame schools in the ladies' homes.

GOVERNING THE YOUNG TOWN

If young men misbehaved, correction was the town's responsibility. When Jonathan, the twenty-three-year-old son of Pastor Phillips, became a problem to his widowed mother and to the town, he and two other youths were reprimanded publicly. The selectmen advised Jonathan to apprentice himself to the master of a trade for a year and ordered him to report to them weekly and in writing.

Public complaints were brought before the selectmen, who were elected each year. They supervised the repair of fence enclosures, the walking of boundaries, and the care of beef cattle. They hired a herdsman, Solomon Johnson, to keep the dry herd from April to October in the cowpen near the Sudbury border and provided a home there for him. However, Johnson was so lax that eventually they discharged him and hired another herdsman. Finally they abandoned the communal cowpen and ordered the cattle to be divided into four herds, one in each of the four sections of the town. Year after year complaints came in about livestock which roved at will and caused damage. The selectmen imposed fines for offenses such as the failure of an owner to put noserings in his hogs, while other citizens were fined for not paying their taxes. By order of the General Court the wearing of silk goods, gold or silver, lace, buttons, or ribbons was forbidden. Clothing and housing were furnished for widows, orphans, and those who had no source of support, but strangers were forced to leave town if they were unable to support themselves. The selectmen ordered the molding of gunshot, and Lt. Richard Beers was permitted to produce saltpeter for ammunition. In early years this powder was stored in the meetinghouse as the place least likely to catch fire, but later a powderhouse was provided for the purpose. Lieutenant Beers, John Sherman, Nathaniel Biscoe, Capt. Hugh Mason, John Whitney, and Ephraim Child were among the selectmen during this period.

Besides the selectmen's meetings, general public meetings were held to approve the raising of taxes for the town and the colony. The town meeting elected two constables to collect the taxes, appointed the pastor and the schoolmaster, and set the salaries for each. They chose surveyors of highways and viewers of fences and hogs. At one meeting a vote was taken to allow fireworks for a general drill at Cambridge, in which the Watertown military company planned to participate. A certain John Spring was awarded a prize for shooting closest to the bull's-eye. To call the people to town meeting, the selectmen drew up a warrant of articles to be voted upon, which they then gave to the two constables who were to inform the people about them. A typical warrant of 1728 began, "In his Majesty's name you are hereby required to warn the freeholders and other inhabitants in Watertown to meet . . . ."

Bills were ordinarily paid partly with corn at a price set by the court. Musket bullets were used in exchange as equal to half a cent. Because coins were scarce, the colony minted the pine-tree shilling in 1652 and continued to do so for thirty years, when such minting was prohibited by the English government. It was said that a man was paid twenty-five pennies (seventy-five cents) a day for carpentry, and a ha'penny would buy a quart of milk or four eggs.

In his book, *Wonderworking Providence*, published about this time, Captain Johnson wrote:

Watertown is situate upon . . . the Charles, a fruitful plot and of large extent, watered with many pleasant springs and small rivulets, running like veins through-out her body; which has caused her inhabitants to scatter in such manner that their Sabbath assemblies prove very thin if the season favour not, and hath made this great town consisting of 160 families, to show nothing delightful to the eye . . . This town abounds in several sorts of fish at their seasons, bass, shad, alewives, frost-fish, and smelts. Their herd of cattle are about 450, with some store of sheep and goats. Their land in tillage is near upon 1800 acres. This church is increased to near upon 250 souls in church fellowship.

The town fathers voted money for galleries in the meetinghouse to seat the youth and erected a tower to serve as a lookout. A caretaker was appointed whose pay was an excuse from his tax.

1885 photograph of the first Parsonage, built in 1685 and demolished in 1888.

RELIGIOUS MATTERS

So populous had the town become that for two years the Reverend John Sherman was engaged as pastor to help Mr. Knowles. He came from Connecticut, having turned down invitations from both Boston and London. Many years earlier, as a bright young man, he had substituted several times for Pastor Phillips and had proved so able conducting a service of thanksgiving held outdoors under a tree that his listeners marveled.

Pastor Knowles exerted himself to such an extent in his preaching that he occasionally fell exhausted in a faint. He remarked, "I had rather be in a jail where I might have a number of souls to whom I might preach than to live idle in my own house." His duties in Watertown were interrupted by an invitation to go to Virginia. Although Knowles's missionary group made many converts in the South, the authorities of the Church of England there drove them out. In 1650 he departed for England, never to return. He had been in Watertown for ten years.

The third pastor, John Sherman, stayed for thirty-five years, married twice, and fathered twenty-six children. He was a scholar learned in mathematics and astronomy and published several almanacs of pious essays. Perhaps absentminded, he was several times fined for minor infractions of the rules and then excused from paying the fine. A member of the Harvard Corporation, his twice-a-month lectures attracted students from Cambridge, and he was described as the "golden-mouthed preacher." These lectures continued for thirty years. Sherman lectured without notes, depending on his memory. In private, his words were few, helpful, and easy to remember. A talkative person once remarked to him that he must have studied the art of silence, whereupon the minister replied that he might well do the same.

THE MEETINGHOUSE

With so eminent a pastor, the inhabitants became aware of the need for a new place of assembly. The twenty-year-old hall needed repairs and was cramped for space, even with its galleries. The carpenter John Sherman, a cousin of the minister, presented plans and was authorized to build a new

38

meetinghouse like the one in Cambridge, the cost to be 152 pounds. Three men were to decide where it should stand, with preference being given to the north side of Meeting-House Common—somewhere between John Biscoe's land and the property of Sergeant Bright. The old building was to be torn down and its seats reused.

A difference of opinion exists as to the exact location of this meetinghouse. A stone marker at 43 Hillside Road reads, "Site of the Meeting-House 1635-1723," but since this land was sold a dozen years later to raise money for a new bridge, it would hardly seem likely that the meetinghouse stood on it.*

A third meetinghouse may have replaced the second, near the burying ground at the present location of the Coolidge School. A pastor's house was later to be built at that corner, convenient to the meetinghouse.

According to Convers Francis the plan to build "was abandoned for the present, but resumed at different periods till it was accomplished" in 1723. "This subject had been before the Town in 1654; it was now [1685] revived but was again set aside for the present." Later Francis says, "We have already seen that 38 years before this time [1692], some movements had been made toward providing a new place of worship."

THE NEW BRIDGE

To replace the twenty-year-old footbridge near the mill, John Coolidge, Jr., was engaged in 1667 to lay a new foundation. Wooden boxes like upside-down pyramids were filled with stones. The tops met each other, but the bases left triangular openings for water to flow through. John Sherman, the carpenter, sawed trees in two lengthwise and laid them out three abreast with their flat side up. This new bridge was only three feet wide, no wider than was needed for a horse or cow to cross. There were few carts at that time, and most loads were still carried on the backs of horses.

To meet this expense, a portion of Meeting-House Common was sold and a toll was charged those who crossed the bridge. The cost of repairing the bridge was paid by Watertown, although it also benefited neighboring towns. Watertown often appealed to the court for help. After building the new bridge, the town purchased the weir and leased the fishing privilege.

KING PHILIP'S WAR

There now occurred an influx to America of a new religious society, the Quakers, whose disapproval of magistrates, oaths, and military service was repugnant to the colonists. Punishment was imposed on John Warren of Watertown for harboring some Quakers. Boston banished the outspoken ones, and when Mrs. Mary Dyer and two men returned, they were hanged on Boston Common.

This harsh action was considered excessive by even the strictest Puritans and resulted in less severe punitive measures. The government needed the support of the colonists against a new menace, a general uprising of New England tribes under "King" Philip, the Wampanoags' chief. Watertown showed its distrust of the Indians by refusing to let Nathaniel Coolidge sell his weirland across the river to the Indians of Nonantum. The harbor towns, including Watertown, escaped massacre and pillage, but towns along the Merrimack and Connecticut rivers were under constant attack. Watertown sent a number of soldiers to relieve those river towns and also supplied them with ammunition. These costs were supported by a heavy military tax.

In 1675 the governor ordered an attack on the Wampanoags at Swansea. King Philip's fort, located in the midst of a frozen swamp, was protected by high walls. Captain Davenport of Watertown led his men up a slippery tree trunk in order to scale the wall but fell from Indian gunfire, and the attack continued until at last the camp was taken. One volunteer from Watertown, on seeing bloodshed, panicked and had

*See footnote on page 29.

to be sent home. A thousand Indians were reported to have been killed in the raid.*

The chiefs convened a great pow-wow at Wachusett. From its height they could look down on the new settlements in the Nashua Valley at Lancaster, Groton, and Still River, all established by Watertown families. Philip, like a panther, sped through New England forests to gather his men. His warriors, not fully understanding his plan, broke loose and burned settlements, killing their inhabitants. Capt. Richard Beers of Fresh Pond, Watertown's first innkeeper and active in town and colony affairs, assembled his company near Northfield. He was trapped and killed by an ambush of Indians and his head and those of his fallen comrades were placed on spikes along the roadway to create terror. Beers Mountain was named for him, and stone inscriptions mark his grave and the location of the skirmish. John Chenery of this company reached home but died the next day. His house has stood since 1654 at 52 Washington Street, Belmont.

During the following March forty Watertown men answered a call from Groton, and a detachment also went to relieve Lancaster, where William Flagg, John Ball, and George Harrington lost their lives. Lancaster was rebuilt after the war by a commission of which Capt. William Bond was a member. Bond's farm on Belmont Street was the later location of Payson Park. Sudbury was also attacked and called for help whereupon Capt. Hugh Mason rushed out with his men and drove the Wampanoags across the Sudbury River. An Indian leader, One-Eye John, threatened to burn Watertown and nearby towns but never carried out his plan.

Finally the desertions of Indians and the death of Philip allowed the colonists to gain the upper hand. After Philip's War trouble with the Indians shifted to the frontiers.

During Quaker and Indian troubles, the old disagreements with England continued. King Charles II restored the line of kings and in 1680

* Philip and his Wampanoag force (thought to be surrounded), escaped from Swansea at the end of July and moved to the Connecticut Valley. The Colonial authorities, believing that the Narragansetts were harboring Philip and many of his men at their great fortified village in a swamp near Kingston, Rhode Island, attacked the fort in a December snowstorm, using the combined forces of the United Colonies (Massachusetts Bay, Plymouth, and Connecticut). This latter battle is the one Hodges describes. Colonial losses were heavy, and many Narragansetts escaped to reinforce Philip in central Massachusetts.

King Philip, or Metacomet, from an engraving by Paul Revere.

demanded the return of the colony's charter. For the first time all assistants were present at the Massachusetts General Court to vote on the matter. Watertown instructed her two representatives to refuse compliance. The charter was actually terminated four years later when a hated royal commissioner took over the province. When the King died the following year, hope of regaining the charter was revived. In May 1689 another town vote on the matter requested an increase in the number of representatives:

The inhabitants do empower their representatives to act in their behalf always provided that the charter rights be maintained . . . and that the number of freemen may be enlarged further than have been the custom of this colony formerly.

Rev. John Bailey, 1686-1690.

The town called John Bailey, a forceful young Boston minister, and he accepted on condition that the parish make him comfortable by being peaceful. After the reception for the new minister, eighty-four-year-old Deacon Henry Bright broke several ribs. In his diary Judge Samuel Sewall records that the deacon, "carrying home chairs, etc., used at Mr. Bailey's is hurt by his cart, none seeing, so that he dies" two days later. A new parsonage, thereafter known as the Bailey House, was built at the corner of Mill Road and Arlington Street. Mr. Bailey began the "Bailey Book," which was continued by his successors and is now printed in the Watertown town records. In it Pastor Bailey recorded 361 baptisms, indicating more than one child born to a family as an average in his seven-year pastorate. He joined 39 couples in marriage and accepted 117 persons into church membership. A good man, Bailey said that he wished not to "live without love, speak without feeling, and act without life." His assistant, his brother Thomas, died while still young. Thomas's marker in the old burying ground bears the inscription, "Here lies the precious dust of Thomas Bailey, a painful preacher, a tender husband, a faithful friend, a cheerful dier . . . [who] lived much in a little time."

A Boston minister, Henry Gibbs, served briefly as a helper to Bailey, whose spirits were often low and whose health was poor, due to his having been incarcerated in an Irish prison because of his seditious preaching. In 1692, without giving a reason, Bailey left Watertown and returned to Boston. His wife is buried in the old graveyard.

7

New Trends

N THE FIRST HALF of the eighteenth century, important changes were taking place in the colonies. There were border wars with the Indians, allies of the French, as the French claimed Canada and the vast stretches west of the English coastal provinces. Watertown contributed both money and men to help England and when the fighting ceased, England repaid this expense to the Massachusetts Bay Colony whereupon a brief period of prosperity ensued.

While the French-Indian Wars lasted, however, times were bad. The scarcity of money fostered the bartering of goods so that a householder wishing to buy dishes might pay for them with a length of home-spun cloth. More goods were exported to the Bay Colony from England than vice versa, leaving a trade balance to be paid in silver. The General Court issued paper certificates which were to be redeemed in silver coin at a later time; still more paper money in large quantities was printed until it came to be worth only one third of its face value when exchanged for silver, and silver coins almost disappeared. Seth Storer, the town pastor in the 1750s, agreed to a cut in his salary from 180 to 66 pounds.*

Caleb Church owned the old mill and a lodging-house at the bridge. His business was assessed 140 pounds to pay the minister. In 1686 it was enlarged into a fulling mill to cleanse and shrink cloth by means of hot water and pressure. He kept the inn for a quarter century, then sold it to Thomas Learned in 1712, after which it was run by the Learned family for nearly sixty years. An unusual event which took place at the mill was the marriage of the miller's daughter Lydia. Most of the marriages, however, were performed at the minister's house after the banns had been posted for three consecutive Sundays.

*As a result of the Louisbourg expedition, a paper money inflation raged in Massachusetts in the mid-1750s. A shipment of specie from England in payment for the province's expenditures in that campaign permitted the resumption of metallic currency, and outstanding paper money was outlawed and redeemed at a reduced rate. The record shows increases in the minister's salary and some payments in firewood to meet the falling value of money. The reduction was to bring the salary into line with the new currency.

THE BRIDGE IS REPLACED

A bridge for the passage of horse carts was constructed in 1719 at the corn mill, the fifty-year-old foot-and-horse bridge a short distance downstream having by now become too old and narrow.

Construction was entrusted to Thomas Learned and Capt. Thomas Prentice, for which they were promised 160 pounds. Although they received an additional sum from private gifts and from farmers at the West End, they were losers by 125 pounds. Watertown Street was laid out soon afterward on the south bank.

Watertown was at the crossroads of traffic then as it is today, and a great deal of traffic crossed the river here carrying men and goods from the coastal towns to the settlements upstream. Watertown not only paid for and maintained the bridge, but also benefited by being a center for trade and industry. Besides the fishing resources, there was easy access for transportation and for trade. Because the responsibility for building and repair was assigned to Watertown, the Court finally relinquished claim to the bridge.

A CHANGING SCENE

Upriver towns reported to the Court that Watertown was stopping fish from going upstream beyond the rapids. Part of the catch was salted down in barrels and shipped south to be used in soup for slaves. A new corn mill was put into operation on Stony Brook to serve the farmers in the western part of town. They were already meeting to transact their own affairs, and they were now freed from support of the schools.

By 1700 the cattle business was declining and there were half as many animals as there had been in 1650. Inasmuch as milk was not pasteurized, there was a high rate of infant mortality. The community turned increasingly to sheep raising, since wool could be spun and woven in the home. Wool not needed locally could be shipped to English factories. Hogs were raised in town as well.

Wealth came largely from the ownership of land, production of foodstuffs, and illegal trade or smuggling. Merchants were experiencing a period of prosperity after the war with Canada. They shipped fish and small saddle horses to the West Indies, from which they brought back wine and sugar products, particularly molasses for making rum. They bought outlying lands and settled tenants on them but remained in comfortable houses and grew rich while their tenant farmers remained poor. They sent lumbermen into the King's Woods and shipped logs to England or used them for shipbuilding along the coast. Logging was carried on in timberland south of Mill Bridge. Logs were chained together and drawn by oxen across the new bridge. In time the chains wore the bridge planks badly, making regular repairs necessary.

The town made several appeals to the Court for more land on which to settle the younger population. The Court had promised two thousand acres of homestead land and fifteen hundred acres of meadow land. This last grant was in exchange for a piece of land six miles square, which had been taken many years earlier when Concord was laid out.

Land was increasing in value. East End people who no longer used the common land for feeding cattle, sold their share and pooled the proceeds, using it to provide a new house for their preacher and a stone wall around the graveyard. The remaining common land was sold by the town a short time afterward. The roads became narrower, for the width was not needed for herding droves of cattle. The money was used to improve the schools.

Watertown traders were located well inland and their business was conducted mainly within the colony. Vegetables from their gardens were taken by cart or river barge to Boston. Boston set aside four markets where traders were required to conduct their business. Watertown merchants protested the restriction to no avail; they were of independent mind and resented interference.

North Square in Boston was the location of one of the markets. Paul Revere, whose house was in the square and who was clerk of this market, later had the responsibility of opening and closing the market by ringing a church bell. Watertown traders may well have sent their produce to this market via the Boston Road, their carts rolling along the narrow streets of Boston on two wooden wheels.

In this period Boston had several severe outbreaks of smallpox. Cases in Watertown were often kept in isolation, and many inhabitants objected to the new practice of inoculation. Boston was crowded and, like all cities of the time, suffered from poor sanitation. Drinking water was boiled and used for tea and rum. So pervasive was the tea-drinking habit that it was blamed for the loss of teeth in young people.

The Abraham Browne house, built in 1694, prior to restoration.

Watertown inhabitants were hard workers and frowned on idleness. Some of the rich families used Indian servants but considered them unreliable, and few owned black slaves. Time for leisure reading was spent on the *Boston Newsletter* and the *Boston Gazette.* The Cambridge press published religious tracts and school texts.

SCHOOL PROBLEMS AND "SAM THE MASTER"

Mr. Norcross had taught writing, arithmetic, and Latin for thirty years, but now Watertown had difficulty in finding a schoolmaster. In 1696 the court fined the town for failing to keep a school. For five or six years discussions were held in town meetings over the relative merits of building two schools at either end of the town. Land was chosen and money was voted, but the vote was reversed, and the old schoolhouses were repaired. Lieutenant Sherman taught for a time and other masters were Harvard students named Angier, Goddard, Shattuck, Ward, Fessenden, and Livermore. Their salary remained at thirty pounds.

Following the sale of public lands by East End citizens in 1736, the teacher's pay was increased to double and more. Nathaniel Harrington, who was hired for several terms, received sixty, seventy-five, and even ninety pounds. A second master was secured as a result of recommendations from the General Court.

The most colorful of the teachers was Mr. Coolidge, commonly referred to as "Sam the Master." He was hired to teach in Watertown in 1725, just a year after receiving his Harvard College degree. He had been chaplain of a garrison on Castle Island in Boston Harbor, and had also worked at the Harvard College Library for a year. Although he was an intelligent man, he drank and was often intoxicated. Complaints came in from Charlestown, Roxbury, and Dorchester where he was found wandering, sleeping in barns, and muttering to himself in Latin. One day, soaked by the rain, he was walking through Watertown marketplace when a voice from a drugstore called out in Latin, "Master Coolidge, it has rained very hard. I don't know how hard, do you?" He seized a stone and flung it through the window breaking several bottles. Back in Latin came his reply, "I have broken a great many things. I don't know how many, do you?" Although he had a salary of thirty pounds, he was so poorly clad that on Thanksgiving Day a church collection was taken to outfit him. He was called before the selectmen to answer for his gypsy ways and promised improvement. Desperate, the selectmen threatened to put him in chains if he continued his wild behavior. He asked for a bearskin coat to be tailor fitted, and his request was granted.*

The schoolhouse of Sam the Master was the same one built in 1649 on Strawberry Hill. It was a Latin School, preparing boys for higher study. For North Side children there was a little 25 by 20 foot building built in 1709 near today's Lowell School. In 1769 a one-story schoolhouse was constructed at the corner of School and Belmont streets, giving a name to School Street and serving the East End. Four dame schools were held in private homes.

It is hard to locate the first West End school, since information about early schoolhouses is scant. Town records indicate that the taxpayers were reluctant to pay for new buildings. Pupils had long distances to walk and were often needed for work at home. Terms were short and teachers changed often. Sometimes in winter the same teacher served both ends of town for short terms. After 1766 the selectmen delegated their responsibility for maintaining schools to a school committee, which was required to report to the town annually.

THE BROWNE FAMILY

The tower of the Strawberry Hill School was used as a lookout for Indians where Capt. Abraham Browne stood guard. In 1694 Abraham Browne built the house which now stands at 562 Main Street (next to the present Browne School) on land inherited from his grandfather, the surveyor, Abraham Browne. It is the oldest house in Watertown and was occupied until 1900 by descendants of the original family. The first Abraham Browne, who had been a signer of the 1630 church covenant, was a nephew of Elder Richard Browne and had surveyed the farms and meadows, laid out the roads, and superintended their repair. His original grant of sixty acres ran west of Howard Street and south of Main Street.

After Elder Browne's death in 1650, his widow Lydia gave the eastern half of her estate near Howard Street to her son Jonathan; the west half she gave to her son Abraham. Abraham's half is described in a letter as follows:

wilderness land without any improvement or mowable ground, upon which Abraham Browne built, fenced, broke up, and lived till his death and then left it to his wife [Mary] and two children.

Mary's second husband recorded that the house on this west section was burned. Its heirs sold the land to their cousin, Capt. Abraham Browne, who, already part owner of the east half, built the Browne house which still stands on West Main Street. Only that part of his house which is farthest from the street is original. There were two rooms, a living room with a tiny winding stairway leading to a large chamber above. The seventeenth-century triple windows with their small diamond panes, the huge hand-hewn beams, and original plaster are well worth seeing. The fireplace is large enough to walk into. Another living room was added later and contains a fireplace with an enormous brick oven. Finally a third part was added on the north. When the house was restored in 1924 by the Society for

*The errant schoolmaster appears in the town records over a considerable period. He was discharged from the school and became a town charge, boarded at town expense by relatives and others. The town sought unsuccessfully to get him confined in Boston, Watertown having no place of confinement, and his keepers were authorized to chain him if necessary. The town accounts show the item "A lock for Samuel Coolidge." He reformed periodically, and after lecturing by the selectmen was restored to his position as teacher, the town retaining his wages against the amounts spent to support him. After several reforms and relapses he apparently became hopeless. He last appears in the record when the selectmen provided for his funeral and auctioned his clothes against his debt to the town.

45

the Preservation of New England Antiquities, a scrap of paper was found tucked behind a beam. Signed "B.B.," for Benjamin Browne, brother of Abraham, the note reads:

Brother, pray let sister have a little money if you can buy me three or four hundred clapboard nails pray you take care of my drink that is at Goodman Harrington's if it be not yet made, pray straighten the hoops of the barrel and get a little hot water put in it. Bespeak Goodman Harrington very hard about my beverage. Pray get my thousand bricks told out, for I am a-covering my house and much straightened for time if you can do this you will oblige me to remain your loving brother.

SOCIAL UNREST

The Jacob Caldwell house, circa 1742, is characteristic of small house design of the period incorporating the beverly jog at left.

The manners of youth in those times worried the orderly inhabitants of the neighborhood of Angier's Corner. Oakes Angier, son of the minister of the middle meetinghouse, ran one of the two taverns in a neighborhood of only a dozen homes and a store at today's Newton Corner. So disgusting were the antics said to have been at one tavern that the hamlet earned the nickname of "Hell's Corner." The villagers signed a petition to bring it under the control of Watertown but without success.

Small dwellings of this period were built close to the street, with shallow cellars, snug roofs, and a beverly jog on the outside for extra space and light.

A generation of farmers who drew their living from the soil held the West End, while moneyed families of the East End formed a more refined class. The favored folks dressed in color and lace and wore powdered wigs under their three-cornered hats. A rivalry arose between socialites and frontiersmen. All over the provinces and even in England the gap widened between farmers and the privileged merchants and clergy. Frequent clashes occurred between the Tories, who were loyal to the king, and the Whigs, who supported greater independence and fought against involuntary taxation.

Interest in religion declined. Weekday lectures became popular because they afforded people an opportunity to unbend. With the increased interest in politics, government, and individual rights, college graduates turned from studying for the ministry to legal training.

The people of Massachusetts Colony* had been forced to surrender their charter in 1684 and could no longer elect their own governor, being subject to the control of one royal governor after another. In 1691 they were granted a new charter which permitted non-church members the right to vote. A voter had to be a property owner but did not need to be a church member and this new enfranchisement ended the Puritan domination.

Greater participation in government did not lessen the people's resentment of British taxation. Their complaint was not that the taxes were excessive or that they went to England, but that the taxpayers were not represented in Parliament where the decisions were made. Communication was too slow to make their plan of representation in Parliament practical, and their requests were turned down.

With the new charter, Watertown was organized into three military precincts. The citizens underwent military drill and although discipline was poor, they became crack shots and wasted few bullets. Cannon and heavy arms were used for defense

*Under the pre-1684 Charter Massachusetts Bay and Plymouth were Colonies. Under the 1691 Charter Massachusetts Bay and Plymouth were combined and formally known as the "Province of the Massachusetts Bay."

Benj^a Brown

from the earliest times. In 1639 William Jennison had organized the Ancient and Honorable Artillery Company at Watertown (also called the Great Artillery Company of Watertown).

WATERTOWN LOSES TERRITORY

The new half century found Watertown torn by stormy meetings that divided the town and resulted in a loss of territory. With Pastor Bailey gone, a general town meeting was called in 1692 to discuss what to do, particularly where to build a new meetinghouse. The meeting broke up with no decision, but an appeal was made to the royal governor, Sir William Phipps, to appoint a committee to settle the matter. When the committee submitted its report there was opposition first from the selectmen, then from 120 farmers in the western part of the town. Another town meeting failed even to appoint a moderator. A new meetinghouse was finally constructed in the late winter of 1696 at Knowles delta (at the intersection of Orchard and Lexington streets), a location more convenient for the western farmers. It was to be used as an assembly hall for the whole town. Jonathan Phillips, who had been in trouble as a young man, was hired as sexton. He had now become a justice of the peace and had been keeper of the dog pound. So stubborn were the East End people that they refused to enter the new building and continued to use their old meetinghouse for another thirty years.

The town fathers sent several invitations to the Reverend Henry Gibbs to accept the post of minister. Son of a Boston merchant, Gibbs was a young Harvard graduate who had worked for several months as helper to Pastor Bailey. He had preached at Watertown but hesitated to accept while parish feelings were running so high. He turned down an invitation to come to the new middle church, which then called Rev. Samuel Angier. The East Enders even offered to move Mr. Gibbs's goods from Boston. He finally consented and arrived for his installation ceremony, but the East meetinghouse was found locked, its key in the possession of the selectmen, who favored the middle-church faction. Although it was a cold October afternoon the service was held outdoors.

The town was now supporting two pastors, Mr. Angier and Mr. Gibbs. The extreme western farmers were excused from paying a church tax and went ahead with plans to build their own meetinghouse. Thus at the end of the seventeenth century Watertown had three places of worship: the west, the middle, and the east, although interest in religion was declining. The western farmers were becoming more and more of an independent community and in 1713 formed the town of Weston. The new town occupied nearly one half of the territory but agreed to continue to support repairs to the bridge.*

Next, the town was officially divided into two precincts, of east and west. The Waltham farms became the West Precinct. When the formation of two separate towns was considered the clerk wrote in his records: "We humbly pray there may be no further procedure upon the order for dividing the Town into two townships."

With no cooperation from the East Enders, the middle meetinghouse fell into disrepair and was abandoned. The farmers of the West Precinct bought a meetinghouse from Newton for four hundred dollars, moved it four miles, and set it up as ordered by the General Court. After the death of Mr. Angier, they called Rev. Wareham Williams, who in his boyhood had witnessed the Indians attack his hometown of Deerfield. He saw them kill members of his family and he was taken with other captives to Canada.

At last in 1723 the East End inhabitants erected a new meetinghouse on Common Street Hill. The west church quarreled over a schoolhouse and pulled away in 1738. One of the three leaders of the movement for a separate church town was Sam Livermore. At the age of thirty-four he was already clerk, road surveyor, and constable of the West Precinct. He served as tithingman and sexton for the meetinghouse. His great-uncle, John, had built the Livermore homestead on the land which was to become the Lyman estate and, retiring to his cowpen farm on the Sudbury line, died just before Governor Belcher granted the nephew's petition for a town to be called Waltham after a town parish

*Weston and later Waltham shared in the fishery and in the expense of maintaining the bridge until 1820 when they gave up their share in the fishery and Watertown assumed the full cost of the maintenance of the bridge. The income from the fishery at that time covered the town's cost for schools.

First Parish Church silver. The mugs in the foreground were made by Jonathan Edwards and the one on the right was the gift of Rev. Henry Gibbs in 1677.

in England. The Livermore property was inherited by Sam, who married four times; Sam served Waltham for many years as selectman, treasurer, clerk, assessor, and representative. Because the west meetinghouse stood on his land, he was granted a free seat near the pulpit.

With the separation the new east building was the only meetinghouse in Watertown and took another bite from the original town, which had shrunk to one sixth of its original size. Residents who attended church in Cambridge petitioned the Court successfully to add their part to Cambridge. In another hundred years, the same action formed Belmont on the north. The town was left at its present size of four and one half square miles, about three miles long and one mile wide. Prospect Hill, in the center of the early settlement, was now in Waltham.

The colonists had survived Indian wars and religious persecutions. Now came the madness of the witchcraft trials. However, there was little excitement in Watertown. A child died in the Jennison

home apparently from a natural cause, but blame for its death was placed by a woman of low character upon a woman known as "Goody Kendall." Goody was tried and judged guilty. Of the Salem madness, Mr. Gibbs left in his diary the note:

May 31st [1692] *I spent this day in Salem village to attend examination of criminals and observed remarkable passages there in. Wonder'd at what I saw but how to judge I am at a loss.*

A few months after the new meetinghouse on the hill was finished, Pastor Gibbs died and was buried in the Arlington Street Cemetery. He left one hundred pounds to Harvard College and his "silver bowl with the leg" to the Watertown church. Later, when his widow died, the town furnished the mourners with gloves and wine,* as it had done for the funeral of the widow of Pastor Sherman, plus a black burial cloth for the occasion, as was the custom.

*Footnote page 49.

48

Watertown had celebrated its one hundredth birthday. Many of the founders are buried in the old Arlington Street graveyard. In it are the graves of John and Mary Coolidge, the American heads of the family from which President Coolidge was descended. As the years passed, among those buried were ancestors of Presidents John and John Quincy Adams, of James A. Garfield, and of Franklin D. Roosevelt. Forebears of Presidents Pierce and Taft also lived in Watertown.

New Trends

*Rum and wine were considered so essential at funerals that it was the regular practice of the selectmen to vote money for them at the funerals of paupers buried at town expense. The selectmen observed on one such occasion that four gallons of wine, also sugar and spices were to be provided, "so the said Bless may have a decent funeral, all at the Town's expense and charge." Another time six shillings were voted for a coffin, eight shillings for rum (at a shilling a quart). Abuse of liquor at funerals became so serious that the General Court in 1742 passed a law regulating the cost of funerals, and forbidding the serving of wine, rum, or spirits, the fine to be fifty pounds (approximately a minister's annual salary). Liquor was no longer provided for funerals until the law lapsed in the 1770s, when the cheerful manner of celebrating the rites of passage was resumed, at least in the case of ministers.

49

Years of Turmoil

1750/1800

The death of Dr. Joseph Warren as depicted in John Trumbull's famous "Battle of Bunker Hill." Courtesy Museum of Fine Arts, Boston /Fund, Estate of Joseph Warren.

8

Away With British Taxes

THE REVEREND Seth Storer came to Watertown at the age of twenty-one, having graduated from Harvard three years earlier. He stayed for half a century. His family home was in Maine, where his father had been a colonel in the French and Indian Wars, and his sister Mary had been taken as captive by Indians to Canada. Shortly he moved into a new house next to the new meeting-house on Common Street Hill. Storer's benign countenance shines still from his portrait in the First Parish Church. Border wars with Canadian Indians and the French caused such a drain on the town's financial resources in 1750 that the town was forced to cut Mr. Storer's salary by two thirds.*

THE MEETINGHOUSE PROBLEM AGAIN

Thirty years later in 1754, the town was again torn by dissension concerning the location of their place of worship. The meetinghouse on the hill was inconvenient for inhabitants who lived near the river; the vote to relocate it nearer the center was passed by a majority of only three votes in the face of stiff opposition from the residents in the northern part of the town. A rich rum dealer, Nathaniel Harris, donated a parcel of land for the purpose at the present location of the Common Street Cemetery.

The town clerk recorded the event:

At a general Town meeting of freeholders and other inhabitants of Watertown qualified to vote in this Town on the 20th of February 1754: Voted that the public meeting-house belonging to this Town be removed from the place where it now stands on School-House Hill to the half acre of land lately given by Nathaniel Harris, Es- *quire, to the Town and that the said house be anew erected there and that sash windows be put into the house in lieu of the windows now in it. This vote passed in the affirmative by three odds. Voted and chose the gentlemen which gave the security to the Town, viz. Josiah Convers, Esq., David Baldwin, Daniel Whitney, Jonathan Bemis, John Brown, Edward Harrington, and Mr. John Hunt, to be the committee for the ends above-said.*

The volunteers immediately set about moving the building in spite of February weather and frozen ground. Convers Francis related what happened: "The old house was accordingly taken down and materials transported to the destined spot, to be set up; but before the work could be completed, the building in its unfinished state was burnt to the ground." The suspicion of foul play

*See note on inflation of money, page 43.

53

Rev. Seth Storer, pastor, 1724-1774, from a portrait by John Smibert.

was directed at various persons, but the culprits were not identified. Pastor Storer invited the Sunday assemblies to meet temporarily at his house on the hill.

The voters came together again in May 1754 to choose a representative to the General Court, "at the place where the meeting-house was burnt," and after electing John Hunt they adjourned to the inn of Mrs. Mary Learned for their unfinished business. They also voted to petition the General Court for "part of Cambridge with part of Newton as an equivalent for what is taken from Watertown for Cambridge" and charged Mr. Hunt, Dr. Josiah Convers, and Capt. John Brown to present the case to the General Court.

The selectmen soon met again, this time at Coolidge's Tavern to prepare for another town meeting:

to know the mind of the Town whether they will come into any measures to procure a convenient place for the in-

habitants of the Town to assemble in, for the public worship of God. So as to ease the Rev. Mr. Storer of meeting in his house. For the Town to manifest their mind, what steps are proper to be taken under the present awful frown of heaven against the Town, that the Divine anger may be removed and the Divine blessing obtained, and the peace of the Town promoted.

Feelings ran so high that a day of fasting and prayer was declared.

Mr. Josiah Convers was moderator of the meeting held to make the final decision on the location of the meetinghouse, and the rancor reflected in the speeches of the north siders echoed down the years:

The great disadvantage we are under by reason of the conduct of a party who dwell on the southerly part of the Town who in order to drive on their schemes in regard to the pulling down and removing the meeting-house, denied a number of persons who were possessed of some of the best estates in the Town from putting in their votes in the most important affair that ever came before a town, and thereby denied them the just rights of English subjects. . . . They pushed on their vote in an illegal manner. Said party proceeded immediately to the pulling or rather breaking down the meeting-house. All such proceedings reflect dishonour on the wisdom of the Great and General Court who were pleased to interpose in fixing the meeting-house more than 30 years since. It is easy to observe how they style themselves Town as if all their votes had the sanction of Town orders. It is well known that those who are opposed to the removal of the meeting-house are owners of much the greater part of the ratable estate in the Town. Therefore we do now give our protest against our paying any part of the cost that is proposed to be raised.

The objectors sought to place the cost of a new building on those men who had guaranteed to move the old one. The meeting finally authorized three hundred pounds to erect a new place of worship on the donated lot and charged a committee including Cpl. Edward Harrington and Capt. Jonathan Browne to carry out the plan. The committee salvaged such materials as they could from the fire and hired an out-of-town company to do the job.

When complete the building stood fifty-six by fifty-two feet with a fourteen-foot-square steeple at the west end. A fourteen-foot-square porch at the east end gave access to the gallery. The main en-

54

trance was on Mt. Auburn Street. The meeting-house contained a circular platform for the presiding officers, and a sounding board over the pulpit projected the preacher's voice. A bell hung in the tower at the Common Street end of the meetinghouse and was used to call the people to arms and to notify them of important events such as funerals. On the spire of this white tower a cock weather vane, believed to have been made in the Revere shop in Boston, glistened in the sunlight. This weather vane is now in the DAR museum in Washington. To the east of the building were sheds for quartering horses and carriages during meet-

ings. Between the sheds and the meetinghouse was the graveyard, surrounded by a stone wall. The town carriage which bore the dead from their homes to the church for burial was kept in a special house.

This meetinghouse, which became famous in the colonists' struggle against British taxation, was the last one built by the town. A commemorative stone listing the names of the last three town pastors stands at the corner of the present Common Street Cemetery. In the cemetery granite posts locate the corners of the building.

THE STAMP TAX

Town patriots united to protect their liberties against King George III and his Parliament. Smugglers of sugar and molasses from the West Indies had eluded customs duties for a long time. George III was determined to put a stop to the disobedience of colonists to the crown and decided to tax various commodities, including tea, by levying a stamp tax.

The imposition of the tax through the sale of stamps precipitated a Stamp Congress at New York. The colonists did not soften their attitude when England refunded the expense for the French and Indian War. Young men banded together in secret clubs called Sons of Liberty and Committees of Correspondence sprang up to send out messages; Paul Revere was a rider for the express from Boston to Philadelphia.

Watertown aligned itself with Boston and other towns in sending messages to its representative, Lt. Daniel Whitney. In January 1768 the following instructions were given to him:

We, your constituents, charge you, sir, as our representative, be upon your guard against measures disrespectful to the best of sovereigns or undutiful to our Mother Country, but join in all measures in ascertaining our charter privileges and for obtaining relief of those grievances which threaten us with impending ruin.

Mr. Whitney helped to word the resolutions:

The Town of Watertown being alarmed at the late imposition on the colonies . . . have considered with pleasure the . . . resolutions many towns have come into for . . . the encouragement of their own manufactures, do also cheer-

fully and unanimously vote that we are ready to join in any patriotic endeavours to . . . prevent our gold and silver from giving us the slip. That we consent to lay aside all foreign teas . . . and whilst by a manly influence we expect our women to make this sacrifice to the good of their country, we hereby declare we shall highly honour the encouragement of our own manufactures, this being in our judgement at this time a necessary means (under God) of rendering us a happy and a free people. [Likewise these gentlemen] who used to regale themselves with the best of liquors have determined to drink only cider and small beer for the future.

Again in the next September a meeting was called

to consider what is proper to be done in the present melancholy circumstances of this province in particular as well as America in general, especially to hear the late resolves of the town of Boston and to choose a committee to join with such other towns as think proper to be done in the present state of affairs.

Here we note that for the first time America was regarded as their country.

The colonists quit their husking bees and frolics to settle down to home manufactures and home-brewed tea. They boycotted British goods. King George's tax impositions were met with violence, the resistance orchestrated by Samuel Adams, a Boston Whig. Stamps were destroyed, tax collectors were insulted; a Harvard College building was burned; and the governor's house was looted. British redcoats from Halifax were stationed in Boston. On March 5, 1770, the "lobster backs" were

The Hunt house, built prior to 1768 by John Hunt, was later known as the Broad Tavern.

heckled until they opened fire in self-defense, and five British soldiers were killed and six wounded at the King Street riot, since known as the Boston Massacre.

Many Whigs in England sympathized with American sentiment, and many Tories in America favored obedience to the crown. As it happened, on that same day when the first blood was shed the English repealed the taxes on all British goods except tea and the garrison was withdrawn. The tax on tea had been an unsuccessful attempt to trick the colonists into obedience.

Indignation meetings were held in New England towns during the winter of 1772-73. After a circular letter from the Boston Committee of Correspondence called them to a meeting, Watertown men responded thus:

Resolved that it is the opinion of the Town that the State of Rights of the colonists in general and of this province in particular, as men, as Christians, and as subjects, are by the town of Boston very properly stated. . . . When we take a view of the numerous instances wherein our constitutional rights and charter privileges are invaded and violently taken from us, and the many particulars wherein we are cruelly oppressed—we are filled with fearful apprehensions that there is a design formed to enslave us, that the plan seems to be carrying into execution with great rapidity.

THE BOSTON TEA PARTY

In 1773 a quantity of surplus tea was shipped by the British East India Company to America to be sold, and three of the ships sailed into Boston Harbor. On December 16, the last day for them to remain in port, Governor Hutchinson finally decided to refuse them permission to leave with their cargo still unloaded. That evening Sons of Liberty by the dozens, dressed as Indians and with painted faces, climbed aboard the ships and dumped the cases of tea into the waters of Boston Harbor.

Three of the young men were from Watertown: Capt. Samuel Barnard; Lt. Phineas Stearns; and John Randall, a civilian.

Paul Revere and Joseph Palmer were also Liberty Boys. They sang "Rally Mohawks, bring out your axes / and tell King George we'll pay no taxes / on his foreign tea." In Betsy Hunt's diary she wrote:

[I was] *sitting rocking the baby* [in Boston] *when I heard the gate and door open. Supposing it my husband returning from club, I opened the parlor door, and there stood three Indians. I screamed and would have fainted out of fright, had I not recognized my husband's voice, "Don't be frightened, Betsy, it is I. We have only been making a little salt water tea."*

Later Betsy added:

Soon after this [the Boston Tea Party], *Secretary Fluker* [secretary to the governor] *called upon my husband and said to him, "Joe you are so obnoxious to the British government that you had better leave town. You can take your personal property but none of your goods." Accordingly we left town and went to live in part of my father's house in Watertown.*

Joseph had two warehouses near the Boston wharfs, and he packed several trunks with merchandise to go with his household goods, wife, and child. On the next day his warehouses were looted and burned down by the king's soldiers.

Less than three weeks after the Tea Party, Watertown drew up a warrant and at town meeting voted unanimously in a long resolution to discourage by every means the sale and use of tea, to withold licenses from any innkeepers who used it, and especially to oppose the distribution of East India tea,

taking into consideration the distressed situation of this province as well as the other British American colonies,

thereby denying us an exclusive right to tax ourselves. . . . The public distress is greatly increased by the late act of Parliament impowering the East India Company to export their teas to America subject to duties upon its being landed.

The voters upheld the action of Bostonians in disposing of the tea and put the blame on the port officials and the governor,

dreading the slavery with which we seem to be threatened and being true friends to liberty to which we have an undoubted right, we would exert ourselves to the utmost of our power.

"Ma'am Coolidge's" Tavern, built between 1740 and 1742 by William Williams, shipbuilder.

Phineas Stearns

9

The Tax Revolt

TWO DAYS after Christmas in 1773 the Watertown selectmen issued a town meeting warrant

for the Town to take into consideration the many evils and difficulties this province in particular, as well as America in general, labour under by the importation of teas into this province subject to duties laid on same by an act of Parliament, and to see if the Town can come into some measures to discourage importation and at last to come into some resolutions that may prevent the trade and consumption of that article within the Town of Watertown until such time as the duty shall be taken off the same.

A week later, on January 3, 1774, the Whig citizens gathered at the meetinghouse here and voted a number of resolutions. The document read in part:

Taking into consideration the distressed situation of this province as well as the other British American colonies occasioned by the British Parliament's claiming a right to tax the colonies and bind them in all cases whatsoever—thereby denying us an exclusive right to tax ourselves and disposing of our own properties and have actually levied a tax upon the colonies by imposing heavy duties on sundry articles imported by the colonies for the express purpose of raising a revenue to the Crown, and the injurious application of the revenues so unjustly extorted from us (viz) for the support of civil government and defraying the charges of the administration of justice—the bad effects whereof are already felt in this colony by rendering one branch of the legislative court entirely independent of the other for its support, and the aspect is no less threatening with respect to the executive part of the government, having a tendency (as we apprehend) of sapping and finally overthrowing our civil constitution of government and introducing an arbitrary one. The public distress is greatly increased by the late act of Parliament impowering the East India Company to export their teas to America subject to duties upon its being landed—and the proceedings of said company in consequence of said act in shipping a very large quantity for the colonists, a large quantity whereof hath lately arrived in Boston Harbor, whereby the inhabitants of Boston and the neighbouring towns have been greatly alarmed, which has occasioned the inhabitants of Boston and the neighbouring towns to assemble and consult how the fatal consequences of landing and vending said teas might be prevented, and we are fully of opinion that the people had a right thus to meet and consult for their common safety . . . And we would be glad to be joined by all our brethren on the continent (in like tribulation) in this laudable attempt, for this purpose we resolve: 1st to endeavour to discourage and as far as it lies in our power prevent the importation or bringing of tea into this province by the East India Company OR ANY OTHERS, AND ACCORDINGLY DECLARE THAT FOR THE FUTURE WE WILL NOT PURCHASE ANY TEA NOR SUFFER IT TO BE USED IN OUR FAMILIES.

William Bond

In England the action taken by the colonists caused grave consequences. Parliament passed the Port Act, and by June 1 the port of Boston had been closed and General Gage had been installed as military governor.

The Tax Revolt

WATERTOWN PREPARES FOR ACTION

The summer of 1774 was busy with talk and preparation against possible British action. Each month brought notice of a town meeting, and the selectmen purchased ammunition and flints. The sum of twenty pounds was voted to pay for this powder from the money families paid for pews in the meetinghouse. A secret place for storing ammunition was found in the meetinghouse, probably under the pulpit.

Officers with military rank such as Ens. John Stratton, Capt. Sam Barnard, and Col. William Bond, were given instructions to train not only the militia but all citizens for two hours each week during the three autumn months. They were ordered to report the names of all who could be instantly ready when called and to supply them with arms and ammunition. A vote was taken to prepare the two Watertown cannon. Each piece of ordnance was to be mounted with a wooden frame on two large wheels and to be made ready for firing. The sixteen cannon which had been kept at Richardson's Tavern were now useless.

Governor General Gage having disbanded the Massachusetts General Court, men from Watertown and six other towns of Middlesex County met at Concord on August 30 to consider appropriate action. Watertown authorized its five selectmen to attend this meeting to discuss ways in which the charter rights of the colony might be preserved. The selectmen were to be paid for their time and expenses.

The outcome of the county meeting was that a congress for the Massachusetts Province would meet at Salem on October 5. A common cause now united the men of the province. Watertown's representatives to the congress were Capt. Jonathan Browne, John Remington, and Samuel Fisk. The tax collectors were directed to pay no more money into the provincial treasury and were promised protection. The Province sent four delegates to Philadelphia for a congress of twelve colonies in September. Resolutions were voted by both congresses and were confirmed by the Watertown voters. Nine men were charged with carrying out the resolutions.

In November 1774, while the townspeople were involved in the resistance to British authority, their beloved pastor, the Reverend Seth Storer, died. Storer had served the town and the people long and well. For three years no one was found to take his place, and therefore preaching was done by visiting clergymen.

In 1775 Betsy Hunt Palmer wrote in her diary:

At my father's house at Watertown, on the 1st of March 1775, my second child Mary was born. When Dr. Spring brought her to me, he said, "Here is the prettiest creature which was ever born into the world." And truly she was a beautiful child, and never cried at all.

The baby was the future Mrs. Royal Tyler. When she was an old lady she wrote *Grandmother Tyler's Book*, describing the events of her life.

Dr. Marshall Spring was active in the Tory cause. Nearly his whole life was spent in Watertown. After graduating from Harvard College he had taught for one year in Watertown; he was liked and respected by his pupils and later, as a doctor, by his patients. Medicine, like law, was learned in apprenticeship to a professional man. Marshall Spring presumably learned medicine under the tutelage of his uncle, Dr. Josiah Convers, who lived in Watertown. In spite of his Tory sympathies, he was popular with the people of Watertown.

On April 5 General Gage disguised two of his men as Yankee workmen and sent them to look for the Watertown cannon. One was twenty-two-year-old Pvt. John Howe, and the other was Col. Francis Smith, a stout, slow man who later commanded the redcoats at the Battles of Lexington and Concord. Early on the morning of the fifth they set out carrying walking sticks and arrived at a Watertown tavern in time for breakfast.

"Where could we find employment?" asked the colonel of a tavern maid.

"Smith," she shot back into his face, "you'll find employment enough for you and all Gage's men in a few months."

The officer, plainly ruffled, complained to the innkeeper about the girl's rudeness, but the landlord replied that she had only recently come from Boston, where she had learned to recognize many British soldiers. Smith swore to bring out his regiment and have the wench shot. He returned to Boston, promising Howe promotion if he would finish the trip alone. The British never found the cannon, which the townspeople had hidden in a barn.

Concord was now under suspicion, for the Congress of Massachusetts province was in session there. Governor Gage had set a price on the heads of Samuel Adams and John Hancock. The British regulars sang:

As for their king, John Hancock.
And Adams, if they're taken,
Their heads for signs shall hang on high
Upon that hill called Beacon.

THE FATEFUL DAY, APRIL 18

On the night of Tuesday, April 18, the countryside was aroused by news that the British were sending an expedition to seize the powder stored at Concord. At midnight Abraham Whitney, thirty-nine years old, mounted his horse at the family homestead where Concord Road (now Lexington Street) joined the Post Road. His horse's panniers were loaded with shoes which his brother wanted delivered in Lynn early the next morning. On his way through Charlestown a man halted him, saying, "Do you know the regulars are landing?" With the training and alertness of a minuteman and Son of Liberty, Whitney threw off his load, wheeled around, and galloped for home, where he had left his four children and their stepmother. On the way he gave the alarm, "The regulars have landed. Assemble on the church green at sunrise."

The next morning the militiamen of Captain Barnard's company gathered at the meetinghouse. During that same night Paul Revere had carried the news by way of Medford, while William Dawes spurred his horse along the south bank of the Charles River with the same message. On Wednesday morning the Newton men marched with their leader, Michael Jackson, in haste to Watertown, where they found Colonel Gardner and his Middlesex regiment readying for action. Jackson declared that the time for shooting had come and that in order to cut off the British he and his men would take the shortest route to get a shot at the enemy. One hundred and thirty-nine Watertown militiamen under Captain Barnard joined with Jackson's men as both companies entered Lexington, sniping at the "lobster backs" who were now in retreat along the road back through Arlington and Cambridge to Charlestown. For this action they received the praise of Dr. Joseph Warren, head of the Provincial Assembly.*

First to appear with his gun on that day was a twenty-year-old volunteer, Leonard Bond. Nineteen-year-old Nathaniel Bemis shouldered a musket marked with his father's name, David Bemis, and the date, January 1775. He is said to have shot a retreating British officer and captured his sword, which the family kept as a memento for many years. Many of the families were represented by more than one family member, for example, the three Sangers and the six Whitneys.

*These were militia, as the Watertown Town Meeting had voted not to form a company of minutemen. One hundred thirty-nine men were paid for two days' service and their mileage, and were issued rum and biscuits. There is some mystery about the action of the Watertown men that day. Joseph Coolidge, the only Watertown man killed, did not accompany the Watertown militia, but went as guide to the Natick company which he found at the center seeking guidance to the scene of action. His name is not on the list of militia who were paid for turning out that day. General Heath, in his account of the day, says that he arrived in Watertown about eleven in the morning and found a militia company (not necessarily the Watertown men) at the center awaiting orders. He sent them to Cambridge to tear up the bridge there and take a position on the Boston side of it to prevent the British from retreating by that road. Since the British actually took the Charlestown road, these men would have seen no action. A speaker at the centennial celebration in 1875 spoke of the remarkable fact that there was not a single tradition of participation by anyone but Joseph Coolidge. Some of his listeners must have known some of the veterans of 1775, and many of their children, and indeed have been their children and grand-children, yet his comment apparently did not bring forth any reminiscences.

Of 134 militiamen and volunteers from Watertown, only one, Joseph Coolidge, lost his life. When the call to arms came to the Coolidge house on Grove Street, Coolidge left his plow, shouldered his gun, and volunteered to guide a Natick company to Lexington. Since Coolidge was one of the town's tax collectors, his wife buried his tax records for safety. His children, Joshua, Joseph, John, Marcy, Elizabeth, Eunice, and Lucy, did not see their father alive again. Beside his body was found a primitive musket; someone had stolen his own fine gun. His descendants honored him by erecting a seventeen-foot shaft over his grave in the old graveyard at the intersection of Arlington and Mt. Auburn streets.

During all of that exciting Wednesday men with firearms, many of whom were in shirtsleeves, were on the march. Dr. Spring, Tory though he was, worked long and hard among the dozens of wounded patriots. School buildings were taken over for storing war supplies. John Draper later submitted to the town his baker's bill for furnishing bread to the soldiers, and the widow Dorothy Coolidge served rum from her tavern at the bridge. Both were paid by the town the next year.

Betsy Hunt Palmer wrote of the day of April 19 in her diary:

My father Hunt was now an invalid and lived in the house with us. He had had, some time before, a turn of bleeding at the nose until he was nearly dead, and of which he never recovered. My mother was also there. My husband was quarter-master general and my father Palmer was a member of the Committee of Safety. On the night of the 18th of April, I heard the drum beat; I waked Mr. Palmer and said, "My dear, I hear the drum." He was out of bed with the rapidity of a bullet from a gun, while he was dressing, his father entered and said, "My son, we must ride. I have received an express message. Three men lie dead at Lexington." My husband was off in an instant. I entreated the old gentleman not to go, but he would not stay. He told me that there would probably be another brigade along soon and that I had better remove out of the way. They had their horses saddled and their pistols loaded in the barn, for they expected some sudden alarm. They were gone immediately. I never saw anything of them until the next night at ten o'clock. In the meantime, I sent my father and mother with my horse and chaise to a Mr. Gibbs' in Newton. Afterwards I took my children and went to the home of Mr. Pidgeon in another part of Newton,

The Coolidge homestead on Grove Street.

and there I took possession of his premises, which were vacant. [The story is continued by her daughter, Mary:] *The family, alarmed at the rumors flying about, had fled farther back into the country, leaving their doors open, as was customary then. By this time the country was aroused. Men with guns in their hands were running in all directions, and some officers who were trying to organize them a little called upon us and urged us to have something cooked for the poor fellows who should survive this day. They would return, probably wounded and hungry, for there had been no time to provide for them, such had been the hasty movements of our treacherous foe. Accordingly I, knowing well the sentiments of Mr. Pidgeon and his wife, hung over the large kitchen fire a five-pail kettle we found there, and, going into the cellar, found barrels of excellent pork and beef and vegetables of all kinds that the season afforded, with which we filled our kettle and set it boiling, and well it was we did so, for long before night, the poor fellows began to return in a dreadful plight, hungry and dirty and weary, some so exhausted as to lie down on the floor and around the door, unable to stand. From them I learned, after they were refreshed a little that the day had been a dreadful one; many brave fellows dead or dying, "but we beat the rascals and have driven them back to Boston."*

Daughter Mary reported more details of her mother's story:

My mother and her friend spent the day, while the kettle was boiling, scraping lint. They received messages almost

Samuel Adams

hourly from the battle-field, and solicitations for more lint and bandages, for which they tore up garments, table cloth, towels, etc., anything my Grandmother Hunt's ample stores provided. Nothing was withheld which was called for, nor were their house or stores more free than those of all the country round. John [a servant] went back and forth continually all that day with the chaise between Newton and Watertown, carrying and bringing messages from Grandfather Hunt, who, being one of the Committee of Safety, was able to keep the ladies informed as well as anyone could of the progress of events; while my grandmother and her unmarried daughters, Catherine, Ruth, and Sally, were themselves also employed in acts of hospitality and mercy to officers and men who were constantly passing and repassing through that eventful day, when, by British orders, the first blood was shed in battle between those who were brother Christians and ought to love each other.

At the Pidgeon house, darkness had come.

Here, [wrote Betsy,] I waited anxiously for the return of my husband and his father. I had begun to despair when they galloped up to the house. They had ridden all day, and my husband had completely ruined a beautiful horse he had given me as a bridal present, called Rising Sun. It was never good for anything afterwards. They rode up to the door, scarcely able to sit their horses and quite unable to dismount *without assistance, which was cheerfully given by several of those who had already rested and partaken of our beef and pork. Two of them helped my father [father-in-law] from his horse, who begged them to lay him on the floor before the fire for his limbs were so cramped he could not stand. He was so exhausted as to be unable to speak or move, and it was many hours, under the most judicious treatment, before he showed any encouraging signs of animation. Nor was my husband so much better off. They had both been in the saddle from daylight till then, riding all the time, especially my husband who was aide to his father.*

A regiment of retreating redcoats found their way back through Watertown.* One of them was passing near the house of Lydia Warren Barnard where a crowd had gathered. As local folklore has it, Mrs. Barnard seized his horse's bridle and commanded him to dismount. He pleaded that he had done no shooting, but on opening his cartridge box she found several cartridges missing. She threatened him with his own sword till he fell on his knees and begged for his life. The story is told that bystanders took the captive to a tavern for safe keeping, and his horse was turned loose.

The war with England was on. The colony, with its coastline from Martha's Vineyard to Nova Scotia, was ready to fight.

THE MASSACHUSETTS PROVINCIAL CONGRESS

The Massachusetts Provincial Congress moved to Watertown from Concord. On the Saturday following the battle the Provincial Congress was granted a permit to use the Watertown meeting-house, and here it resumed the session which had been adjourned in Concord. The representatives met and approved the recruiting of thirty thousand men. They instructed the Committee of Safety to requisition private horses and wagons, the bills for which were to be submitted to the Committee of Supplies.

At the Common Street Cemetery these words are carved in granite:

Here stood the meeting-house in which met the Provincial Congress from April 22 to July 19, 1775. The Great and General Court or Assembly was organized and held its sessions from July 19, 1775 to Nov. 9, 1776.

Watertown was the seat of government for this colony for a year and a half during these eventful times.

A popular Boston physician, Dr. Joseph Warren, was elected president of the assembly. He succeeded John Hancock, who with Sam Adams had gone to Philadelphia, where both men took their places as elected representatives of Massachusetts in the Continental Congress. On Sunday the twenty-third the assembly called for recruits. Dr. Warren issued a proclamation, which read in part:

In Congress at Watertown. Gentleman, the barbarous murders of our innocent brethren on Wednesday the 19th

---

*All accounts state that the line of retreat of the British was along Massachusetts Avenue until the neighborhood of Porter Square was reached. Watertown at that time did reach to Fresh Pond, about a mile from Massachusetts Avenue and it is possible that stragglers may have come that far from the main body, but hardly a regiment.

Portion of town warrant in 1777 listing Dorothy Coolidge's reimbursement for services rendered during the battle of Lexington.

instant, has made it absolutely necessary that we immediately raise an army to defend our wives and our children from the butchering hands of an inhuman soldiery. . . . Our all is at stake; death and destruction are the certain consequences of delay; every moment is infinitely precious; an hour lost may deluge our country in blood. . . . We beg that you will hasten by all possible means, the enlistment of men to form the army, and send them forward to headquarters at Cambridge.

In May Colonel Easton brought the news to Watertown that some New England recruits had captured two forts on Lake Champlain. Two hundred British cannon were captured and some of them would be moved down to join the Cambridge army.

PAUL REVERE AT WATERTOWN

Paul Revere was wanted for arrest, and so he stayed out of Boston after the Lexington affair. In May he slipped a letter past the sentries directing his wife to pack what she could into a horse-drawn cart and take the six children to Watertown by way of Boston Neck. The oldest son, Paul, a youth of sixteen, remained behind to run his father's silver shop.

Rooms were found for the family at John Cooke's house, which stood at the present intersection of Watertown and California streets. Its location is marked by a stone inscribed: "Paul Revere, in a house standing on this lot, made the colonial notes ordered by the Provincial Congress of 1775." The Reveres lived there for nearly a year. The elder Revere was a skilled engraver and silversmith. Many of his copper engravings accompanied the family. Newly engraved plates were used to print money to meet the expenses of the war. He printed 100,000 pounds in Colony notes which the British called "cardboard money." In four-pound denominations,* it guaranteed a loan for two years at the interest rate of 6 percent. Revere was paid fifty pounds for his work. He worked at printing the currency all night, helped by young John Cooke. The Assembly directed him to keep the plates under military guard day and night. An expert horseman as well as a clever craftsman, Paul Revere performed many services for the province of Massachusetts.

---

*He was later ordered to print notes in smaller denominations and eventually printed several hundred thousand pounds' worth. This was the first time in twenty-five years that paper money had been legal tender in Massachusetts, and the issue defied an act of Parliament.

63

Watercolor of the John Cooke house, better known as the Paul Revere house because of the latter's residency during 1775.

OTHER REFUGEES

Revere's friend Benjamin Edes was a printer, and it was at his house that the Tea Party boys had assumed their Indian disguises. Edes left his business in Boston one June night and escaped to Watertown, bringing type and a printing press in a boat up the Charles River. In a room in the Cooke house where the Reveres were boarding, he published the *Boston Gazette,* the date of the first edition being June 5, 1775. Later he moved his business to a shop in the Watertown marketplace. The *Boston Gazette* was read widely throughout the colonies and Edes became official printer for the Provincial Congress. Ink for the *Gazette* had to be imported from England, and there were only three mills in the colony from which paper could be obtained. The masthead carried a picture of Liberty sitting beside a cage, from which she has released a bird. Her spear is topped with a liberty cap. The news published in the *Boston Gazette* consisted of correspondence, public notices, and advertisements: "Good stabling for horses and best of English hay to be had of George Feecham near Watertown Bridge"; "Committee of Donations for the town of Boston are notified that their meeting stands adjourned to Wednesday 24 Jun. 1775 at 12 o'clock at Widow Coolidge's tavern in Watertown near the Great Bridge."

Many Whigs left their Boston homes to seek refuge in Watertown, since this crossroads town had many taverns and inns. In 1775 there were approximately one hundred dwellings with an average of seven persons living in each, hence room could be made for newcomers. Few Tories lived here; in fact, most Tories from the area were fleeing to Boston for the protection of the British soldiers. They took what supplies they could carry, for in Boston they would have to be satisfied with a frugal diet of salt meat and fish.

64

"Hennery" Knox, a plump, jolly bookseller, was among the refugees to arrive in Watertown. In his Boston shop he had sold books on military subjects to British officers. In his spare time he read everything he could find about the workings of cannon, and he learned enough to be made colonel of artillery without ever having seen active duty. The British, puzzled about how he found out so much about their plans, did not know that he planned to marry Lucy, daughter of General Gage's secretary, and was able to obtain information through her efforts. Lucy accompanied her new husband to Watertown and, bravely hiding his sword in the folds of her ample skirt, eluded the guards. They found room at the Cooke house on Watertown Street.

Dr. Joseph Warren stayed with the Hunts while in Watertown and shared a room with Elbridge Gerry, another member of the Committee of Safety, who later became governor of Massachusetts. While at the Hunts' he fell in love with their beautiful daughter Katy, Betsy's sister.

Dr. Warren and his Committee of Safety worked late into the nights on plans for supplying an army at Cambridge. The flicker of their candlelight in an upper room at the Hunt house could be seen by neighbor women who worked late preparing food for the soldiers.

While the Assembly was in session at the meetinghouse, it rented space from nearby householders in their dwellings for the use of its committees. Particularly adaptable for this purpose was the Edmund Fowle house, consisting of four rooms on the first floor and an unfinished garret above. The Assembly commissioned Captain Browne, Captain Dix, and Major Fuller to lay a floor in the large upper room and furnish it with seats for committee meetings. The floorboards, seventeen to nineteen inches wide, are still in use today.

The house was set a little way back from Mt. Auburn Street. Its location is marked by a granite slab, on which are inscribed these words: "Here the Honorable Council met while the Assembly sat in the meeting-house near by, 1775-1776." Beyond the Fowles' house, garden, and orchard a farmstead stretched northward to a brook and included Whitney Hill. In our time the house is standing at 26-28 Marshall Street, having been moved in 1876 from Mt. Auburn Street by a later owner, Charles Brigham. Marshall Street took its name

from Marshall Spring Fowle, grandson of the builder and namesake of the beloved doctor. Marshall lived here in the 1800s and was the last of the family to own the house. He is reported to have been married in his own parlor and never to have slept away from home.

The Fowle house is now owned by the Watertown Historical Society. In it are the original staircase, fireplace materials, and window casings. A "borning room" was where the baby slept. A tablet on the house reads:

During the British occupation of Boston, the seat of government of Massachusetts Bay Colony was in Watertown. Here committees of the second and third Provincial Congress met from April 22, 1775 to July 19, 1775, and the Executive Council from July 19, 1775 to Sept. 18, 1776.

Another tablet reads:

In this house met the council of the Great and General Court of the province of Massachusetts Bay Colony of New England July 1775-Nov. 1776. Members of the council—John Hancock, Samuel Adams, John Adams, Robert Treat Paine, Thomas Cushing, Benjamin Lincoln, John Winthrop, Moses Gill, Dr. Samuel Holton, James Bowdoin and others.

In the summer of 1775 James Warren, a rich merchant and an assembly representative from Plymouth, came to stay in the home of the Fowle family. He wrote to a friend in Philadelphia, "Everyone either eats, drinks, or sleeps in this house." The house must have been a beehive of activity.

On June 12 assembly members gathered at the meetinghouse to hear a proclamation from General Gage declaring martial law for the whole province and advising the people to keep order and to suppress all rebels. The assembly immediately disobeyed the governor, voting money for the support of the soldiers at Fort Ticonderoga and weapons for the Cambridge militia. The Committee of Supplies received 1,065 pieces, and Watertown became a kind of arsenal. A fast day was declared to pray for the success of the Philadelphia congress and for the unity of the colonies. The Harvard College Library was removed from Cambridge for safety. The Assembly supplied the soldiers with rum from Watertown and advised them to attend

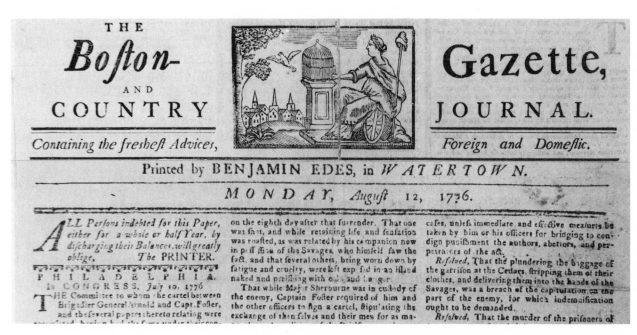

Masthead of "The Boston Gazette" in 1776 when it was printed in Watertown.

public worship and not to swear. In June 1775 the assembly issued an excellent record of the events leading to the rebellion and sent numerous letters to the other colonies.

DEATH OF DR. WARREN

In mid-June Yankee defenses were constructed on Charlestown Heights commanding a view of Boston. On June 17 the British set out to capture the fortification. Betsy Hunt Palmer, who was still staying in Newton, told the story:

I used to go down to Watertown every day, and on the 16 June I met General Warren for the last time. He had been our family physician, and I am sure, next to my husband, I liked him better than anybody. He was a handsome man and wore a tie wig; he had a fine colour in his face and light blue eyes. He dined with us and, while at dinner, said to me, "Come my little girl, drink a glass of wine with me for the last time, for I am going on the Hill tomorrow and I shall never come off."

According to Elbridge Gerry, the doctor occupied himself until late that night with his medical records. His sleep was spoiled by a nervous headache. He had resisted the decision to fortify Charlestown, but the assembly council had overruled him. After a dawn breakfast he took leave of the Hunts, asking the women to prepare lint and bandages "for the poor fellows will want them before night." When he had ridden slowly as far as the bridge, he turned his horse around and galloped back up Galen Street to bid them farewell once more. Although president of the Assembly, he did not appear at the meetinghouse that day. At the army's Cambridge headquarters he rested briefly and on waking set off for Bunker Hill, now a newly appointed major general. When General Putnam offered to turn the command of the battlefield over to him, he replied, "I am here only as a volunteer; tell me where the onset will be most furious." Dressed in his best clothes, he was neat as always but careless of his own safety. When leaving the battle at the end of the fight, the doctor came face to face with a British officer, who greeted him and then shot him through the head. A famous painting by John Trumbull commemorates the death of Dr. Warren at the Battle of Bunker Hill.

James Otis, a brilliant leader of the Whigs who was said to have become mildly insane from a blow on his head, was living with his brother-in-law James Warren. Sensing the excitement, he slipped away, borrowed a gun at a farmhouse, and took part in the fighting, returning late that night unharmed but exhausted.

Saturday, the day of the battle, had dawned blistering hot. Cannonfire burst from British vessels and set Charlestown on fire. The smoke from the burning of three hundred dwellings was carried away from the battlefield by an east wind. In spite of having little powder, the soldiers bravely sang the tune of "Yankee Doodle" with the words, "Father and I went down to camp along with Captain Gooding / There we saw the men and boys as thick as hasty pudding."

On the third British attack the Yankees' powder gave out. To cover the retreat of those who held the defenses, the Watertown company of forty-one men was called into action under the leadership of the innkeeper, Capt. Abner Crafts, who had been their drillmaster at the West School. Their regimental leader, Gardner, received a mortal wound while fighting bravely; his command was taken over by Lt. William Bond. Isaac Baldwin of Watertown also gave his life on that day.

Betsy wrote in her diary:

The next day I rose very early and could distinctly hear the cannon on Bunker's Hill and see the smoke of burning Charlestown. I hastened to Watertown to learn the news. General Warren's servant met me in front of our house, and seeing my horses, he said as the tears ran down his cheeks, *"Ah, Missee, Missee! The devils have killed my master."*

Warren's body was hastily buried on the battlefield with a farmer's body. Later it was identified by Paul Revere, who recognized a gold spring he had furnished Warren to hold a false front tooth. The doctor was deeply mourned; General Gage said that his life was worth the lives of five hundred other Yankees. On April 19 Dr. Warren had raised the alarm and had also taken part in the Lexington fight, where a bullet had grazed his head, cutting off a curl of hair. The Assembly now elected James Warren to succeed Dr. Warren as president. James Warren was not, as some have supposed, a brother of Joseph's.

Although news of the Battle of Bunker Hill took several days to reach Philadelphia, on June 17 the Continental Congress had designated the Cambridge militia as part of the Continental army. The Middlesex regiment with its Watertown company commanded by Lt. Bond then became the Continental 25th Regiment. Congress voted Col. George Washington commander in chief and General Washington set out for Cambridge to take command a week later. The Assembly sent Mr. Moses Gill and Dr. Benjamin Church to greet him in Springfield and escort him to Cambridge. No one suspected at the time that Dr. Church was a British spy.

GENERAL WASHINGTON ARRIVES IN WATERTOWN

On General Washington's arrival in Watertown early on Sunday morning, July 2, the town received him with enthusiasm. Accompanied by his aides, Lee and Schuyler, and a troop of light horse, he was escorted to the Coolidge Tavern at the bridge. There in a public dining room with a view across the river to the marketplace, widow Coolidge set her famous hot johnnycakes before the guests. General Washington was captivated by the widow's twenty-one-year-old daughter, Mary.

The tavern stood at the site of the present trolley terminal where Water and Galen streets meet. A gavel was made from the wood of the old Coolidge Tavern and still exists in the collection of the Historical Society. The tavern was built by a shipwright named William Williams and was purchased by Jonas Coolidge, a brother of the schoolmaster, Sam Coolidge. Eventually it was owned by his grandnephew, Nathaniel, Jr., who left it to his widow when he died in 1770. British officers often patronized the Coolidge Tavern where in the taproom they enjoyed "flip," a concoction of rum mixed with spices and water and served steaming hot. In the winter of 1775-76 the members of the Massachusetts Assembly met in the tavern while the meetinghouse was being prepared for them.

From the Coolidge Tavern, General Washington proceeded to the meetinghouse where the Assembly had gathered to greet him. He mounted the stone steps, and when he entered the main room the Honorable James Warren made the speech of welcome.

"To his excellency George Washington, Esquire, general and commander of the Continental Army," Warren declared, pleased at the opportunity to greet the general and welcome him to Watertown. He apologized for the tattered army of men of whom General Washington was to take command but wished him success in his present undertaking. In reply the general addressed his hearers by speaking briefly of the hurried formation of an army: "Whatever deficiencies there may be, will, I doubt not, soon be made up by the activity and zeal of officers, and the docility and obedience of the men." Both speakers called for divine help in their endeavors; then shouting townspeople thronged around the meetinghouse and cheered Washington.

From Watertown, Washington's company with its impedimenta proceeded to the Cambridge camp where they finally arrived at the headquarters which had been prepared for the new general. On the following day General Washington took formal command. It was now his difficult task to organize the motley, undisciplined troops. They had thirty-two barrels of powder, no uniforms, and were rude and unruly. "And there was Captain Washington with grand folks all about him," they chanted to the tune of "Yankee Doodle." "They say he's grown so tarn-ed proud, he cannot ride without them." A Virginian and a man of property, Washington was expected to entertain at parties in his headquarters, while at the same time as general he had to plan and prepare a nine-mile arc of artillery with which he hoped to besiege Boston and drive out the British army.

THE NEW COURT

Soon after General Washington arrived the Provincial Congress was dissolved. In its place, on July 19, they elected the Great and General Court in Watertown. Its structure was patterned on the old charter which provided for the election of a council of twenty-eight men who would assume the duties of the governor. This structure remained in effect until a new state constitution took effect in 1780.

The new Court continued to meet in Watertown until November 1776 when it moved to the Boston State House. Watertown's representative in the General Court was Capt. Jonathan Browne, who had now been elected to all three provincial congresses in Salem, Cambridge, and Concord, and in 1775 in Watertown. Captain Browne, the great-great-grandson of Abraham Browne, served as town clerk for thirty years, from 1760 to 1791, and also as treasurer, assessor, and justice of the peace.

While sitting in Watertown throughout the years 1775 and 1776 the General Court provided for the relief of refugees from Boston and cared for the wounded. It collected weapons and ships to defend the coast and served as the government of the colony. The women of Watertown molded bullets, spun yarn, and wove cloth to make soldiers' clothing. Metal was stripped from windows and melted down for use as bullets. All available space in homes and stores was put to military use.

DR. BENJAMIN CHURCH, SPY

Several large mansions in Cambridge had been vacated by Tories, many of whom left everything and fled to Canada. Their houses, including Elmwood, later home of the poet James Russell Lowell, were used for an army hospital. Dr. Benjamin Church was surgeon general, and the Henry Vassal mansion, opposite Washington's headquarters on Brattle Street, served as his headquarters and hospital.

In the fall a letter signed "B. Church" was found when a woman spy with whom he was living "an immoral and dissipated life" was searched. Printed in the *Boston Gazette* at Watertown, the letter was read by an astonished public. Here is part of it:

I hope this will reach you. Three attempts have I made without success. The last, the man was discovered in attempting his escape, but fortunately my letter was sewed in the waist-band of his breeches. . . I wish you would write me largely in cyphers . . . to be delivered to me at Watertown. Make use of every precaution or I perish.

Benjamin Church had escorted the Commander from Springfield, and his grandfather had fought the Indians.

A military court was held under the commander, and this trusted patriot was exposed as having been a British spy for ten years.*

He was imprisoned at his own headquarters, and today one may see his initials "B.C." carved into a door in the Vassall house. His punishment was to be determined by the Assembly. On November 7 General Gates took Church in an open carriage to Watertown under guard of twenty men accompanied by a fife and drum corps. The galleries in the meetinghouse were jammed with spectators and below them sat the Assembly. All listened to Dr. Church's plea of innocence. Looking around at his accusers, he declared that not one of them was more loyal to the patriot cause than he. "The warmest bosom here," he stoutly claimed, "does not flame with a brighter zeal for the security, happiness, and liberty of America." His eloquent self-defense caused him to be pitied in spite of the evidence. Abigail Adams, however, reflected, "You may as well bind a hungry tiger with a cobweb."

Church, convicted as a traitor, was deprived of his membership in the Assembly and was sent to a Connecticut jail where he was confined and forbidden pen, ink, and paper. His eloquence in both speech and writing the English language must have been a considerable threat, for he was allowed to speak only in English and within the hearing of an official. Because of illness, the next year he petitioned the Assembly, was released on bond of a thousand pounds, and declared on oath he would not leave the colony. He was later transported to exile in the West Indies. Nothing was ever heard of the ship on which he took passage.

Dr. Church was succeeded by Dr. John Morgan, who as the new surgeon-general made this appeal in the *Gazette*:

To the Public–General Hospital at Cambridge, Jan. 3, 1776. An appeal from John Morgan, chief physician to the army. Returns thanks . . . for gifts of old linen . . . thread, needles, and pins, and would further like old sheets . . . Blankets are greatly needed for the hospitals for which a suitable price will be given.

The year 1775 ended with the arrival of George Washington's wife from Mount Vernon. Her journey was slow as her party had to travel over rough roads worsened by bad weather. Frequent stops were necessary for rest and a change of horses. The cavalcade went by way of the old Boston Post Road (now Main Street in Watertown), one of the most traveled highways in New England. Again the population turned out at noon on December 11 to see Martha Washington. In the vanguard rode a mounted escort, followed by a gilded coach once the property of the exiled Governor Hutchinson and drawn by four horses with tossing plumes, attended by black postillions in scarlet-and-white liveries. Tradition says that Mrs. Washington took tea at the Fowle House with Mercy Warren, but since contemporary accounts make no mention of this incident, the story is probably apocryphal.

The record does show that Mrs. Washington joined her husband at three in the afternoon at his headquarters, now known as the Longfellow house, where he was awaiting her with midday dinner. During that winter she gave and was entertained at many parties, several times coming with the general to Watertown homes.* Washington had been accused of neglecting sociability to concentrate on military planning, and his wife was able to remedy this situation.

Another event soon crowded the Watertown meetinghouse. March 5, 1776, was the sixth anniversary of the King Street Riot (the Boston Massacre). The Watertown celebrators showed their warm approval of that day's oration delivered by a Malden clergyman, who blamed the British for stationing regiments on police duty in a country still at peace. His speech was published by the printer Edes. Prayer was offered by Dr. Samuel Cooper, a refugee who often filled the Watertown pulpit, no pastor having been secured to replace Seth Storer. Dr. Cooper is said to have preached in a loud and sonorous voice in favor of the patriotic cause. An excellent horseman, he was said to show more concern for his animal than for his wife.

---

*The court dealt only with the letter. While various people including Paul Revere suspected Church, the full evidence of his treachery was revealed only when General Gages' correspondence was examined years later.

*Mrs. Washington arrived at Cambridge on December 11 in a modest carriage with two escorts. Mrs. John Adams wrote her husband on November 27 that Colonel Warren was at his farm in Plymouth and would not return to Watertown for a month. Presumably Mrs. Warren was with him.

A Adams

Mercy Otis Warren, 1728-1814, from the painting by John Singleton Copley. Courtesy Museum of Fine Arts, Boston/Fund, Bequest of Winslow Warren.

Meanwhile, the jolly expert on artillery, Gen. Henry Knox, was carrying on an enormous enterprise as he conducted the most unusual procession ever to pass through Watertown. Teams of oxen inched their way toward Cambridge over snow-covered paths or muddy tracks in New York and western Massachusetts. When they reached Watertown they passed along Mt. Auburn Street goaded by the staves of their drivers and dragging fifty-nine cannon captured from the enemy at Fort Ticonderoga. A commemorative tablet in front of the present East Branch Library records the event:

Through this place passed General Henry Knox in the winter of 1775-1776 to deliver to General George Washington at Cambridge the train of artillery from Fort Ticonderoga, used to force the British army to evacuate Boston.

These cannon helped to tighten the noose around Boston. Commander Washington stealthily prepared equipment and militia, hoping to capture Dorchester Heights before the British could secure that last vantage point. Among his reinforcements were 102 Watertown men, including Lt. Edward Harrington; Sgts. Josiah Capen, Jr., and Nathaniel Bright; and Nathaniel Coolidge as clerk. Capt. Phineas Stearns, a Tea Party boy who had fought in the French and Indian War, commanded 95 men. He had subsequently been offered a commission as colonel but declined and resigned from the army to return to his family.

On a March night about two thousand men carrying trench tools and accompanied by wagons and cannon loaded on oxcarts threw up wooden defenses on the Heights. Cannon fire was used to cover the noise of their frenzied preparations. At daybreak the British were completely surprised. "That old fox," as they called General Washington, had trapped them; their days in Boston were numbered. A terrible storm delayed their departure until March 17, now observed as Evacuation Day and also as St. Patrick's Day in Boston.

The British fleet sailed away, carrying both redcoats and Tory sympathizers. Any hope of being reconciled with England was now abandoned. The Massachusetts Assembly submitted to its member townspeople a resolution for independence. At their meetinghouse on May 20, Watertown voters discussed a resolution:

relating to the Congress of the 13 united colonies declaring them independent of Great Britain. The question was put to know the mind of the Town whether they will stand by and defend the same with their lives and estates, and it passed in the affirmative unanimously.

Only a few weeks intervened until the Declaration of Independence was made public in Philadelphia on July 4, Independence Day. A sign in front of Coolidge Tavern on which was painted the visage of King George III was taken down, and on its replacement was painted the likeness of another, Gen. George Washington.

Among the eager patriots at Philadelphia was Elbridge Gerry, who had fallen in love with Catherine Hunt, the illiterate sister of Betsy Hunt Palmer. Gerry had faithfully kept his promise to write to her during his long months of absence but received no replies, for Kate was ashamed to admit her ignorance. He returned to see her twice and continued to write more letters, but not receiving any answers, he stopped writing. Eventually an announcement appeared in the newspapers of his marriage to another Catherine, a Miss Thompson of New York. Katy never did marry, though she was a brilliant and charming woman. After the war she renewed her friendship with the Gerrys, who were then living at Elmwood in Cambridge, and she took her niece, Mary, Betsy's little daughter, to work there as a nursemaid. Years later Catherine Thompson became first lady of Massachusetts when Gerry became governor. Governor Gerry gave his name to Gerry's Landing near the present Eliot Bridge in Cambridge as well as to the word "gerrymander."

The British now carried the war from Boston to the Hudson River area, and in March Lt. William Bond's regiment was sent up Lake George toward Canada. His son Henry and Lt. Edward Harrington also took part in this expedition. When a remnant of their unit returned to Fort Ticonderoga, desperately ill with camp sickness, the two elder men died and were buried opposite the fort. The *Boston Gazette* carried this notice: "On 31st ult. [August 1776] departed this life Col. William Bond. He met the last enemy with great calmness and intrepidity. In his death, our country has lost a rare patriot, and a most vigilant officer of tried bravery." Burial took place before his regiment marked by the discharge of three 24-pound cannon and with volleys of muskets. He was the grandfather of Dr. Henry Bond, author of a book on Watertown genealogy, and a descendant of William Bond, who had been appointed captain of the East Precinct when the town was divided into military precincts in 1692.

A meeting held in Watertown during the summer dealt with plans for recruiting:

To agree upon some proper method for raising Watertown's part of 5,000 men ordered for the defense of this country, and to grant a sum of money to forward the affair. Voted sum of 6 pounds 6 shillings 8 pence to each person that shall enlist into the service for the Town for the present service till Watertown's proportion is complete.

At the conclusion of the Hudson River campaign, General Burgoyne's army surrendered to the Americans at Saratoga, New York. None of the soldiers was allowed to return to England. They were quartered in Somerville and Cambridge. Officers were sent to Boston and Cambridge to be quartered, a very unpopular move. Watertown's meeting declared that "The quartering of British officers among the inhabitants at this time is very dangerous to the peace and safety of the Town . . . and therefore we cannot give our consent thereto." Several, however, were housed at the Richardson Tavern.

Watertown sent 302 men into the war. Among them was Capt. John Fowle, who fought valiantly and efficiently under General Lafayette in Virginia. To the end of his life he complained of the low pay he received for his service. Long war records are recorded for Asa Stearns and for Capt. William Bemis, Capt. Christopher Grant, and Capt. Samuel Bowman. Bowman was captain of the guards who led Maj. John Andre to the gallows. On each side of the culprit walked Thomas and Ephraim Hunt, brothers of Betsy Hunt Palmer. David Cutting, another Watertown soldier, was burned to death in a barn where he lay with a broken leg.

The end of the war with Britain left the country with hard and far from peaceful times. Before the war ended an epidemic of smallpox raged in Boston, and again refugees found shelter in Watertown.

During three of the war years after the Reverend Seth Storer died, the preaching was done by visiting ministers. Finally the youthful Daniel Adams was secured to be town pastor. He had a good singing voice and was popular, especially with young people, but he died prematurely. His successor was Rev. Richard Rosewell Eliot, a descendant of the John Eliot who had been missionary to the Nonantum Indians. The schools reopened in October 1775, and by 1776 the school system was divided into three districts. Two or three persons were made responsible in each district for making repairs with money allotted to them for the purpose by the town.

The east schoolhouse was located at the corner of Belmont and School streets; the west schoolhouse stood on Howard Street, then only a roadway leading to the river. John Stratton, the master, taught in both schools. For the middle district a one-story "Brick School" was constructed in 1798 on Mt. Auburn Street near the market. At last the old schoolhouse on Common Street Hill was abandoned and the building was sold. It was the first school built by the town in 1649 and was used for more than 150 years. In more remote parts of town four or five dame schools for small children were still being operated. On the South Side such a class was held in the home of Capt. Abner Crafts.

The town endorsed the new government of Massachusetts, the articles for a new national government, and the payment of its soldiers. By 1779 inflation had caused prices to soar, and the town attempted to control the economy by publishing a list of fixed prices for goods and labor. For a day's work a man could earn sixty shillings. Candles cost eight shillings a pound and milk two shillings a quart. Shippers charged eighteen pounds, fifteen shillings to carry a boatload of goods between Watertown and Boston; those who charged more were "cryed" by the clerk at town meetings for six months. In the next year the pound was devalued and Watertown accepted a new currency which made seventy-five dollars in old paper money equal to one silver dollar. To raise money for the repair of the bridge, a town lottery was tried but failed.

GEORGE WASHINGTON RETURNS

On October 17, 1789, the town once again welcomed the leader of the new nation, "His Highness, the President-General of the United States." Washington traveled to Boston by carriage from the new capital, New York City, accompanied by secretaries and servants. Upon arriving in Watertown he changed his traveling suit of brown cloth to a military uniform. As the procession continued handkerchiefs fluttered from local windows, and Watertown's war veterans lined up before the meetinghouse. Bells rang and cannon boomed. All of the local town militia marched to Boston Neck via the South Road. There they engaged in rivalry for priority with the Massachusetts State Militia.

On November 5 Washington came back to Watertown from Boston, following nearly the same route taken by the patriots returning from the Battle of Lexington in April 1775. He came without escort to the Coolidge Tavern for a rest. The daughters of local families, in order to obtain a close-up view of the President, arranged to serve his supper in relays in the public dining room.

Learning that Mary Coolidge, whom he had enjoyed meeting on a previous occasion, was ill, the President drew up his horse in front of her house facing the marketplace. Now Mrs. William Hunt, Mary appeared at an upper window overlooking the elm-shaded garden and graciously received the President's salute.*

*In his diary the General wrote that he had never had worse entertainment; he complained about the food, untidy servants, and buggy beds.

Years of Industrial Growth

1800/1900

INTERIOR VIEW OF THE UNITED STATES ARSENAL, AT WATERTOWN, MASS.

BOSTON, SATURDAY, JANUARY 5, 1856.

10

The New Freedom

ATERTOWN entered the nineteenth century happy with the new American freedom, its population about two thousand. The people were learning to produce their own goods instead of importing them, with manufacturing and cattle raising being two of the chief occupations. Several men made money, built fine houses, and enjoyed their newfound leisure.

The new government carried heavy debts. Merchants had difficulty obtaining credit, but in spite of hard times a few citizens in the East End started a subscription library by pledging to purchase shares at three dollars apiece. This money bought the first sixty books, which were to be loaned to the shareholders for a fee, with which more books could then be acquired. A room in Bird's Tavern at the junction of Mt. Auburn and Belmont streets, formerly Richardson's Tavern, housed the collection. The library shareholders exchanged books once a month. Founding members included persons from the Bird, Bond, Bright, Chenery, Clark, Coolidge, Livermore, Stone, and Whitney families. The Union Social Library supplied books of travel, history, animal husbandry, essays, and fiction to the town for forty years from its inception in 1779.

In the same December the town was saddened by the death of the president. The people gathered at the meetinghouse to hold a memorial service with special music composed by Mr. Babcock, the choir leader. For several weeks afterward a black man named Prince, a former servant of William Hunt's, continued to mourn in his own way by standing throughout each service, wearing a black band on a scarlet coat bedecked with the brass buttons he had worn at the Battle of Bunker Hill. Prince had served the general when Washington had been a guest at the Hunts' house.

DR. MARSHALL SPRING

When the new form of government was first proposed, the town meeting had opposed it. Among those in opposition to the new Constitution was Dr. Marshall Spring, the same Tory who had cared for veterans wounded at Lexington. Spring distrusted the ability of the common people to govern themselves, and at the state convention which approved this new document he voted against it.

For several years he served on the Governor's Council as a representative from Watertown under Governor John Hancock.

Dr. Spring made his calls on horseback. A generous man, he never exacted payment for his services from those unable to pay. On the present Gore property, there stood at that time an old building in which he inoculated people against

The Richardson Tavern, built before 1700 by Dr. Palgrave Wellington, later became Birds' Tavern.

smallpox. Because there had been a smallpox epidemic in Watertown in 1792, others now submitted to this new method of prevention. Such was the controversy surrounding the question that two special town meetings were held, with the result that inoculation was forbidden but quarantine was imposed on those who were sick.

When Jefferson was voted into the presidency, Dr. Spring changed his vote to favor the party in power, asserting that he wished to secure his real estate, and trusted in the ownership of property to protect his wealth. After his death money was found hidden under cushions in his home, and he left his son an estate worth more than two hundred thousand dollars, one of the largest bequests in Massachusetts during the century.

FINE MANSIONS ARE BUILT

Jonas White's farm on Main Street stretched northward at that time to include Whitney Hill. In 1804 Jonas White's son Abijah, who married the daughter of a Tea Party boy, built a brick mansion on this property. Abijah became rich by raising, slaughtering, and selling cattle. His herds of cattle were pastured in outlying towns, then shipped to the West Indies.

A neighbor to the west of the Whites was Nathaniel Bemis, who lived in a big dwelling at the corner of Lexington Street. He had been born in the house a year after his father, David, built it in 1765. A great elm tree on the boundary was referred to for years as the Whitney elm. John Whitney and his son John, Jr., were early emigrant settlers, smoke from the father's house could be seen over the trees from the home of John, Jr., on Lexington Street. The Whitneys cleared the land and planted fruit trees, from which came the name of Orchard Street. Their successors included Benjamin, who fought the French in 1690; John, a blacksmith; Captain Daniel; Deacon Daniel; and Abraham, a shoemaker who fought the British on April 19, 1775.

78

In 1804, the Honorable Christopher Gore returned from an assignment by President Washington which had kept him in Europe for eight years. During this absence he observed house designs abroad and made his plans to build a summer residence on the large tract he owned on the present Watertown-Waltham boundary. This land had belonged as pasturage to Pastor Phillips and Sir Richard Saltonstall and had then passed into the hands of ancestors of President Garfield. A large house on the land had burned while Mr. Gore was abroad. His new mansion was completed in 1806 and has since become famous for its beauty and architectural simplicity. It is now owned by the Society for the Preservation of New England Antiquities. The Gore house contains two oval rooms, an elaborate state reception room, a flying staircase, and a room on the top floor fitted out as a nursery. The house is furnished with antiques and contains books from Christopher Gore's library. Bricks, fireplace marble, and wood for the building were imported, and much of the material was brought upriver by barge. It is said to have cost twenty thousand dollars, a great deal of money at that time. Gore wrote,"Although built with greatest economy, it will keep me at the Bar longer than my love of indulgence would desire." Riders dismounted and coaches unloaded onto a stone platform by the two front entrances. A nearby deer park was famous for its forest trees and for a mile-long walk.

Mr. Gore was shrewd in business, honest, and proud of his wealth, but he was not popular in Watertown. His elegant coach with its uniformed attendants was considered showy. A Waltham resident was heard to say that Mr. Gore and his lady had a haughty way of sweeping down the center aisle of their meetinghouse to the governor's pew at the front. Gore was the first attorney general of Massachusetts and in 1809 became governor for one term; he was defeated for a second term by Elbridge Gerry.

Northeast from the Gore place was the widespreading land of Theodore Lyman, called The Vale. Mr. Lyman built his splendid residence a few years before the Gore mansion was erected. Lyman had become rich by fur trade in the Pacific Northwest. A Watertown settler, William Paine, had owned part of the future Lyman property as his allotment in the great divides. He sold this property

William Abijah White, 1818-1856.

to John Livermore of Watertown, who bequeathed it to a grandnephew, Capt. Sam Livermore, also of Watertown. Both John and Sam were maltmen, producing barley malt for brewing beer. Sam's son founded the town of Livermore, Maine, and sold his Waltham holdings to the Dix family. Theodore Lyman brought his family to the former Dix estate.

The West Precinct meetinghouse also stood here, and because he owned the land, the elder Lyman was entitled to a free pew in the church. His son, Theodore, bought the Gore estate on the death of its owner and lived there for five years. The mansion and grounds of The Vale have been preserved for some 150 years by the Lymans and are now on display to the public. The Vale is now owned by the Society for the Preservation of New England Antiquities.

A short time after the new White, Gore, and Lyman mansions were erected, another fine residence was built as a summer home by Harrison Gray Otis, a wealthy Boston lawyer and friend of Governor Gore. Charles Bulfinch, architect of the Boston State House, had built a city home for the

Otis family at 45 Beacon Street. The new Otis property was on Strawberry or Common Street Hill, the highest point in town, and the house was enlarged under the supervision of Bulfinch and renamed The Oakley. It featured an oval reception room and an unusually fine flying staircase. Surrounding it were forty-five acres skillfully landscaped to command distant views, including Boston to the east.

Otis, known to friends as Harry, was a charming and jovial gentleman who had a large family. As mayor of Boston for three consecutive terms, he entertained many rich and famous guests. After Otis's death in 1825 William H. Pratt purchased the mansion and took pains to preserve its former dignity. His art gallery and plant cultivation were famous; he introduced many varieties of shrubs and trees. The estate later became the Oakley Country Club, and the grounds became a golf course. The mansion burned in a spectacular fire in 1913.

"Oakley" as a name was suggested by the abundance of oak trees in the vicinity (now called Waverley Oaks). Twenty-six of them predated any American settlement, and it is said that when one of them fell it showed evidence of being eight hundred years old. In "The Oak," the poet James Russell Lowell painted a word picture:

*His boughs make music of the winter air,
Jeweled with sleet, like some cathedral front.*

The spiral staircase of the Gore mansion.

OTHER PROMINENT BUILDINGS

Richardson's Tavern, which was first built on Belmont Street by Dr. Palgrave Wellington and later moved to the junction with Mt. Auburn Street, became the Jonathan Bird Tavern about 1800. With a big addition at the front, the house had thirty guest rooms, a bar, and an upstairs ballroom. Here Jonathan's son Joseph was custodian of the Union Social Library. Joseph's six children, including Joseph, Jr., and Horace, lived here.

The Birds were singers and lovers of music. The singing school had been in existence for thirty-five years by the time Joseph and Horace became teachers there. The town appropriated one hundred dollars for expenses and also furnished candles.

The land of Capt. Moses Stone was near the tavern. A brave fighting patriot, the captain's profession was medicine, but he spent his time caring for his six thousand acres, part of it in Jay, Maine, where he encouraged settlement. His death about 1800 ended the line of Stones residing in the big house at the corner of Coolidge Avenue. Near it grew a famous pear tree, said to be 285 years old when it was cut down in 1921. A shady hill known as Stone's Woods (Mt. Auburn Cemetery) was a favorite resort for picnickers. In 1831 the Massachusetts Horticultural Society paid six thousand dollars for the land in order to create an arboretum; later it became the first garden cemetery in America, most of its grounds lying within Watertown bounds.

Next to Captain Stone's house, his cousins inhabited the original homestead of their common ancestors, Simon and Jane. These forebears were settlers whose holdings comprised the later location of Mt. Auburn Cemetery. The family burial plot is less than two hundred yards from the location of their early dwelling. Seven generations of this family line worked the land in orchards and gardens.

The Coolidge home where the grandchildren of Joseph lived stood on Grove Street in the year 1800. This was the family of his son Joshua. Coolidges also occupied the Bailey House on Mt. Auburn Street, the property including much of old Meeting-House Common. From there on to Fresh Pond and around it stretched large market gardens.

The South Side, which Thomas Mayhew had first owned, came into possession of Gregory Cooke and his heirs. The Cookes owned property to the west of Galen Street until well after 1800. One member, Stephen, had claimed all the South Side plus land beyond the Newton line. He built a gristmill on Smelt Brook, which crossed his land and ran through Boyd and Howard ponds before reaching the river. Later John Cooke lived in the house with brick ends on Watertown Street where Paul Revere had printed colonial money. John's cousin, Capt. Phineas Cooke, came to own the major part of the family inheritance, and his land, well wooded with chestnut trees, originated the name of Chestnut Street in Newton. Phineas Cooke's two daughters married Dr. Walter Hunnewell and Capt. John Fowle of Watertown. Phineas sold his land to William Hull (later a general), who built a malthouse by the river and a large dwelling called the Nonantum at Angier's Corner. Hull wanted to develop this area, now known as Newton Corner, into a thriving village but met with money troubles and was obliged to sell out to Dr. Eliakim Morse in 1805.

Dr. Morse had moved from Connecticut to Boston where he became rich manufacturing and selling drugs. His second wife was Mary Hunt, daughter of Mary Coolidge of the tavern. He lived in the Nonantum house while erecting a colonial mansion on the highest part of his land, facing Galen Street. For its impressiveness and position overlooking the valley, it was one of the finest for miles around. Morse renamed the Boston or Country Road after the Roman physician Galen. The road was widened and became an elm-shaded thoroughfare. Morse outfitted a trading vessel, also named *Galen,* which met disaster in the sea war with Britain.

The Coolidge Tavern and a wharf near the bridge were used by a lumberman, John Brigham. Nearby, on Water Street, was the house of Abraham Sanger, who ferried passengers by rowboat from his Watertown wharf to Charlestown or Boston. He loaded flat barges with various goods and poled them along with the tide. Abraham's father, David, had occupied this house, and before that his grandfather, Sam, had operated a smithy and potter's shop in the 1770s.

Sounds of hammers and saws came from boatbuilders. Some of the boats were sturdy enough for coastwise trading. The river front was alive with activity. A short distance up Galen Street was the Hunt homestead, built in 1715. Sam Hunt, a

Oakley, as rebuilt in 1808 by Charles Bulfinch as a summer home for Harrison Gray Otis.

brother of Betsy Hunt Palmer and a master of Boston Latin School, ran his father's distillery.

William, another brother of Betsy, was a housebuilder who had built a mansion on the former Oldham farm at the head of Riverside Place; the estate passed to his grandson and finally to the Perkins School.

At 77 Riverside Street the brick house of Tyler Bigelow faces the river, having four stalwart chimneys, a fireplace in every room, and a wide central hall running from front to back on the first floor. It was erected about 1800 and was of about the same age as the Gregg-Rockwell house which formerly stood at no. 50.

81

Simon Stone

The home of Capt. John Fowle stood on the present site of the Main Library, and it was to this house that he brought his bride, Mary Cooke, in 1782. Mary was descended from George Durant, who came from England to Middletown, Connecticut, in 1663. The Fowles had five children while they lived on Main Street, and later, when they had moved to 49 Mt. Auburn Street, three more. Captain Fowle served as a selectman for several terms and was active in town affairs. A trader, he declared that he was "fortunate by land and unfortunate by sea." After the Revolutionary War he became one of the charter members of the Order of the Cincinnati, an officers' benefit society.

Mary Cooke Fowle's sister Susanna also lived on Main Street with her husband Dr. Walter Hunnewell, whom she married in 1800. Hunnewell was for many years the town's only physician. Their son, Horatio Hollis Hunnewell, became a prosperous banker in the firm of Samuel Welles and married Isabella Pratt Welles. He purchased an estate in West Needham which he named "Wellesley" in

honor of his wife's family for whom also the new town of Wellesley was named in 1881. In 1898 he gave a wing to the public library in memory of his father.

Captain Fowle's brother Edmund lived in the colonial house which had served several committees of the Provincial Congress. Edmund's farm extended northward beyond Whitney Hill. One of his eight children, Rebecca, only thirteen when President Washington died, later recalled paying her respects to his memory by marching through the streets of Watertown with her friends, wearing mourning badges on her shoulders.

The elder daughters of John and Mary Fowle, Charlotte, Harriet, and Maria, became famous beauties who inspired the often-quoted toast (attributed to the poet Robert Treat Paine), "To the fair of every town, and the Fowle of Watertown!" Adeline Fowle married twice; her first husband was a wealthy banker twenty years her senior, by whom she had one child. After Samuel Welles' death she married Charles Jean Marie Felix, Mar-

Adeline, daughter of
Capt. John Fowle.

John, son of
Capt. John Fowle.

Pauline Adeline, daughter
of John Fowle, Jr.

quis de La Valette, who subsequently adopted her son. During the Civil War Adeline used her influence to ensure France's sympathy with the Union cause. At her grandson's baptism, the Emperor Napoleon III and the Empress Eugenie were god-parents. Although she lived in France for many years, Adeline cherished her family connections and remained close to her sister Eliza, who was married to Charles Smith of Boston.

Charlotte Fowle married Benjamin Wiggin, a successful banker of Boston and London. When she and her husband returned home to Boston in 1845, Mrs. Wiggin provided a home for her nephew, Henry Welles Smith, the son of her sister Harriet, considered the most intellectual of the Fowle sisters. Harriet married a lawyer, William Smith, and lived at first in Hanover, New Hampshire, where their son was born in 1822. John Fowle married Paulina Cazenove whose home was in Alexandria, Virginia. Descended from Huguenots who had left France after the revocation of the Edict of Nantes to live in Geneva, Paulina had attended a French boarding school in Philadelphia and had met Major Jack Fowle on a visit to Boston. They were married in 1831, lived in Chicago, and later at West Point. Major Fowle was killed in the explosion of a river steamboat in Cincinnati, but was survived by his wife and daughter, Pauline.

John and Mary Fowle's younger son Charles had joined the new American Navy at the age of nineteen. Inspired by his father's motto, "Never take the lie; decide it by sword or pistol," Charles responded to a challenge to duel with a British sailor in New London in 1823 and was mortally wounded. Maria Fowle married Abiathar G. Britton, a talented New Hampshire lawyer and friend of Daniel Webster.

Henry Welles Smith, the son of Harriet, married Pauline Fowle, the daughter of Paulina Cazenove and Major Jack Fowle, in 1854. Henry had been educated by his mother and his paternal aunt, who was a pupil and admirer of Mary Lyon, the founder of Mt. Holyoke Female Seminary, and by Mrs. Samuel Ripley, at whose home in Waltham he had lived for three years while attending school. Mrs. Ripley, a clergyman's wife, mother of seven, a friend of Emerson and an accomplished Greek scholar, was living proof of the intellectual as well as the social and domestic gifts of women, and made a profound impression on Henry. In later

Moses Stone, Jr., 1749-1803, from a copy of a pastel portrait.

Primitive painting of the Stone farm.

George Tyler Bigelow, Chief Justice of the Massachusetts
Supreme Court, 1860-1867.

Henry Fowle Durant, 1822-1881.

years he said, "I have seen her holding the baby, shelling peas, and listening to a recitation in Greek, all at the same moment, without dropping an accent, or particle, or boy, or peapod, or the baby." Henry Smith graduated from Harvard in 1841 at the age of nineteen, and practiced law with his father in Lowell for five years before moving to Boston, where, finding eleven other lawyers with the name of Smith, three of them Henry Smith and one other Henry W., he changed his name to Henry Fowle Durant, adopting his own and his wife's family names.

Henry and Pauline Durant were an unusual couple. Henry was extremely successful as a lawyer and won many cases with his gift for elucidation of difficult and complex cases. In the Eliot School case, Durant argued in favor of the reading of the Bible in public schools. Pauline Durant had had a deeply religious upbringing and had also the advantage of a fine education, having attended schools in New York and Paris. In the south of France she had visited her aunt Adeline, now the Marchioness de La Valette, and in Rome had become known as "la bella Americana."

The Durants had a son, Harry, and a daughter, Pauline. When the baby, Pauline, died at the age of six weeks in the fall of 1857, Mrs. Durant took refuge in her faith, but her husband found solace in re-reading Scott's Waverley novels. After Harry's death of diptheria at the age of eight, in 1863, however, Henry Durant experienced a religious conversion, and he and his wife turned their attention to carrying out God's work as they interpreted it for themselves. This led to the founding of Wellesley College in 1870.

The education of women had become necessary when the Civil War removed young men teachers from the secondary schools of the nation. The positions were filled by young women who were often pitifully unprepared for their tasks. Mount Holyoke had been founded as a female seminary in 1837 and became a college in 1893, and Vassar College accepted its first students in 1865. In 1867, Henry and Pauline Durant decided to found an institution for the education of women, to be called "Wellesley" after the estate of their neighbor and cousin, Horatio Hollis Hunnewell. Durant abandoned the practice of law, although he retained his

84

interest in his investments, and he and his wife devoted the rest of their lives to the establishment and nurturing of the college. Fired with religious zeal and with a consuming interest in poetry and Greek, Henry Fowle Durant said, "Women can do the work. I give them the chance." Durant lived only six years after the formal opening of the college in 1875, but Mrs. Durant was a guiding hand and strong supporter of Wellesley College until her death in 1917.

EARLY MANUFACTURING

The old corn mill stood for many years near the dam, but about 1800 was relocated near the bridge. On the island thus vacated, a chocolate factory was built which later became the Walter Baker Chocolate Company of Dorchester. Operation of the corn mill was moved to the rear of a building close to the river, and a cotton factory occupied first the second floor and later the whole building. Several other mills straddled the canal, manufacturing paper, dyes and medicines; three other factories manufactured soap and candles.

A mile upriver Seth Bemis manufactured cotton cloth. Seth inherited the mill from his father David, a descendant of early settlers. David Bemis had dammed the river at this point to turn millwheels on both sides of the stream. On a knoll near the mills the father built a large house where Seth and his three brothers grew up.

Seth had an inventive mind and set to work on raw cotton. Using a crude whipping frame, women and girls worked at home earning a comfortable living preparing this material for carding at four cents a pound. The raw cotton was beaten with a stick in the frame for two or three minutes to force the seeds and dirt out through the bottom. Manufacturers in the North, slow to accept the new cotton gin which had recently been invented by Eli Whitney, a descendant of Watertown settlers, now converted to Seth Bemis's ugly machine. The "devil" replaced the women's work with thousands of steel fingers.

Bemis converted his mills to manufacture combed cotton. His finer thread, called Bemis's warp, was used on hand looms in the home for weaving blankets and rugs. English weavers were imported to make cotton cloth on hand looms for the manufacture of sheets and shirts. The looms also wove bed ticking and cotton bagging for the South.

Quarrels with England cut off the importation of sailcloth to America in 1807. Winslow Lewis, a Boston merchant, took his problem to Seth Bemis. Lewis promised to market the cloth if the Bemis

Seth Bemis, 1775-1851, from a portrait by Francis Alexander.

mills could manufacture it. A Bemis workman devised a twisting machine with forty-eight spindles and success came in six months. The cloth was probably the first duck or sailcloth manufactured in America. It sold in Boston for sixty-five cents a yard and furnished the sails for the frigate *Constitution*. Bemis wagons carried the duck to Baltimore and returned filled with raw cotton and tobacco. The tobacco was powdered into snuff at the mills.

During the years of the sea war with Britain from 1812 to 1815, Watertown sent fourteen men to do coast guard duty. In the winter of 1812 Seth Bemis produced illuminating gas from burning

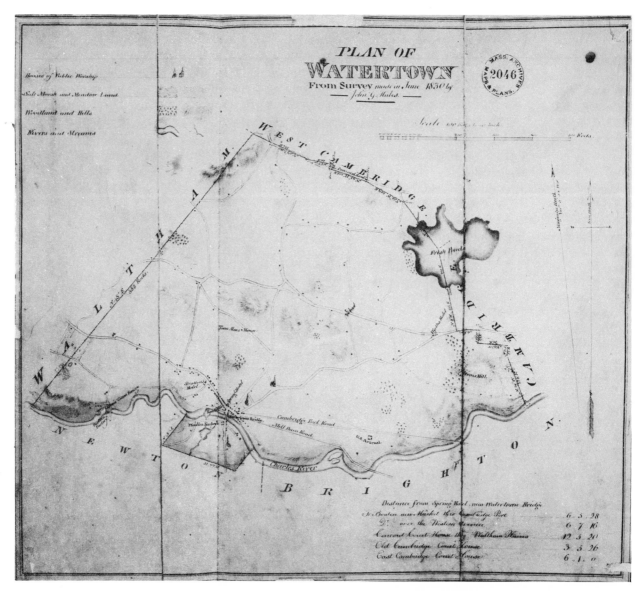

Plan of Watertown from a survey made in 1830 by John G. Hales.

coal, thus furnishing light for the mills. Although the first to use gas for lighting, the tin tubes leaked, and the use of gas in the Bemis mills ceased after a few years.

"Tin Horn" was the name given to the little settlement of workers' houses on both banks of the river near the mills, so called because a horn summoned them to work at seven on winter mornings, at five in the summer. They were called to breakfast and to noon dinner at the house of Capt. Luke Bemis, brother and partner of Seth for a time. Work ended at 7:30 P.M. and at dusk on Saturday.

Girls came from surrounding farms to work at the mills, saving their earnings for marriage. Working conditions were clean and comfortable, and those were the days of paternalism among factory owners.

In another experiment Seth Bemis laid a rolling stone dam in front of his wooden dam, a curiosity which seemed to find no imitators. He made one mistake when the Boston Manufacturing Company, located two miles above the Bemis dam in Waltham, offered him twelve thousand dollars to lower his dam twelve feet. Waltham then developed cotton and wool manufacture to such an extent that the town became a thriving industrial center and three of the old mill buildings are in use today. Because there was not sufficient power in Waltham, several mills were started in Lowell, which then became one of the world's largest manufacturers of cotton textiles.

For thirty-eight years the Reverend Richard Rosewell Eliot preached from the famous meetinghouse pulpit. He was tall and slender and dressed in the colonial style of wig and breeches. His health was delicate but his speaking voice was strong. In 1818 both Pastor Eliot and Dr. Spring

died. The widow Eliot then took in boarders, for whom she is said to have made fresh sponge cake every evening. Later she moved in with her relative, Luke Bemis, at Tin Horn.

"Began to board at Dr. Bemis' June 21st, 1819," comments the new town pastor, Convers Francis, in his diary. Dr. Bemis was a nephew of the mill owner, and his house stood near the corner of Main and Lexington streets. The newcomer fresh from Harvard College was named Convers after his mother's maiden name. This was his only parish and he was the last town pastor.

THE CURTIS BROTHERS

Meanwhile two brothers, Benjamin and George Curtis, came of school age in their grandfather Robbins's house at the northern end of the Great Bridge. Their grandfather had died leaving a large family. Their father, master of a merchant ship, having died at sea, their mother Lois earned a living by keeping a variety shop and a lending library. Mrs. Curtis was said to be beautiful and beloved by all for her kindness. Among Mrs. Curtis's customers were Dr. Eliakim Morse, Mrs. Luke Bemis, Joseph Palmer (Betsy's husband), and Nathaniel R. Whitney. (This Whitney became the new owner and occupant of the Hunt house.)

Friendly ladies from Newton patronized the shop of Lois Curtis and stopped to chat. Dr. Spring's son was among those who contributed books for the lending library. Her son Ben hungrily read these, fearing that someone would want the one he was reading before he could finish it. In this way he was able to retell to his younger brother the stories of Sir Walter Scott and Washington Irving. The books were loaned at a charge of nine cents.

The brothers learned their letters from Ma'am Gerrish, an elderly maiden lady who had taught their mother and many other Watertown children.

Ben was also taught to knit a pair of woolen mittens for himself. He was adept at putting a neat leather cover over a ball. For geography and arithmetic he went to a Newton master, and he took Latin lessons at the new parsonage and, like Henry Fowle Durant, at the Ripleys' school on Pleasant Street in Waltham. Mrs. Ripley gave lessons, knitting and rocking her baby's cradle while she listened to translations of the Latin poets, which she knew by memory.

The two Curtis brothers lived much outdoors; they loved sports and knew every cove and boulder of "dear old Charles," as George wrote in a life story of Benjamin. Their room first looked out on the river and its tumbling falls. Twice daily the salty tide flooded the banks as far as the falls, then receded, leaving marshy flats on each side of the channel. They waded into the water to catch minnows to use for bait when they went fishing for pickerel. Ben watched the use of flashboards above the dam and saw how the waterpower was controlled for the millwheels. His powers of observation later helped him in the practice of law. Sometimes he went hunting with his uncles James and Isaac. These uncles and one other, George Robbins, were selectmen several times.

THE WATERTOWN ARSENAL

The brothers must have wandered downriver and watched buildings rise for the new U.S. Arsenal about 1820. Capt. George Talcott was in command, and a Boston architect, Alexander Parris, was employed for the design. The captain had

commanded the Charlestown Arsenal when scarcely more than a dozen men worked there. After the War of 1812 the Charlestown Arsenal was needed for the exclusive use of the navy. The captain was authorized by President Madison and the

87

1817 engraving of rectangular stone magazine at the Arsenal.

Commonwealth to seek another location for the army's equipment. He sounded the depth of the Charles River for schooners and reported his chosen site in Watertown to be "well situated for supplying the forts in Boston Harbor and vicinity, and for receiving arms and equipment manufactured in Massachusetts and intended for distribution in the eastern States." The site had been used as a camping ground by fifty Indians during the British siege of Boston.

On this land in 1816 the captain erected a brick storehouse. Soon thousands of pounds of saltpeter and brimstone for ammunition arrived for storage. About 1820 a quadrangle of two-and-one-half-story buildings was erected, besides storehouses; magazines for powder; officers' quarters; barracks for enlisted men; and various shops for smiths, carpenters, and other workers. In addition to being a storehouse, the Arsenal workshops were used for minor repairs and cleaning and for manufacturing small parts for hand weapons and wooden mounts

for seacoast guns. A lumberhouse was built near the wharf. The sight of masted freighters bringing lumber from Maine forests to unload on the Arsenal shoreline became a familiar one in Watertown. The first forty acres cost the government fifty-six hundred dollars; thereafter, the value of adjacent land increased. When the government, twenty years later, wanted more space, it paid thirty-five hundred dollars to Col. Thomas Learned for his land.

About the same time the soap factory burned to the ground in a big blaze which brought out the town's two horse-drawn water tubs, manned by eighteen volunteer firefighters. Refreshments were supplied by the town.*

The same year which marked the new Arsenal and the fire also brought a new mill. It stood near

*Liquid. Some years later the town meeting voted to discontinue the practice of furnishing rum to firefighters at town expense.

the Newton boundary on Williams Street and was called the New England Lace Factory, unique in America in making lace by machine. Benjamin Fewkes, the owner, had sought to compete with existing lacemakers in Nottingham, England, in the production of pillow or handmade lace. He and his associates packed his lacemaking machine deep in salt and smuggled it to the New World. They located their factory in a brick building on the Charles. From 1820 to 1823 Fewkes employed young women from the town; later he moved his business to Ipswich.

The Curtis boys were twelve and ten years old when they saw the construction of a private school, paid for by parents who purchased shares. In other New England towns Phillips Academy, in Andover, Massachusetts, and Phillips Exeter Academy in Exeter, New Hampshire, were founded by descendants of the Reverend George Phillips. The Watertown school was known as the Academy; it faced what is now Saltonstall Park on Main Street, on a shaded rise of land called Church Hill which had belonged to James Robbins. One of its first masters was John Appleton, who later became a Maine judge.

Evening lessons with the young pastor, Convers Francis, prepared Benjamin Curtis for Harvard. Francis was now married and lived in his own house, constructed of brick at the corner of Riverside Place, a few steps from Ben Curtis's home. The same house now faces Watertown Square and retains its early features: old window casings with inside blinds, original stairway and fireplaces.

The marketplace took on a new look as masons laid bricks for a three-story hotel in 1822. The Spring Hotel stood on the site of Learned's Tavern facing the bridge; it was planned by Dr. Spring's son to induce his friend Col. Edward Richardson to remain in Watertown as an innkeeper.

A stretch of young Marshall Spring's land extended from the marketplace northward for some distance, through which a new road called Spring Street had been cut ten years earlier. Spring Street followed Treadaway Brook, starting opposite the factory of the Watertown Cotton Company at the bridge. The brook coursed through farmland belonging to the old parsonage and then through the Jonas White and Edmund Fowle properties. The brook received its water from two sources—one on the hill near the present Garfield Street, the other near Orchard Street. Another brook had its two sources at Whitney Hill and near the corner of Main and Lexington streets, then followed an easterly direction and joined the Treadaway near the Spring Hotel. The full flood passed under a planking at Main Street and entered the river at the bridge.

When Benjamin Curtis entered Harvard, Mrs. Curtis and George took up residence with him near the college. Benjamin became a lawyer and Supreme Court justice, his brother George became a lawyer in New York City, and they remained close friends all their lives.

LYDIA MARIA FRANCIS

Lydia Maria Francis was born in Medford, Massachusetts, in 1802, the daughter of Convers and Susannah Rand Francis. Her father was a baker who became famous through the production of his famous "Medford crackers." The father also of Convers Francis, who became the minister of the First Parish in Watertown, the elder Francis was a staunch foe of slavery. Convers' and Lydia Maria's paternal grandfather had fought at the Battle of Concord in 1775. Convers attended Harvard and Lydia Maria was educated at the local Dame School and Medford Academy. When her mother died, Maria (as she preferred to be called), only twelve, was sent to live with her newly married sister in

Maine; at the age of eighteen she left to teach school in Gardiner, Maine. When Convers Francis was married in 1822, he and his wife invited the twenty-year-old Maria to live with them in Watertown. The love of books formed a strong bond between brother and sister. When only fifteen, Lydia had written to Convers at college that she was "busily engaged in reading *Paradise Lost*," and complained that the author caused Eve to humble herself before Adam. Her belief in the equality of women and blacks marked Maria's life. At her brother's house, Maria plunged into writing for publication. "The writing of her first book, in a little chamber of my house," noted her brother, "I

Rev. Convers Francis, 1795-1863.

At her school in Watertown, Maria taught the older girls of the town. Martha Robbins, an aunt of Benjamin and George Curtis, also taught in the school, where French, drawing, and gentle manners prepared girls to become ladies. Boys attended the Academy. It was well into the nineteenth century before girls were allowed to attend public schools with boys, and many years before they attended schools of higher education. The girls who were taught by Katy Hunt, Ruth Wellington, and Eliza Stratton were trained in such homemaking skills as sewing and embroidery, and Maria and Martha carried on the tradition of separate education for females.

During the time she taught school in Watertown, Maria wrote in a letter,

I come home from school tired to death from nouns and verbs, and find the house empty, swept, and garnished, with not a single indication of animated existence except the cat, who sits in the window from morning till night, winking at the sun. That is to say, when the sun is to be winked at; for during the whole of this equinoctial week, the skies have looked like a tub of cold suds.

From her teaching experience Lydia Maria Francis conceived the idea of publishing a children's magazine. In 1826 the first issue of *Juvenile Miscellany* appeared, and she continued to publish and do most of the writing for the magazine after her marriage to David Child in 1828. In 1829 Lydia Maria Child published *The Frugal Housewife,* a book of shrewd household hints and cost-cutting information. An instant success, the book went into twenty editions within seven years.

Maria's deep loathing for racial prejudice led to her writing in support of Indians and against slavery in *The First Settlers of New England* and *That Class of American Called Africans.* Meanwhile, David became engrossed in the project of raising beets for the production of sugar as a substitute for sugar cane, a product of southern slave states. In 1837 he and Maria settled on a farm in Northampton. David's project, however, never succeeded, and since he stubbornly refused to undertake the job himself, Maria accepted William Lloyd Garrison's offer to edit his weekly, *The National Anti-Slavery Standard,* for a salary of $1,000 a year. She was a prolific writer for many years and was the author of the popular verse, "Over the River and Through the Wood," often quoted as a Thanksgiving poem.

shall never forget. A dear, blessed sister has she been to me; would that I had been half as good a brother." This book was an Indian tale, *Hobomok,* published in 1821. It was followed by *The Rebels, or Boston Before the Revolution.* The popularity of Maria's books secured her entrance into the literary and intellectual circles of Boston, where she became known as the "brilliant Miss Francis." Not content with her literary accomplishments, however, Maria opened a private school in Watertown.

During her stay in Watertown, Maria became acquainted with David Child, a guest of her brother's. David was a law student in the office of his uncle, Tyler Bigelow, who lived on nearby Riverside Street. Of David Maria commented, "He is the most gallant man that has lived since the 16th century and needs nothing but helmet, shield, and chain armor to make him a complete knight of chivalry." Courtship meant many delightful evenings spent together. David, however, proved incapable of earning a living, and Lydia Maria Child, as she became in 1828, spent her life attempting to support them both.

Her anti-slavery polemics and David's inability to earn a living led to hard times for the Childs, and after an unsuccessful period at a rented farm in West Newton following the failure of the Northampton experiment, they moved in with Maria's father in Wayland. There she completed a massive work, *The Progress of Religious Ideas Through Successive Ages,* a survey of the world's religions.

John Brown's raid at Harper's Ferry elicited an offer from Mrs. Child to nurse Brown when he became a prisoner. When her offer was rejected, she replied with an eloquent condemnation of the slave system which was published in the New York *Tribune* and reprinted as a pamphlet by the Anti-Slavery Society, quickly selling over three million copies. In 1860 Maria published three more pamphlets urging immediate emancipation of the slaves, and in 1865 she published *The Freedman's Book* to instruct and motivate former slaves through the writings of eminent blacks. During the 1864 Presidential election campaign, Maria wrote angrily concerning the lack of female suffrage, "To think that . . .I, who have so long and carefully watched all the springs in the machinery of the state, would be contemptuously thrust from the polls! What a burlesque on human institutions!" Mrs. Child inherited her father's farm in Wayland and lived there quietly until her death in 1880.

During her whole life Maria remained a loving and loyal wife to her husband. Once when he remarked, "I wish for your sake, dear, I were as rich as Croesus," she answered, "You are Croesus, for you are king of Lydia." Her friend the poet Whittier collected her letters into a book with the comment, "It is not too much to say that she was the most popular literary woman in the United States." Her admirer, James Russell Lowell, wrote of Maria:

*Yes, a great heart is hers, one that dares to go in
To the prison, the slave-hut, the alleys of sin,*

Lydia Maria Francis Child, 1802-1880.

*And to bring into each, or to find there, some line
Of the never completely out-trampled divine;
If her heart at high floods swamps her brain now and then,
'Tis but richer for that when the tide ebbs agen.
What a wealth could it bring to the narrow and sour,
Could they be as a Child but for one little hour!*

Watertown celebrated its two hundredth birthday in 1830. Pastor Francis' historical address celebrating the occasion was enlarged and printed as a *Historical Sketch of Watertown,* and was chiefly concerned with the history of the First Parish Church.

EARLY SCHOOLS

In 1815 a public census was taken to list all children of school age. It reported 87 at the east district, 142 at the west district, and 230 in the middle district. The largest district then became known as the "double district" and was allotted six hundred dollars a year of the twelve hundred dollars school appropriation. A second floor was added to the Brick School, and a little wooden room was added in the yard for the highest class. Rooms for dame schools were provided in Deacon Tucker's house at 72 Mt. Auburn Street and at

91

William Earl's house. Firewood for the schools was purchased and delivered by the town.

A new Coolidge School was built in the east section; it faced Mt. Auburn Street at the corner of School Lane and remained in use for many years.

The west district school on Howard Street was used until the Marshall Spring School was built. Its only neighbor was Henry Bright's house. The school consisted of a single room entered by two doors, between which were the master's desk and platform; there was a stove in front of the master's desk. A sloping floor held three tiers of double desks. The smallest pupils, seated in the front row, had no desks, and they toed parallel chalk lines. Christmas was not celebrated in the eighteenth and nineteenth centuries, and school was in session until July. The work consisted of penmanship, geography, and spelling. The children coasted on sleds down the hill behind the school, and there was rifle practice on Bacon Hill across the street. A branch railroad ran by the school; an engine roared by, interrupting class and showering soot on the pupils six times a day. Seth Bemis rode by on horseback or in his chaise, and Edward Everett lived in Dr. Spring's house nearby. As seventy children crowded the room, tiers were added and a new floor was laid in 1843. Among the pupils of the 1840s was Robert Murray, later a minister whose description of the school is in Rand Scrapbook IV.*

THE FRANCIS FAMILY AND THEODORE PARKER

Dr. Hiram Hosmer, 1798-1862.

Land adjoining the Francis home was bought by Dr. Hiram Hosmer. A Harvard classmate of David Child's, he had practiced medicine as a bachelor in Watertown. His marriage took place in the same year as that of the Childs, 1828, and he made his

family home in the spacious house next door to them at 12 Riverside Street. His daughter Harriet was born there in 1830, endowed with an artistic genius that would make her famous in America and Europe.

Convers Francis's collection of books was one of the finest private libraries in the country. On encountering a friend he often would draw a prized book from his pocket to show him. He did not enjoy preaching, being modest and self-effacing. He said he felt "shut up, that the audience had no sympathy with me," but his conversation in a social group was easy and animated. He stimulated others to express their thoughts. Among these was a group of young writers in the Boston area. Some of them, such as Ralph Waldo Emerson, often visited the Francis home: there he spent time in the study, which extended the length of the house with windows looking upon North Beacon Street (then called Market Street). Francis's house became the center for the development of liberal opinions.

One afternoon in April 1832 a young man, dressed casually and carrying a small bundle, arrived at the Francis house. When he entered the study, he looked happily around at the well-filled shelves and said:

I am told that you welcome young people, and I am come to ask if you will be kind to me and help me, for I have come to

*The scrapbooks compiled by the Reverand Edward Rand, the Episcopal minister, for the Watertown Historical Society.

Watertown to try and keep a school. I long for books, and I long to know how to study.

The young man was Theodore Parker, for whom the Parker School is named. Encouraged by the pastor, he borrowed books in German, Greek, Hebrew, and Latin. Thus commenced a long and intimate friendship.

Parker found lodging at the tavern-home of Nathaniel Broad, which then occupied the southern corner of Galen and upper Water streets. It faced the estate of Dr. Morse and the newer house of the townsman Abraham Lincoln. The Broad house had been built sixty years previously by John Hunt with an adjoining shop, which was used as a bakery in Parker's time. Over the bakery was a large unfinished room Parker used as a school. The twenty-two-year-old teacher set about making this room into a school by boarding the floor and lining the lower part of the walls with a rough wainscot. He built twelve desks, but had thirty-five scholars at the end of the first year and fifty-four in the second year. He charged by the quarter year, four dollars for elementary pupils and five dollars for the upper class. He asked the children many questions and taught them to think and to discover things for themselves. He earned the respect of his pupils and enjoyed entering into their games at recess.

Parker spent many hours in preparation for college, burning his oil lamp until late at night. Twice a week he walked to Cambridge for Hebrew lessons.

The Francis family introduced Parker to other local people. There were the Whites of the Elms, their cousins the Thaxters, and the Bigelows. Sometimes he walked along Common Street to North Watertown to visit his uncle, Peter Clarke. Peter's father had built the house in 1760, and the family had listened to and watched the British retreat from Lexington from a vantage point in their yard.

Lydia Cabot also boarded at the Broads'. Parker became leader of the church school and walked home with Lydia. Lydia's manner was different from Parker's impulsive one; he appreciated her understanding companionship. When they became engaged Parker wrote, "I love my books the more, my school the more, mankind the more, and even God the more, for loving you." He gathered outdoor specimens for his pupils with zest. Four years of study and waiting passed before he obtained a parish and the couple could be married.

He jokingly said that he would be so sparing of expense as to save ink by not crossing his *t*'s or dotting his *i*'s. At the end of his second year of teaching in Watertown, he had saved enough money for college. Parker entered Harvard in 1830.

On Parker's last day in his little school young Briggs delivered a farewell speech and presented him with a silver cup from the school. This was too much for Parker, and he bolted out the door in embarrassment. On graduation from Harvard, Parker preached his first sermon in the Watertown meetinghouse. Theodore Parker became a leader in the two great movements of the mid-1800s, abolitionism and liberal Protestantism.

Parker had been born in Lexington in 1810. His grandfather, Capt. John Parker, had lined up a

Theodore Parker, 1810-1860.

company of Minute Men on Lexington Green on April 19, 1775, and ordered them to load their muskets. Then he shouted, "Don't fire unless fired upon; but if they mean to have war, let it begin here!" Theodore inherited his grandfather's independent spirit; at his christening, tradition held

Sketch of 1754 meeting house made by Charles Brigham in 1886.

Theodore Parker was ordained a minister of the Unitarian church in 1841. During the age of transcendentalism in Massachusetts, a group of liberal thinkers led by Emerson, Hawthorne, Margaret Fuller and others was attempting to establish a system of religion based simply on a belief in God and the immortality of the soul. Parker espoused these humanistic beliefs, and adopted the cause of abolitionism. He worked and wrote for peace, temperance, the rights of labor, and on behalf of those who suffered from poverty and injustice. He preached in favor of John Brown and corresponded with the abolitionist Charles Sumner and with leaders of the Union cause, and is said to have influenced Abraham Lincoln in the derivation of his concept of "government of the people, by the people, for the people."

Ungainly and awkward in bearing and unmusical in voice, Parker yet managed to exert great influence on his audiences by the eloquence of his speech and the reason of his arguments. His exertions of speaking and writing exhausted him and he became ill on a lecture tour in 1857; from this he recovered somewhat after a sojourn in Switzerland, but died in Florence in May 1860.

that Theodore resisted the minister's efforts, demanding to know the reason for "being wetted."

RELIGIOUS PROBLEMS

A century of debate on the location of the meetinghouse had divided the town in the seventeenth and eighteenth centuries, reducing it to one sixth of its early size. In the thirty-year period (1825-55) the village again was engaged in a dispute over religious beliefs. This religious questioning was going on throughout New England. The Puritan faith had undergone a change. The Unitarians reacted against the orthodoxy of the state church, believing in a single personality of God and denying that the Bible was inspired by God. Pastor Francis was himself a seeker for truth and encouraged freedom of thought, but at the same time he encouraged the peaceful settlement of disputes. The change to a Unitarian parish in Watertown was, thanks to him, so gradual during the early 1800s as not to be dated by any definite year. During this period the parish continued to use the old meetinghouse.

Twice on Sundays, Col. Tom Learned could be seen striding from his home on Mt. Auburn Street toward the meetinghouse, his cello tucked under his arm. At the last stroke of the church bell he would tune his instrument. His seat was in the center of the singers' gallery at the rear of the room. The Reverend Convers Francis, stocky in his silk robe, stood under the sounding board, and always read his sermon without embellishment.

Between the extremes of Puritan and Unitarian beliefs several religious groups favored neither view. One of these groups, the Baptists, objected to being taxed for the town church. Accordingly, those who could present proof of their Baptist membership were excused from paying the church tax.* Their belief required baptism by immersion. They did not believe in infant baptism, reviving the ancient dispute between Pastor Phillips and the rich tanner Biscoe. The Baptists were also strongly op-

*By State law, evidence of membership in an organized Church (other than Congregational) was required in order to avoid the church tax.

posed to the use of liquor, with some justification, for at this time there was a good deal of public drunkenness.

Taverns were numerous, and liquor flowed freely, especially after the sea war with Britain. A local rhymster had this to say:

Many a flimsy old hovel, deep sunk in the mud
Greets the eye as you enter the village,
Where the young and the old topers swallow their drink
Seeking the foulest of ruins, the brink.

The Baptists got their start by teaching a group of children who met at Deacon Tucker's at 72 Mt. Auburn Street. The deacon was a wheelwright and a strict teetotaler, who would do no work on a wagon which carried liquor. In 1830 these Baptist families built their first meetinghouse,* and the passage between Mt. Auburn and Spring streets is still called Baptist Walk.

In 1828 Universalists who lived on the South Side had constructed their house of worship at the upper end of Water Street. It was on the opposite corner at the Broads' that Parker later started his school. This Universalist church was the first new meetinghouse outside of the town parish.

The First Parish had been incorporated with a charter from the state, which provided for the support of the minister. Residents who no longer considered themselves members of the parish petitioned the General Court that the minister's fund be either returned to the town treasury or distributed among all religious groups. The matter was finally settled in 1835 by separating church and town money, property, and business.

Being no longer a town church with a town-supported pastor, the First Parish made plans for a new wooden meetinghouse. The site was on Church Street, and its design was a more ornate one than the former lantern-type church had been. Its tower had four pinnacles, and it was approached from the marketplace by a new road, Church Street, which had been laid out the year before. The same road accommodated another new structure facing the meetinghouse, an academy to replace the one on Main Street where Oliver Wellington had been the last schoolmaster.

*Its present site is occupied by a liquor store.

It was Wellington who had built the two-story private school with its row of pillars.

On a spring morning of 1837 Mr. Francis wrote:

In passing the site of our old meeting house, I observed that yesterday and today the last remains of it had been levelled with the ground. The old spire came down, and the cock bowed his head to the dust, after having for so many years stood manfully up midst the winds of heaven, and turned himself round with silent significance to the various points of the compass. So my old church has vanished from the list of existing things and is henceforth to be only a remembrance.

The weathercock was preserved, but the meetinghouse which had been the birthplace of the state legislature was gone. May Day added another note in the Francis diary: "I helped to plant several trees on the hill around our new church."

Even while the old house of worship was being used another religious group was meeting in a home across the road. The Methodists, like their church brethren in England, were precise in their methods and church duties. Among them was George Tyler Bigelow, a cousin of David Child's and later chief justice of Massachusetts.

The leader of the Methodists, Leonard Whitney, was descended from original Watertown settlers and had moved from Sudbury in the 1820s to take work in a papermill. He soon bought it from its owner, William May, a selectman. The factory stood behind Lewando's on the site of the old corn mill. The Methodists first held meetings in Leonard Whitney's home on Mt. Auburn Street; later they bought the Main Street Academy for four hundred dollars when Wellington built his new school.

In 1841 fire broke out in a bakery and spread to the Unitarian church. Francis's diary reads:

Our beautiful church is laid in ashes. The fire went on with incredible rapidity, and the assistance was late in coming, so that it was impossible to save anything. I must say that I wept like a child to see a sanctuary so dear to my affections, and bound to all my thoughts by such pleasant and hallowed associations, going down in the flames.

The *Boston Traveler* printed an account of this worst blaze in Watertown's history to that date. It said that fire broke out in a bakery between midnight and one in the morning. The stables of the

Antipas Jackson's blacksmith shop with the old Baptist Church in the background.

Spring Hotel also burned. At 3:00 A.M. the fire was still burning. Citizens appeared to have met the danger as lines of "females" formed soon after it began and were still passing buckets when the newspaper went to press.

Nothing could be done except to shoulder the burden of building another meetinghouse. The new one followed the same design and became the meetinghouse of the First Parish Unitarian, until its demolition in 1975. It was a notable example of Victorian Gothic architecture. Francis gave the ded-

ication address but did not remain as its leader. He left Watertown for Harvard Divinity School, where he became professor of theology. He and his family are buried in Common Street Cemetery.

Leathe's bakery at the corner of Church and Main streets, where the fire had started, was rebuilt. For years it housed a barbershop. On Pleasant Street a small dyehouse business was opened by James McGarvey, which was later enlarged to become Lewando's laundry.

THE CUSHINGS

Traces of an old cellar on Townsend Street in Belmont mark the birthplace of John Perkins Cushing. His mother's kin, the Perkinses, were sea merchants. Their stories of doing business in the West Indies dated back before the Revolution, and at one time seventy of the company's ships plied the seas. John Cushing went to sea at the age of

sixteen. On his way out the ship's master died, and John took charge of the ship. He lived in Canton, China, for twenty-five years and returned to Boston a wealthy man, at the age of forty-one.

In spite of his business success and wide travels, Cushing was somewhat reclusive, seeing only his close friends. He married and, desiring to build a

96

First Parish Church Meeting House, erected 1842.

more were spent for adorning the already handsome landscape.

When a later occupant of the palace was asked how many rooms it had, he replied, "I don't know, but there are fifty fireplaces." First-floor rooms opened upon a large central rotunda, which had walls that could be removed in summer. A curving stairway led to a gallery from which one could look down into the rotunda. On two sides of the house large fluted marble pillars with Ionic capitals rose to a blue-slated roof. Incoming carriages passed a thirty-acre lawn closely clipped and circled by trees, approached the house over an oyster-shell driveway, and stopped under a porte cochere at the main entrance.

An upstairs conservatory for plants overlooked a vegetable garden in the back. Beyond this was a deer park and a winding path to a rustic summer house on Pequossette Hill, giving a magnificent view over broad fields.* Fifteen other buildings included a sixty-foot conservatory, a large greenhouse, and special rooms for palms, grapes, peaches, figs, and vegetables, stables for horses, and barns for cows. All this went by the name of Cushing Gardens or "The Bellmont." Later "Belmont" was taken as a name for the street and the town, and Cushing Square now marks one corner of the former estate.

Once a week in summer the public was invited to walk along avenues of elms and purple beeches, old oaks, tulip trees, and cypress. The estate became the most famous one of its kind in New England. There were rare trees brought home by Cushing from his travels, and in May visitors came to admire the magnolia bloom at its height. Cushing's favorite diversion was to entertain children with elaborate parties, for which he supplied Chinese firecrackers, ponies, music, and processions.

house, asked the price of Whitney Hill. Its owner, the strong-minded country squire Abijah White, replied, "Mr. Cushing, you have not enough money to buy that hill." Cushing turned to North Watertown, where he chose a beautiful expanse of slopes and fields. From several owners he bought a total of two hundred acres, including a house and land which a Portland merchant, Eben Preble, had acquired in 1805. Preble's son-in-law Nathaniel Amory sold the property to Cushing. Mr. Cushing lived in the Amory house until 1840. With $115,000, he built a new mansion; thousands

JOSIAH STICKNEY

Another self-made man bought about thirty-five acres of the first Oldham farm where the Georgian mansion built by William Hunt stood. The grounds of Perkins School are on the former Stickney estate. Josiah Stickney was the youngest of eleven children whose parents had settled in the village of Grafton, Vermont. Almost unschooled except by his parents, at nineteen he set out on foot to walk the one hundred miles to Boston in December. He found work with his brother Isaac, and on Isaac's death he took charge of the business. Stickney became prosperous by his activities in trading, whaling, and the sugar business. He held

*The chapel remains as a branch of the Belmont Public Library.

many positions on the boards of banks and rail-roads.

In 1845 Stickney purchased the riverbank property in Watertown. The view over the valley was excellent. The soil favored the growth of fruit and flowers at a time when horticulture was popular. He specialized in dahlias, then a new variety of flower, and his pear orchards were the finest in the state. He raised a family of three sons and four daughters. Stickney donated land for the first building of the Massachusetts Horticultural Society in Boston. In his first will he bequeathed his estate to the society for experimental gardening, then changed his mind and gave the society twelve thousand dollars instead to be spent on books for a "Stickney library."

In 1846, the town having been without a town hall for ten years, a wooden frame structure was built close to the corner of Main and Church streets on part of Dr. Spring's property. The town paid twenty-five cents a square foot for the land. Stone steps ran the full width of the front, and tall fluted Corinthian columns with capitals of carved acanthus leaves furnished a perch for pigeons. A hall on the second floor was capable of seating three hundred persons. The first floor was used for town offices and a jail and for a time by the public library. The fire station was behind the new town hall.

THE FIRST CATHOLIC CHURCH

At first, Catholics belonged to parishes in neighboring towns, but when the Catholic church in Waltham burned, worshipers who lived in Watertown obtained their own parish. Social and religious differences caused occasional friction between Watertown's old-timers and the newcomers, who were arriving in increasing numbers. When the Academy on Main Street became available in 1847, the Catholics offered to buy it. The Methodists, who had been using it, closed the deal on the understanding that the building was to be used for a bonnet factory.

The Methodists were building a new church; in the meantime they were obliged to hold their meetings in the new town hall. On the steeple of their new meetinghouse was mounted the bronze weathercock which had survived the burning of one meetinghouse and the demolition of another. The Methodists' prohibition of singing and dancing caused them to reject the request of the singing school to meet in their new building, and one of their members was expelled for not repenting that he had taken part in a dance.

In 1848 the Catholics built St. Patrick's Hall, their first church, capable of seating eight hundred. Their population doubled in thirty years, and their children caused a further increase in population.

CONGREGATIONALISTS VS. UNITARIANS

Six new buildings—Universalist, Baptist, two Unitarian, Methodist, and Catholic—had now been added, and the Congregationalists moved to build their own. The Watertown congregation which had started under Pastor Phillips was divided between the liberal Unitarians, who claimed the church property, and the more orthodox Congregationalists, who claimed adherence to the traditional faith.

Morning and evening services were held by the Congregationalists in the town hall, and Lyman Beecher served as interim pastor until they could secure a permanent minister. Dr. Beecher's daughter, Harriet Beecher Stowe, was the author of *Uncle Tom's Cabin* which President Lincoln jokingly referred to as having started the Civil War. Beecher was the father of seven sons, all of whom became ministers. Between Dr. Beecher's morning and evening sermons, the town hall was used by a liberal group of Unitarians for Theodore Parker's afternoon lectures. Often Parker's earnest listeners returned in the evening to hear Dr. Beecher's resounding oratory. The evils of drink and slavery were the burning issues of the day.

The Congregationalists, joined by families from Newton and other nearby towns, bought land on Mt. Auburn Street. Believing that their faith preserved the early tradition, they named their new building the Phillips Church after Watertown's first pastor.

The question of the ownership of church edifices between Unitarians and Congregationalists arose in many New England communities. In the *Dedham* case the Massachusetts Supreme Court ruled that the Unitarian group, which had occupied the church building continuously, was entitled to ownership and that the group which broke away had no claim to the property. Apparently the Congregationalists in Watertown made no claims on the church building, and the Unitarians offered the use of the meetinghouse for a reception for the new Congregational pastor.

The nineteenth century saw the construction of a number of public buildings: a town hall, a hotel, seven churches, a district school, and two academies, besides several pretentious mansions. By the middle of the century Watertown was no longer a sleepy New England village. It was ready for industrialization and the introduction of cultural pursuits.

The New Freedom

The Town Hall on election day, 1902.

Cultural Concerns and Town Affairs

THE MID-CENTURY SOCIAL SET

EFORE the railroad intruded upon the White estate in 1846, James Russell Lowell was introduced to the inmates of the Elms by a college classmate, William White, and began courting William's sister, Maria. He wrote to a friend:

I went up to Watertown on Saturday with William White and spent the Sabbath with him. You ought to see his father, the most perfect specimen of a bluff, honest, hospitable country squire you can possibly imagine. His mother too is a very pleasant woman.

Writing of one of his twenty-minute walks along Mt. Auburn Street to Watertown from Elmwood, his Cambridge home, he said:

Last night I walked to Watertown over the snow with a new moon before me. As I stood on the hill just before you enter the village, the stillness of the fields around me was delicious, broken only by the tinkle of a little brook which runs too swiftly for frost to catch it. My picture of the brook in "Sir Launfal" was drawn from it. I believe that I have done better than the world knows yet.

These are the lines to which he referred:

The little brook heard it [chill wind] *and built a roof
'Neath which he could house him winter-proof;
All night by the white stars' frosty gleams
He groined his arches and matched his beams.*

The poem referred to Treadaway Brook, which rose where Garfield Street joins Mt. Auburn Street.
Again Lowell wrote:

I had a time, I tell you, and made a fool of myself. Maria seems half of earth and more of heaven. . . . I walked back from Watertown with her on my arm . . . a glorious girl with spirit eyes . . . This morning I drove her up to Waltham. They tell me I shall be in love with her.

Once when on his way to Watertown the poet was given a ride by Joseph Bird of the singing school. Bird told Lowell how tears came to his eyes when he saw Maria, wearing an oakleaf wreath, present a banner to the temperance society at an outdoor event on the hill behind her home. She was, he said, as lovely as an angel. Maria and her brother William were active in the abolitionist and temperance movements. A town wag rhymed of William White: "Thou Temperance Champion! of WHITE and spotless name; in thine own heart thou need'st no higher fame." Perhaps the Whites and their friends formed a social clique, for Water-

James Russell Lowell, from a daguerreotype taken in 1844.

*With earthquake shudderings oft the mould
Would gape; I saw keen spears of gold
Thrusting red hearts down, not yet cold*

*But throbbing wildly; dreadful groans
Stole upward through Earth's ribbed stones
And crept along through all my zones . . .*

Maria, dressed in a blue uniform, had attended a convent school in Charlestown until a fanatical mob burned it down. For a wedding gift her father gave her a parcel of land, which later was given to the town; on it now stands the North Branch Library and the Lowell School. As the wife of James Russell Lowell, she lived from 1844 to 1856 at Elmwood, the former home of Elbridge Gerry in Cambridge. Hoping to improve her failing health, Maria journeyed to Europe, but died soon after her return.

Celia Thaxter, Poetess

Maria White Lowell's cousin Levi Lincoln Thaxter lived in the yellow house opposite the Elms. The

town was accused of being an "Unsociable Town, with your hoarded-up wealth, for money neglectful of virtue and health—for money you struggle and labor."

The young people organized a "Band of Brothers and Sisters" which met at the Elms so they could give dances and present plays and poetry recitations. At one of the club's parties, James and Maria were crowned king and queen. Lowell said of Maria that she could repeat more poetry than anyone else he knew; she was indeed a poet in her own right. In her poem, "Africa," Maria wrote of the slave traders:

*There came a change. They took my free,
My careless ones, and the great sea
Blew back their endless sighs to me:*

Ann Maria White, wife of James Russell Lowell.

101

Celia Thaxter with her two sons in 1856.

O happy river, could I follow thee!
O yearning heart, that never can be still!
O wistful eyes, that watch the steadfast hill,
Longing for level line of solemn sea,

Have patience,—here are flowers and songs of birds,
Beauty and fragrance, wealth of sound and sight,
All summer's glory thine from morn till night,
And life too full of joy for uttered words . . .

In 1856 the Thaxters, with their two sons, Karl and John, moved to Newtonville, where in 1858 a third son, Roland, was born. Celia's life was saddened by the illness of her eldest son, Karl, and by her husband's reluctance to return to New Hampshire. Levi did, however, encourage her to write, and she saw her poems published in the *Atlantic, Harper's, St. Nicholas* and other magazines. In 1872 her book *Poems* was published, and in 1873 a collection of articles on the islands appeared in the *Atlantic Monthly*. Five others followed during her lifetime. In 1880 the Thaxters moved to Kittery Point, Maine. Levi Thaxter died in 1884, but Celia lived for another ten years, during which she gained recognition as a poet whose work reflected a

Thaxter house stood on what is now Saltonstall Park until 1882 when it was moved across Main Street to the corner of Cuba Street. In 1852 Levi married Celia Laighton, the sixteen-year-old daughter of Thomas and Eliza Laighton of the Isles of Shoals near Portsmouth, New Hampshire. Levi Thaxter had graduated from Harvard and in partnership with Celia's father built a summer hotel on Appledore Island which opened in 1848. Although Thaxter himself soon left the job of innkeeper, the hotel prospered and became popular with New England writers and artists, numbering among its guests Nathaniel Hawthorne, Ralph Waldo Emerson, James Russell Lowell and the painters Childe Hassam and William Morris Hunt.

At the time of her marriage Celia had seldom left her island home. During their early married life the Thaxters lived first on Star Island in the Isles of Shoals, where Levi assumed a temporary post as preacher and teacher to the fishermen's children, and later in Watertown with Levi's family. As a result of nearly losing his life during a storm Levi came to dislike the sea, but Celia retained her love of seacoast life and found an outlet in writing verse. In 1851 James Russell Lowell sent her poem, "Land-Locked," to the *Atlantic Monthly,* which printed it without her knowledge. In it Celia, perhaps inspired by the Charles, wrote of a river:

Black lie the hills; swiftly doth daylight flee,
And catching gleams of sunset's dying smile,
Through the dusk land for many a changing mile
The river runneth softly to the sea.

Levi Lincoln Thaxter, from a photograph taken by his son, Roland.

deep love of the sea, the flowers and the creatures of the New England coast.

Ellen Robbins's World

There were many cousins among the White, Robbins, Thaxter, Curtis, and Fowle families. Maria White's cousin Ellen Robbins lived in a Pleasant Street house facing the river near the dam. From her windows she watched fishermen draw in their shad-filled nets or saw them spearing eels through holes in the ice. She had a view of a blackened old paper mill, surrounded by trees, situated on a promontory jutting into the stream. The great new brick mill of the Whitney paper bag company stood farther along the street. Her father James was a small manufacturer whose nearby soap factory had burned. Her mother had wept when Ellen was born lame. As a small girl traveling by stagecoach to visit an aunt in Boston, she had overheard some unfeeling person remark that she was a "very plain child," but Ellen overcame her handicaps and developed a sensitivity for color and form. She became a well-known watercolorist, specializing in the painting of natural subjects.

Fortunately her ability was recognized and she attended several different schools, finally studying under the artist and writer, Stephen Tuckerman, in Boston. Encouraged by her friends Harriet Hosmer and Margaret Foley, both sculptresses, Ellen Robbins offered her water colors for sale at a Boston art gallery; her success was sufficient to win her a considerable reputation as a painter of water colors, particularly of flowers and fruit. She moved to Boston where she taught art and maintained three studios. Like other artists of her day, Ellen Robbins traveled widely in Europe and America; she became a good friend of the actress Charlotte Cushman, whom she met through Harriet Hosmer. In later life she is said to have commented, "Few people have enjoyed life more than I have."

According to a local story, once when Miss Robbins fell ill, Rector Edward Rand of the Episcopal church mistakenly reported that "Miss Ellen Robbins—whose flowers are so natural, the bees might light on them—is lying ill at her house tonight." He called at her house, apparently expecting her to be dead, but found her sitting up quite alive. A friend attended what she thought was going to be Ellen Robbins's funeral at the Unitarian Building, but it turned out to be the funeral of an old man. When she saw him lying in his coffin, bald as a billiard ball, with thin carroty locks over his ears, the friend exclaimed, "Oh, how changed! I don't see any of Miss Robbins' sisters here. Whose funeral is this?"

The Unpredictable Harriet Hosmer

East of the marketplace Dr. Hiram Hosmer's land dipped down to the banks of the river where there was a boathouse and a bathhouse for his daughter Harriet, the only survivor of his wife and six children. By encouraging outdoor exercise he helped to lay a foundation for a life of healthy activity for his daughter. Harriet attained fame as

Miss Robbins in her studio, from a photograph by J. Appleton Brown.

an artist, and was also an accomplished horsewoman and retained an interest in sports. Life for her was full of zest.

She attended the Bird Singing School with Ellen Robbins and walked the riverbank looking for flowers, the tiniest of which she named "giganticus." The two women were lifelong friends. Harriet encouraged Ellen to paint and paid fifty dollars for one of Ellen's books of flowers. Harriet, famous for her pranks, decided to try to reach Boston before a friend could by removing a coupling pin between her railroad coach and that of the friend

103

Harriet Hosmer, from a painting by Sir William Boxall.

though she was not allowed to participate in medical school classes with men. Wayman Crowe, her classmate's father, was one of Harriet's patrons, and she made a plaster study of Crowe's head, one of the few sculptures Harriet did of a male subject. Before her return home she sailed the length of the Mississippi River, smoked a peace pipe with Indians, and brought up lead from a mine to add to her collection of oddities.

At twenty Harriet decided that she wanted to carve marble, and Dr. Hosmer had a studio built for her on his grounds. Her first marble sculpture

"Hesper" was sculpted by Harriet Hosmer in 1852.

just as the train stopped at the Cambridge depot. The engineer, however, realizing what had happened, reversed the train to recouple it with the stranded coach, and Dr. Hosmer had to pay the bill for Harriet's exploit. On a dare, Harriet crept the length of one of the new town hall's hollow columns as it lay in the marketplace. After Harriet had posted a false funeral notice of the death of Dr. Eliakim Morse to a Boston newspaper, her father, no longer amused, sent her to a boarding school in the Berkshires.

Blessed with natural curiosity, Harriet entertained herself by studying a skeleton in Dr. Hosmer's office and even draped it in her cousin Alfred's clothes. The study of anatomy by women was unheard of in those days, but Harriet had a classmate whose home was in St. Louis, and Harriet made special arrangements to study there, even

was a bust of Hesper, the *Evening Star*. After her workman had cut off the corners of a marble block, Harriet swung a four-and-a-half-pound hammer for eight to ten hours a day until Hesper's form emerged. The sculpture was given to the public library by her friend Dr. Julian Mead, a trustee of the library.

In 1852 father and daughter sailed for Italy, where expatriate artists had formed a colony. There Harriet began seven intensive years of study in the Rome studio of the English sculptor John

104

Harriet Hosmer and her workmen at her studio in Rome.

Gibson. Harriet made many friends in Rome and was celebrated in England and on the Continent. The Prince of Wales became one of her patrons. Her neoclassical sculptures became fashionable, and she made many copies of Robert and Elizabeth Barrett Browning's clasped hands and carved a gigantic statue of Thomas Hart Benton wearing a toga, for the city of St. Louis. Lydia Maria Francis Child, her former neighbor, wrote to Harriet in Rome:

Three weeks ago we spent a night at your father's. You know he and my husband were comrades in their bachelor days, and the meeting made them both young again. Such peals of laughter I have not heard for many a day. All the intimate fixtures in your studio remain as when you left them. Your father takes an affectionate pride in leaving them undisturbed.

Dr. Hosmer wholeheartedly supported Harriet in her studies. Later in life he met with financial difficulties and died a lonely man.

Harriet Hosmer was a celebrated artist of the Victorian era. After her return to the United States she traveled a good deal and lectured on the subject of art to enthusiastic audiences. She wrote poetry and articles for magazines, and worked on the perfection of a method she had developed for transforming limestone into marble. In her old age she lived in the family home in Watertown and spent her time studying and experimenting with the theory of perpetual motion. To the end she retained her zest for life and her gift for friendship.

With its quiet view upon noisy Watertown Square, the family home was occupied by Hosmers until 1922, when it was purchased by Walter Gregg. Among its original features were an outside balcony, purple glass in several of the south windows, a period front door and stairway, three-part solid inside window blinds, hand carvings around the fireplaces, and a mahogany dining-room mantel. In the kitchen were Dutch ovens, an enormous icebox, and food storage bins. The bedrooms featured arched lavatories, bell ropes for summoning

Anne Whitney, 1821-1915.

talent, Barnard encouraged Anne to undertake the formal study of art. Her brother Edward built her a studio which she called "The Shanty," and later in Boston she rented a studio adjacent to that of her teacher, William Rimmer. Her works include the bronze statue of Leif Ericson on Commonwealth Avenue in Boston and the figure of Samuel Adams in Adams Square. After the death of Senator Charles Sumner, a famous abolitionist, a Boston committee planned to honor him by erecting a statue in his memory and held a contest for the best design. They chose the design submitted anonymously by Miss Whitney, but when they learned that the winner was a woman, they reversed themselves and refused her the commission. Miss Whitney, outraged by this injustice, resolved never again to enter a contest, but her reward was yet to come. Years later a group of friends commissioned the work, and the bronze statue of Charles Sumner was placed in Harvard Square in front of the Harvard Law School.

Lucy Stone—Feminist, Abolitionist, Suffragist

Anne Whitney's cousin Lucy Stone was born in West Brookfield, Massachusetts, the descendant of Gregory Stone, who with his brother Simon had left England in 1635 to settle in Watertown. A marker records the event at the former location of the Stone farm in East Watertown; the farm eventually became a part of Mount Auburn Cemetery.

Lucy early became aware of discrimination against women in education. When she read in the Bible that men should rule women, she resolved to go to college to learn Greek and Hebrew in order to find out if the translation, as she suspected, was inaccurate. She became interested in the abolitionist movement from reading William Lloyd Garrison's *Liberator*. In 1839 she entered Mount Holyoke Female Seminary and in 1843 enrolled at Oberlin College, where she studied Greek and Hebrew. In 1847 Lucy graduated from Oberlin, the first Massachusetts woman to receive a college degree.

Lucy Stone became a champion of women's rights as well as those of Negro slaves. In 1850 she called the first national women's rights convention in Worcester, where her eloquence converted Susan B. Anthony to the cause. In 1855 she mar-

servants, and floorboards sixteen feet long. The bath tub was of copper, and there was a basement cistern for the storage of rainwater.

Anne Whitney—Sculptress

Anne Whitney was born in Watertown, the second daughter and youngest of the seven children of Nathaniel Ruggles Whitney, Jr. and Sarah Stone Whitney, both descendants of Watertown settlers. She was educated at home and spent a year in New York and Philadelphia modeling and drawing from life and studying anatomy at a Brooklyn hospital. In 1867 she realized her dream of going to Rome, where she lived and worked for four years. Her talent for sculpture was discovered by accident, as the story goes; when the family was living on Belmont Street near the farm of Capt. "Sam" Barnard, she was watching him work in his garden one day. Idly scooping up a handful of garden sand when a watering pot overturned, she shaped it into the likeness of a familiar face. Recognizing her

106

ried Henry Blackwell, an abolitionist and brother of the pioneer women physicians Elizabeth and Emily Blackwell, but she kept her maiden name. In 1857 the couple became the parents of Alice Stone Blackwell. In 1856 Lucy Stone presided over the Seventh National Women Rights Convention in New York, and supported the Women's Loyal National League, established in 1863 by Elizabeth Cady Stanton and Susan B. Anthony to mobilize support for the proposed Thirteenth Amendment to abolish slavery. During this time she left the Congregational Church and became a Unitarian. Mrs. Stone traveled and lectured widely in the West, the South, and in Canada, wearing the costume popularized by Amelia Bloomer. Often in danger from hostile audiences, Lucy always retained her calm demeanor.

In 1856 Lucy Stone helped organize the American Equal Rights Association to press for suffrage for Negroes and women. In 1868 she assisted in founding the New England Woman Suffrage Association under the presidency of Julia Ward Howe, and the next year she and her husband moved to Boston where Mrs. Stone became the leader of the suffrage movement.

During the late eighteen-sixties the women's suffrage movement divided because of a disagreement on policy and tactics, in addition to personal conflicts, between Mrs. Stone on the one side and Mrs. Stanton and Miss Anthony on the other. Both groups, however, continued to work toward women's suffrage, and in 1890 the infusion of younger workers led to the healing of the breach, and the two groups united to become the National American Woman Suffrage Association.

During the interim Lucy Stone became, in 1872, the editor, with her husband, of the *Woman's Journal,* the voice of the woman's movement, in which she was followed by her daughter, Alice Stone Blackwell. During her later years she continued to appear in public although her voice had failed. Her disposition was kind and her temperament mellowed with age. She was said by her husband always

Portrait bust of Lucy Stone by Anne Whitney. Courtesy Trustees of the Boston Public Library.

to have suffered from headaches and depression. During their marriage Lucy and Henry were often separated for long periods, for Lucy continued to travel extensively and her husband, like David Child, was interested in the efforts (later proved unsuccessful) to raise sugar beets and sorghum in Maine and Western Massachusetts.

In 1893 Mrs. Stone delivered her last lectures in Chicago at the Columbian Exposition. She died in Dorchester at the age of seventy-seven, to the end an innovator, and was the first person to be cremated in New England. Her portrait bust by Anne Whitney was exhibited in the Woman's Building at the Chicago Exposition.

OTHER PROMINENT RESIDENTS

The Locke family lived for three generations in a large house at the southwest corner of Belmont and Common streets. The William Pratt family lived in the Oakley, and across the green slope from

their spacious veranda a mansion was built by Charles Davenport, a Cambridge manufacturer of steam engines and coaches. Davenport's square house and two-story barn were surrounded by

Fountain Hill Estate, built by the Davenport family and later expanded by Alvin Adams.

spacious grounds and a summer house. There was a fountain on the front lawn from which the estate derived the name "Fountain Hill."

Nathaniel Whiting

Nathaniel Whiting was already a wealthy man when he came to live in Watertown. In 1845 he built a mansion which faced south on Marshall Street and here he entertained Charles Dickens when the famous novelist made his second visit to the United States. Whiting was gruff and outspoken, with a strong personality. He loved nature and made many fine improvements to his property, notably planting a row of beech trees between Hawthorne and Palfrey streets. In his old age Whiting was often seen walking on his spacious grounds alone, for one of his sons had died in a fall from an upstairs window, and the other went to California where he became an ostrich farmer.

WATERTOWN'S HAUNTED HOUSE

The "haunted house," as it came to be known, was the subject of an article in *Harper's New Monthly Magazine* in September 1867 and has since become an interesting town legend. The house, built by a Colonel Winthrop who was said to be a descendant of the first governor of the Massachusetts Bay Colony, stood facing Belmont Street. It was a large, low-roofed rambling structure, reached by a curving driveway and surrounded by a grove of hemlocks. According to local gossip the house became uninhabitable, a place of emanations, ghostly visitors, and things that went bump in the night.

The house was indeed built by a G. T. Winthrop in the eighteen-forties. It was said that he had as a student at Harvard led a dissolute life, but after marrying the daughter of a Massachusetts Supreme Court judge, settled down on his Watertown estate and for a number of years led an aimless life. He appeared to have plenty of money, and as time went on he and his wife had three children. With them lived an elderly servant named Molly, who was apparently the source of much of the information that caused the family and house to become notorious.

According to old Molly the trouble began when Alice Morrow, a young woman without family connections, came from Philadelphia to serve as governess to the children. Young, beautiful, and possessed of a mane of waving chestnut hair, she soon became Winthrop's mistress. They went for long rides in his carriage, returning late at night, when

quickly turning the bolt with the latch-key, the governess would enter the house, and, with a light step and a furtive look, pass swiftly up the front stairway to her chamber in a remote part of the upper-story. On such occasions she always wore a dress of black silk, a heavily-fringed black mantle, and a black lace bonnet, with a veil of green barege, thrown back so as to fully disclose her features.

According to Molly's version of the story, the mistress of the house tolerated the situation until she could endure no more and eventually left her husband and went to live with her mother. Although the lovers were now free to do as they pleased, things went from bad to worse. "Conscience had begun its work, or sin had wrought a surfeit," according to the chronicler in *Harper's*. In any case, Winthrop drank heavily and spent much of his time barricaded in his library in a state of "beastly intoxication," while Alice Morrow, the governess, became "pale and emaciated." Winthrop's financial affairs deteriorated, and he was said to be desperate for money. At this point his mother-in-law stepped in and paid off the mortgage to prevent his losing the property. Soon after this Alice Morrow left, supposedly sent away by the penitent husband, and was never seen again in Watertown.

Mrs. Winthrop now returned home, and "gradually . . . the long-suffering woman lured him from his evil ways, and won him back to herself and his children." Apparently, however, not having learned from experience, she permitted another hapless young woman to enter the household, this time the "portionless child of a widowed sister" of the Colonel's, and again young, beautiful, and innocent. Claire, like Alice, was employed as governess to the children, and "ensnared by the arts of this wicked man, she too fell from true womanhood." Once more Mrs. Winthrop left her hus-

Nathaniel Whiting, 1802-1871.

band, and once again the estate was mortgaged and Winthrop was said to be on the verge of bankruptcy.

Suddenly, however, Winthrop was observed to be in possession of plenty of money, and this time it was not due to the generosity of his wife's mother. An itinerant peddler by the name of Carroll, who was known to carry with him large quantities of money and jewelry, vanished at the same time. Claire and Winthrop were overheard by the housekeeper quarreling in the library, and when she returned from market, the girl had left "to live with relations." The children were taken away to live with their grandmother, and Winthrop apparently drank himself to death in his lonely mansion.

The house was sold to pay Winthrop's creditors and passed through the hands of several owners until purchased by a financier to house his farm manager, Thomas King. King lived in the house with his wife and children for several years, apparently unafraid of the ghostly apparitions and nocturnal manifestations that had, since Winthrop's death, given it a sinister reputation. Since the house was larger than he and his family needed for themselves, he let out several of the rooms, but

109

neighbors said that all the inhabitants except the Kings themselves were driven out by loud knocks, the sounds of ghostly presences in the upper rooms, the opening and closing of doors in the night, and the house rocking on its foundation. One night, responding to a pounding on the door of the woodshed, King arose and lighting a candle, crept down to the kitchen, thinking that burglars were attempting to break into the house. He thought he heard voices and the quick, sharp blows of an ax, but when he unbolted and opened the kitchen door, no one was there and everything was in its accustomed place. Subsequently he was aroused by the ringing of the doorbell, and when he again ventured downstairs to investigate, he saw standing in the driveway in the clear moonlight a carriage drawn by a white horse. Other manifestations included a chill wind, the sound of earth being shoveled in the cellar, footsteps in the hall, and the sound of a woman weeping. A medium who came to investigate the ghostly occurrences reported that a spirit temporarily inhabited her body, and claiming to be Claire told her that Winthrop had murdered the peddler for his money and that the deadly deed had been peformed in the woodshed. According to Claire, the guilty man and his paramour, the lovely Alice, were condemned to reenact their guilty lives until their sins could be expiated.

The Kings lived in the "haunted house" for several years. After they moved to Connecticut the owner sold the property and eventually the house was torn down. According to the story, in a vault near the haunted building searchers found a luxuriant head of wavy, golden-brown hair with remnants of flesh still clinging to its roots.

12

Business, Industry and Agriculture

COMING OF THE RAILROAD

Early Opposition to the Iron Horse

RAILROAD LINES were laid in the mid-century from Boston to Lowell and Fitchburg. The Fitchburg Railroad ran from the Charlestown wharves past Fresh Pond in North Watertown and thence via Beaver Brook to Waltham. Later its roadbed was laid parallel to the tracks of the Massachusetts Central Railroad, which ran to the west through the Hoosac Tunnel.

The building of a short line to Fresh Pond on the Fitchburg branch of the Boston & Maine was encouraged by Jacob Hittinger. He lived beyond Pequossette Hill or Cushing Gardens and, in season, cut ice from Fresh Pond to be hauled to merchant vessels and shipped to tropical lands. In the winter of 1844 his ice cutter broke open a way for harbor-locked ships of the Cunard ocean-bound service. The ice trade and access by rail to tidewater shippers were important in maintaining Boston as a seaport.

Some shortsighted citizens could not see that the railroad would benefit Watertown's cotton and cattle industries as well as affording a convenient means of travel for townspeople. Among these were Abijah White of the Elms and his brother-in-law, Levi Thaxter, who contended that the railroad would ruin the town. He believed that sparks belching from engine stacks would set fire to their fields. The Boston & Albany Railroad was forced to locate on the south side of the river, thus driving away both residential and business development from the village. Said Mr. White to men of the Fitchburg Railroad who wished to build a six-mile Watertown branch, "You may take as much land as you need for your proposed road, but my grandchildren will plow up the tracks." He refused to bargain, and the matter was left to be settled by the courts. The line was laid in 1846, one year after his death, and was subsequently extended to Waltham.* In 1852 the Elms with the land its master had acquired was sold at public auction, valued at twenty thousand dollars.

Charles Davenport

Jacob Hittinger, who promoted the branch railroad, and Charles Davenport, builder of the first coaches for the Erie Railroad, became associated both by business and by the marriage of their children. Davenport designed railroad coaches which were entered from each end instead of from doors along the sides of the cars. He was a leader in coach

*The tracks were removed in the 1950s.

111

construction for twenty years. His passenger engines drew five coaches at forty-five miles per hour without losing steam, and his freight engines made fifteen miles per hour hauling a hundred cars, each containing five tons of coal. A rail line was laid directly to his shops in Cambridge where it connected with other lines. He invested heavily in rail stocks and lost most of his investment when the railroad boom ended, but he recovered his losses sufficiently to retire at the age of forty-five.

PAPER, PAPER BAGS, AND UNDERWEAR

Whitney Paper Mill

The Civil War brought changes to Watertown's factories, churches, and schools. The marketplace was astir with four-horse drays, loaded either with wood pulp from Maine or with finished paper, clattering to and from the Whitney Paper Mill. The factory stood astride the canal. Leonard Whitney, Jr. became an associate of his father. He married Caroline Russell and purchased the Elms, the former residence of Abijah White.

In 1857 a mill employee invented a device to shape wrapping paper into a bag, and this crude machine revolutionized the packaging of American merchandise. Grocers who had wrapped a pound of tea in a sheet of paper and tied it with twine now used the practical paper bag. Production soared and so did profits. Because water pressure was inadequate, a shift was made to steampower. With a new partner, E. A. Hollingsworth, the firm name became Hollingsworth and Whitney, and a two-hundred-foot-long building was added to the plant.

The Bemis Mills

This company changed its production from cotton to wool with the retirement of Seth Bemis, Jr., who had been a partner with his inventor father in the manufacture of cloth and dyestuffs. His brother George, a successful Boston lawyer, endowed a professorship of International Law at Harvard University. The new company, Aetna Mills, did a thriving business in fine woolen cloth for women's clothing. Not long afterward A. O. Davidson of Lowell became the new manager and a leader in town. He built his own mansion on the site of Luke Bemis's house. The Bemis School was built in 1885.

A knitting mill stood near the Bemis Mills and the Bemis railway station on Bridge Street. The mill's operator, Thomas Dalby, was a weaver from the English Midlands, as was Benjamin Fewkes of the lace factory. As his business in fine underwear prospered, Dalby built a brick factory on Morse Street.

Meanwhile the Whitney Paper Mill's daily output grew to eight tons of paper and two million paper bags. Wood pulp was brought from Maine, where the company had the rights to hundreds of square miles of timber. In the 1880s, the company received highest prizes at exhibitions, and the name of Hollingsworth and Whitney of Boston became famous for quality. At the close of the century, when the owners had died, the company moved to Maine, and the new owners sold the Watertown plant to the Union Bag & Paper Com-

George Bemis, 1816-1878.

Mansion of Alvin Adams on School Street.

pany of New York. The Whitney family, however, remained in Watertown and continued to be influential in town affairs.

In 1911, beset by financial reverses, the Union Paper Bag Company left Watertown to centralize its operation in New York. Its departure presaged a time of change in the Watertown Square business community.

ALVIN ADAMS' SUCCESS STORY

Railroad investments brought wealth to several local investors, including Alvin Adams. Like Josiah Stickney, he came from a large family in Vermont, and prospered as a self-made man. During a trip to New York City he hit upon the idea of transporting packages for individuals. Adams took a train from Boston to New York, while an associate traveled in the opposite direction; each was responsible for delivering parcels and cash entrusted to him by either individuals or banks. The next day both men made return trips; each continued traveling back and forth until he had used up his season ticket. With this start, Adams extended his business until it reached the Pacific coast and Australia. In 1854 Adams and Company absorbed the Harnden Express Company (founded by William F. Harnden who died at the age of thirty-three), Thompson and Company, and Kinsley and Company. Adams was elected president and the company became the Adams Express Company. The eastern business became a competitor to the American Railway Express Company. The Adams Express service was used during the Civil War by the families of men serving in the Union Army, and Adams delivered the first gold sent back to Boston from the California Gold Rush of 1849.

Adams purchased Fountain Hill, the Davenport estate, and extended his property to include what is today's Adams Avenue, to Hillside Road between Belmont and Mt. Auburn Streets, and the present

113

Hosmer and East Junior High School yards. In 1860, Alvin Adams, now a very rich man, built in a former pasture on School Street a splendid house which he named "Fairlawn." The house contained a gallery which he regularly opened to the public. From the house a private road led to a great barn which stood at the top of the present Hillside Road between the Winsor Clubhouse and Mt. Auburn Street. The barn had marble walls and housed a herd of fine Jersey cows. After Adams' death in 1877, six hundred persons attended a public auction of his cattle, which fetched prices as high as four hundred dollars a head. The Adams house burned in 1886 but was rebuilt by Ralph Warner, whose new house had ceilings decorated with paintings. The house built by Warner also burned.*

LEWANDO'S CLEANSING AND DYEING BUSINESS

The Lewando's cleansing and dyeing business was at one time the largest in the country, serving the eastern seaboard as far as Maryland. It succeeded McGarvey's dyehouse on Pleasant Street, where dyed materials had been hung to dry in the open air near the river. When McGarvey had been in the business about forty years, Adolphus Lewando moved out from Boston where he had been in a similar enterprise since 1828, and bought out McGarvey. Lewando's fortunes survived a fire and the removal of the company first to Maine, then to Dedham. It was relocated in Watertown during the Civil War. Adolphus Lewando died in 1871. The Harwood family then acquired the plant and controlled it for three generations. One employee was said to have worked at Lewando's for sixty-four years, and many others had long terms of service.

The accuracy in marking articles sent to be cleaned and the great care taken to prevent shrinkage earned Lewando's a fine reputation. In advertising, Lewando's quoted Shakespeare's Lady Macbeth's cry: "Out, damned spot!" ("Lewando's" had now become "Lewandos.") Before the advent of dry cleaning with chemicals, steam scouring was employed in the cleaning of silks and woolen materials. Garments were taken apart and laid out on large tables. With the introduction of chemicals the dry cleaning process changed. Stubborn stains were removed by expert "spotters," and each garment was cleaned intact. Laundry and cleansing machinery manufactured in the Empire factory across the river, and later imported from England, consisted of huge washers, a dryer, and machines to add starch and polish to collars and cuffs. Water was drawn from six artesian wells and from the town water supply; waste water was emptied into the river. Local wheat starch was utilized to stiffen shirts.

W. L. Crosby, at one time the Lewandos manager, amused himself by drawing cartoons. From this pastime came the Lewandos trademark showing a yellow cat in an apron tubbing her chicks and hanging them out on a clothesline to dry.

MIDCENTURY AGRICULTURE

About 125 fruit and vegetable farms were located on Watertown's north boundary with Belmont and in Arlington and Waltham. This neighborhood of prosperous farmers provided food for the Boston markets. Their orchards produced between twenty thousand and eighty thousand barrels of apples annually, with winter deliveries of hay, potatoes, and celery as late as

*In its last years the mansion became the Commonwealth Motor and Driving Club, a resort of the sporting element of Boston, and was often raided by the police of a no-liquor, no-gambling town.

January. Bees in attics and in outdoor hives produced honey.

Fruit, vegetable, and dairy farms, occupied a valley between two ranges of hills, along which ran the Fitchburg Railroad. The new Concord Turnpike connecting Harvard Square with Concord, designed by Jeduthan O. Wellington, was built next to the railroad. Colonel Wellington enticed travelers to use the new shorter highway by providing his oxen to help the stagecoach over the southern border of Wellington Hill.

THE SECESSION OF BELMONT

Residents of North Watertown and West Cambridge had to travel a long way to a meetinghouse, a store or a school; and in 1855, Jacob Hittinger, who had interests in the ice business and the railroad, decided to petition for a charter for a new community. Opposition to his plan came from political interests in West Cambridge and from Strawberry Hill property owners in Watertown. Failing in 1855, Hittinger resubmitted petitions with greater numbers of advocates, in 1856, 1857, and 1858, and finally succeeded in 1859. Among his associates were Samuel Mead, Jonas Chenery, Edwin Locke, and William Underwood. During this period a church was erected and was soon followed with the building of schools.

The new town took its name from the Bellmont, at the request of John Cushing, the heaviest taxpayer and supporter of the movement for incorporation. Peter Clarke, aged ninety, was the first Belmont citizen to cast his ballot. Victory was declared with joy, and there was a holiday featuring bonfires and cannon salutes. The new community of Belmont was larger in area than the mother town, having subtracted from Watertown nearly half of its property valuation and one third of its farmland. The birth of Belmont came at the same time as the completion of the railroad as far as the Hoosac Tunnel in the Berkshires, and a Belmont depot was built, called Wellington Station. The iron horse took credit for a steady increase in the new town's population.

Seven Hittinger sons transformed marshes into extensive truck gardens. They hauled as many as fourteen thousand cucumbers a day by wagon to Faneuil Hall market in Boston. At the same time Joshua and John, Jr., great-grandsons of the patriot, Joshua Coolidge, built their own houses across the border in Watertown. Joshua Coolidge's new house stood near the Second Baptist Church.

Lovell Bros. farm and market gardens.

In 1852 John, Jr., built his house next to the old burying ground. His fruit and vegetable market carried the name Vineyard Market carrying on the tradition of the patriot Joshua Coolidge, who had plowed the land between Arlington Street and Bigelow Avenue.

THE CATTLE YARDS

In the 1870s Watertown became the center of a thriving cattle trade in the triangular area of thirty-five acres formed between the tracks of the Fitchburg Railroad and the protecting hill along Walnut Street. A stone retaining wall half a mile long shored up the earth, permitting the cattle to

Joshua Coolidge, 1813-1908.

Most of the cattle came on Monday's trains, sometimes as many as a thousand head arriving by Grand Trunk Railroad from Chicago. On Tuesdays the residents of the Union Market area would hear and see the cattle bellowing and the drovers yelling and brandishing their staves as they herded the animals across the river to the slaughterhouse. Cattle came also from northern New England, where they had been bred and fattened, then driven over the roads to Watertown for sale to down-country milk dealers, a journey which could take weeks. A trick practiced at the Stockyards was to let a cow go unmilked for a day so that when milked the next day her yield per day would appear to be double what it actually was and would thus raise her value. Small dealers such as Cheney, who owned a slaughtering shed near the river, and Lacker, who sold milk which was poured directly into the tin pails provided by his customers, earned their living by locating their businesses in close proximity to the stockyards.

The railroad company built three sheds of similar design for cattle, sheep, and swine. They were well lighted and ventilated and were kept clean with water drawn from a reservoir at Fresh Pond. The three-story Union Market Hotel, with fifty rooms for the use of cattlemen, stood on the site later occupied by the Lewis-Shepard Company. The Lewis-Shepard offices were built on the stone walls of a former horse stable, and several cottages remain from the time when, painted alike in red and gray, they housed the railroad workers. The retaining wall along the tracks can still be seen.

pass directly from the cattle cars into the pens. The law required that the herds leave the trains, be fed, and then be kept in the open for twenty-four hours. They were then driven across the river to the Brighton abattoir or shipped on the hoof to England. John Hathaway of Brighton was manager of the Union Market Stockyards, which became the largest in the country in the volume of animals exported from the port of Boston.

SOAP, SHIRTS AND UNDERWEAR

The Soap Factory

On the south bank of the Charles in 1880 in two buildings near the dam, the three Porter brothers produced bobbins and needles for sewing machine companies, the only such specialists in the country. Their building was later occupied also by Empire Laundry Machine Company, which, in 1883 began manufacturing washing machine wringers and starchers. Downstream, the Newton and Watertown Gas Light Company installed a generator to

meet the new demand for electric lighting. In one of its buildings was the Warren Soap Factory, where great kettles frothed with boiling mixtures. In the space of six months the company shipped two million barrels containing forty kinds of textile soap to cloth and hosiery mills from Maine to Texas. Robbins' Starch Works (once Hunt's Distillery) was sold to Hiram Barker. On Pleasant Street, the Crystal Springs Starch Factory made transparent starch from flour. The factory burned in 1902.

116

Barker Shirts

A shirt factory under another Barker operated on Spring Street, and shirt-making became a Watertown industry. In 1830, to supply the new Boston shirt market, Mrs. Silas Bates hired girls to make shirts by hand in a house in the present location of the public library. Her business prospered and when a new factory was built on Spring Street opposite Fayette Street, it was bought out by J. G. Barker for the manufacture of "Barker shirts" through the second half of the 1800s. A competing factory at 127 Spring Street did a thriving trade under the management of C. F. Hathaway. Between the two establishments, Hathaway set up a laundry and equipped it with machines purchased from the Empire Company across the river. The Metropolitan Laundry Company bought out Hathaway's interests in both laundry and shirt factory, and in turn sold the factory to Simons, Hatch, & Whitten about 1880. The new company drew power from the laundry to drive its fifty sewing machines and two buttoners, the first such to be steam driven. Fifty workers turned out 100 dozen shirts a week.

On Morse Street, Dalby & Son produced underwear from 150 knitting machines. The work was done on an upper floor, from which the great rolls dropped to a bleaching department, then were cut into patterns, stitched, steam pressed, and marketed on the company's newly devised mill-to-store plan.

OF BICYCLES AND STEAMERS

The Elliott Factory

Sterling Elliott of Michigan and the Stanley brothers of Maine were mechanical geniuses who were neighbors and friends. In 1882 Sterling Elliott arrived in Watertown and bought a factory in which to manufacture bicycles. The Elliott home faced Maple Street, and a tunnel connected it with his bicycle factory, located on the lower level near the river.

In 1886 Elliott invented a quadricycle, and while he was working to perfect it, he built a large hall with a hardwood floor where people could practice riding his cycles. One evening the Elliott employees gave a party in the hall and in preparation waxed the floor for dancing. The next day as the wheels of a quadricycle were being turned, its hard rubber tires produced a loud screeching noise on the newly waxed floor. Sterling Elliott's study of the cause of the noise resulted in the development of the automobile steering mechanism. Every problem of the four-wheel automobile chassis—the nonturning front axle, the differential rear axle, self-equalizing brakes, the two-wheel steering mechanism, and its ability to keep all four wheels in contact with the road regardless of the quality of its surface—was solved by the Elliott quadricycle.

In 1894 the Elliott factory's twenty-five workmen built the first bicycle with inflatable tires. The raw rubber used to make these tires was harvested

Sterling Elliott's quadricycle.

in South Africa and shipped to the factory. Sterling Elliott substituted these rubber tires for the large iron-rimmed wheels on a racing sulky at a Waltham racetrack. The world's champion trotting mare Nancy Hanks, with her jockey on the seat behind her, beat her own world record by more than seven seconds. Elliott's factory was inundated with orders and temporarily abandoned the pro-

South side of Main Street, 1865.

duction of bicycles. Rival manufacturers copied his invention, and Robert Ingersoll, a famous attorney, was engaged at $1,000 a day to defend this patent against infringements.

In discussing the new racing record Ingersoll, an agnostic, exclaimed, "That was a hell of a fast gait." Elliott answered, "I thought you did not believe in Hell." Ingersoll smiled and replied, "I don't, but the more I see of some people the more I realize the need of a Hell."

Sterling Elliott spent nine years perfecting a pamphlet-stitching machine that tied the thread automatically on each pamphlet. To do this he had to invent a new and much simpler way to tie a double square knot. He said it was during a sermon at the First Unitarian Church of Watertown that in experimenting with a piece of string he devised a new way to tie the knot. These stitching machines are still extensively manufactured and used in Great Britain.

From 1885 through 1896 Sterling Elliott's principle products were bicycles and trotting sulkies. As a sideline he published *Bicycling World,* a magazine for cycling enthusiasts. In order to mail ten thousand copies a week to subscribers, Elliott invented an addressing system which he and his son Harmon continued to improve upon and perfect until the machines had a secure market. The Elliott Addressing Machine Company later moved to Cambridge and is today located in Randolph, Massachusetts.

In 1896 Sterling Elliott sold his bicycle factory to the Stanley Brothers who derived their inspiration for the design of their steam automobile from the Elliott quadricycle.

The Stanley Steamer

A stone's throw from the Elliott factory was the Stanley twins' factory. Freeland O. and Francis E. Stanley were about the same age as Sterling Elliott. With only limited education they came from Maine and set up a business to manufacture dry plates for cameras, their plant being near the corner of Maple and Hunt streets. The two men were identical twins and wore derby hats slanted over their eyes. They were seated at the factory entrance when their employees arrived at 7:00 A.M. and were inveterate whittlers, always fortified with jackknife and stick. One of them whittled his first violin at age eleven, his last at the age of ninety-one. While manufacturing dry plates they invented an early form of X ray.

It was the steam automobile, however, which brought fame to the Stanley brothers. They were inspired to outstrip a French steam carriage, and this they set out to do. In 1897 they amazed the local populace with their first car. Bearded and sitting high in their open carriage with a lap robe

First horse car from Boston to Watertown, 1857.

Tongue-in-cheek cartoon which first appeared in the Sterling Elliott bicycle catalog of 1888.

over their knees, the brothers steamed along the dirt roads. The engine required a few minutes' time to build up a head of steam. Driving the first model, Mr. and Mrs. F. O. Stanley ascended to the top of Mount Washington in two hours and ten minutes, a distance of more than eight miles of carriage road with a twelve-degree grade. This feat made headlines around the world and set a record for the first automobile to reach the top of Mount Washington.

After two more steamers followed this model, the brothers started manufacturing the necessary parts for the production of two hundred cars. So great was the demand for their patent that they set the price at $250,000, which was met by the Locomobile Company, and for two years it manufactured steamers in the Stanley dry plate building. The Stanley brothers then developed a new design, using a chain drive for axle rotation. For this alleged infringement of patent, they were threatened with court action. In later models the steam was superheated and, under the control of the throttle valve, entered a two-cylinder engine, the power being transmitted through cranks to the gear shaft. The motor was more easily oiled so that

it would not be necessary to stop every few miles to "butter" it. So marked was this improvement that the owners of the old patent sold out at a fraction of the purchase price.

The Stanleys sold their dry plate interests to Eastman Kodak Company and decided to construct a large brick factory, having changed the name of the company to the Stanley Steam Vehicle Company. Because the excavators were nonunion, members of the bricklayers' union refused to work on the building. The Stanleys sold the bricks, hired laborers off the street, and taught them to mix and pour cement. The result was the first factory in New England constructed of reinforced concrete. The building still stands overlooking the Charles River.

The Stanleys did not advertise their cars. They sold for cash to customers as orders arrived, and offered no written guarantee. They would sell no stock in their business, declaring that they had enough trouble just getting along with each other. Their employees were nonunion workers who stayed with them for many years.

The Stanley Steamer automobile enjoyed brisk sales until the outbreak of World War I. Simple,

119

CAR THAT CLIMBED—First car to ascend Mt. Washington, Aug. 30, 1899. This was the first Stanley steamer built by the Stanley twins, one of whom is still living. F. O. Stanley, left, is driving, and F. E. Stanley is seated beside him. The car was put on the road in 1897 and the type was the speediest of cars of all description built about that time. Mr. F. O. Stanley has survived his brother.

News photo of the Stanley twins and their famous Stanley Steamer.

engine. In 1906 the steamer was shipped to Florida where it was entered in a road race against a number of foreign models and established a record of running a mile in twenty-eight and two-fifths seconds. The Stanley Rocket, or "Flying Teapot," was the fastest model, and the Stanley brothers enjoyed racing against each other—so much that they were often arrested for speeding on their many trips between Maine and Massachusetts. After the gasoline engine became popular, people teased them about the appearance of their old-fashioned vehicle and the brothers would reply, "Just the same, steamers are a lot more fun."

Few steamers were built after the beginning of World War I, and in 1918 Francis E. Stanley was killed in a motoring accident on the Newburyport Turnpike. In order to avoid colliding with two farm wagons, Stanley turned the steering wheel of his steamer and collided instead with a pile of wood. Freeland O., prostrated with grief, sold his interest in the business, and the manufacture of Stanley Steamers ended in 1925; Freeland Stanley devoted his remaining years to manufacturing violins in partnership with his nephew and lived to the age of ninety-one.

sturdy, and fast, the steamer was the most economical car until the advent of the internal-combustion

BANKING KEEPS PACE WITH TOWN GROWTH

The Watertown Savings Bank

Charles Barry came to live in Watertown in 1852 when he married Abby Vose Bemis. He and his wife made their home at the corner of Main and Lexington Streets. Barry was in the wholesale coal business and had been one of the first to produce kerosene from Scotch coal before coal was discovered in Pennsylvania. He entered wholeheartedly into local civic activities, becoming a library trustee in 1868 and serving as chairman from 1877 to 1883. Barry was respected by townspeople for his business acumen, his encouragement of thrift, and his dedication to good reading. During this period immediately following the Civil War the need for a savings bank led Barry, Nathaniel Whiting and Joshua Coolidge to apply for a charter from the state. Each of the founding members of the governing board of the new bank invested $100, and when the bank opened in 1870 in an upper room of the Noyes Block, deposits amounted to $924.

The Noyes Block had been built to house Samuel Noyes' grocery store. Noyes, a "temperance" Baptist, moved his store from the east end of Watertown Square, where he had had to compete with three other grocery stores which traded heavily in alcoholic beverages, into available space on the ground level of the Town Hall, and in 1870 moved again into the new Noyes Block opposite. He built the house at the corner of Main and Green Streets for his own residence, and the building later was purchased by the Gallagher family who used it as a funeral home.

In 1892 the bank moved into a $21,000 building designed by Charles Brigham. In 1928 the Watertown Savings Bank replaced the Brigham structure on the same location and expanded its services, making mortgage money available in Watertown and providing a full range of savings bank service to the Watertown Community. In 1976 an addition was built at the 60 Main Street premises and a drive-up branch was also constructed at the corner

Union Market National Bank billboard in Watertown Square, 1920.

of Church and Summer Streets on the former site of the First Parish Church edifice.

The Union Market National Bank

Until the Civil War period the economy thrived on the exchange of goods and currency, but with industrialization and the development of trade and commerce, the banking business expanded to serve the needs of business. A Federal Bank Act was passed by Congress to facilitate the exchange of money by commercial banks. In 1873 in Watertown Charles J. Barry and his associates obtained a charter for a national bank with a capital of $100,000. The Union Market National Bank opened for business in the Bond Building; the bulk of its business was done with the Union Market Stockyards. Barry, having failed to win election to the office of president, left the board of directors, but retained a lively interest in the local savings bank.

In 1921 the space formerly occupied by a dry goods store, a Chinese laundry, and the Noyes Block, in the triangular space at the junction of Main and Pleasant Streets, was cleared and a new bank building was constructed of Indiana limestone for the Union Market National Bank. The

Charles J. Barry, first president of the Watertown Savings Bank.

121

Ceiling mural in the Union Market National Bank was installed in 1921.

122

vault was located in the adjacent Noyes Block, the former home of the bank. The lobby of the new building boasted a ceiling painted with figures representing agriculture, finance, and manufacture; a gun, a beehive, and a lamp symbolized military affairs, industry, and education. The bank's officers and its history reflected its identity with the establishment of first the stockyards and then many other businesses. Among these men were Charles Brigham, H.C. Derby, Oliver Shaw, Alfred Glidden, George Chamberlain, and many others. Starting with checking accounts and business loans and later with savings accounts, the bank provided an immense amount of cash for payrolls and for liberty bonds during the first World War. Through the years it has continued to expand, and in 1979 became part of BayBank Middlesex.

The Watertown Co-operative Bank

The Watertown Co-operative Bank opened for business in 1888 in the upper-floor real estate office of Sam Gleason and Fred Critchett. With a capital of one million dollars the bank sold shares at one dollar each on an orderly monthly pay-plan earning 6 percent interest. Shareholders could withdraw their shares on reaching a certain amount, and mortgages were available on residences.

The Watertown Cooperative Bank took over the old building of the Union Market Bank next to the Watertown Savings Bank in 1921; it underwent several reorganizations and now stands across the street in a new building under the name of the Freedom Federal.

The Coolidge Bank

The Coolidge Bank, founded by a group of East Watertown businessmen in 1960, constructed its present headquarters at the corner of Church and Main in 1970. Pioneering in the establishment of service-charge-free checking accounts, this bank has been responsive to the needs of many local investors.

13

The Civil War Period
and Its Aftermath

THE ROOTS OF THE CONFLICT

URING the years immediately preceding the Civil War the political climate was reaching the boiling point. Abolitionism in the North had estranged the South. Magazines described new western territories: would they become slave or free states? Would the Missouri Compromise continue to maintain the balance of power in Congress? Stormy meetings disrupted the town. George Robbins, the uncle of the Curtis brothers, was a Democrat and the leader of the workers in his starch factory at the old Hunt distillery on Water Street. The Democrats emphasized the rights of the common man. Luke Robinson of the Spring Hotel in Watertown Square led the opposition Whig party in Watertown which represented property interests. Torchlight parades were held and led to fights. Luke Robinson's son William, however, fell in love with the daughter of his rival, George Robbins, and so young William and Abigail were married and found quarters in the Hunt house, the same house where the sculptress Anne Whitney had been born. In 1860 they became the parents of George Frederick Robinson who later became involved in Watertown

politics. "G. Fred," as he was called, eventually wrote a popular history, *Great Little Watertown,* in partnership with his daughter Ruth Wheeler.

Maria White Lowell and Lydia Maria Child contributed to the climate of unrest with their abolitionist tracts, and Theodore Parker lectured vehemently on the subject. Unitarian Pastor John Weiss's strongly held opinions and liberalism led to his twice resigning from his church and twice being invited to return.

Leaders in both the South and the North were stirring public opinion into a frenzy over the question of slavery. Isaac Robbins, another uncle of Benjamin Curtis, received a letter from his brother Josiah in Kentucky. Josiah wrote:

Are you an abolitionist? If you are, don't let me know it, for I shall not like you half so well. Who the Duce is Miss Thaxter, whose name I see coupled in the papers with J. Q. Adams? I understand she is to be appointed Lieut. Genl. of the Abolition forces that are to march to liberate the slaves, under the ex-Pres. & that your cousin Abomelich [Abijah] White is to be Commissary Genl. and that he made a trip to Indiana, trying to collect Swine for the Expedition. I wish you Yankees would mind your own soap and can-

*dles, and [let] the Southern folks alone, with pork & flour
& rice & cotton.*

The Fugitive Slave Act of 1850 raised questions as to the responsibilities of states to each other and questioned the power of Congress to force states to recapture and return runaways. Benjamin Curtis, an able lawyer, gave a welcoming speech in honor of Senator Daniel Webster which impressed Webster by its eloquence and clarity of expression and thought. A Whig representative to the General Court, he exposed secret political bargaining. Subsequently, President Fillmore appointed him to the U. S. Supreme Court. A sheriff, seeing a Bible open on Curtis's desk, is said to have remarked that it was "a strange book for a lawyer to read in his office."

Appointed to the Supreme Court in 1851, Curtis's great moment came in 1857. Dred Scott, a black slave, was taken by his master from Missouri (a slave state) to Illinois and then to Wisconsin (both free states), and finally back to the original slave state of Missouri. Dred Scott claimed the rights of citizenship from having been a resident in free territory. A Missouri court denied his claim, and he appealed his case to the U.S. Supreme Court. George Ticknor Curtis, Benjamin's brother, argued the case on behalf of Dred Scott. Chief Justice Taney read the majority opinion, declaring that Congress had no authority to abolish slavery in the territories. Then Judge Curtis read a minority opinion (representing his own opinion and that of one colleague) supporting the power of Congress to regulate slavery. Curtis's written opinion was given to the press in advance of the publication of the majority opinion. Chief Justice Taney then revised his original opinion to counter Curtis's arguments. When it was printed at last, the majority opinion had been much changed and enlarged. Curtis resigned in protest and returned to private practice, the first justice ever to do so. His resignation drew a cool, formal letter from Taney. Benjamin Curtis later served as leader for the defense in the impeachment trial of President Andrew Johnson. A renowned trial lawyer, he died a rich man in 1874 in his villa at Newport, Rhode Island.

The firing of guns on Fort Sumter brought the issues of slavery and states' rights to a head in April 1861. The war was on, and seceding southern states formed the Confederacy.

The Watertown Arsenal was prepared to furnish equipment to the Union army. A machine

Benjamin Robbins Curtis, 1809-1874.

shop and forge were built, as well as two storage and dry buildings for lumber. Most of the large brick buildings were constructed under the supervision of the Arsenal master mechanic, Thomas French. Older schoolboys and women were employed to manufacture ammunition for hand weapons at seven to nine cents per one hundred. The high quality of iron in the castings produced at the Arsenal, as well as the design of the cannon, earned the admiration of the world. The Arsenal itself served also as a center for experimentation and for the storage of arms; much of the production was subcontracted to nearby foundries.

One such foundry had been built in 1855 next to the gristmill. Its molding room was flush with the Main Street sidewalk; a long brick storage warehouse fronted on Galen Street; it had wharves on the river. Its owner was Miles Pratt, an enterprising young stovemaker. His investment in construction and operation soon took all of Pratt's money,

THE EXECUTION OF JOHN BROWN!

The citizens of Watertown are hereby invited to assemble in the

TOWN HALL,

On Friday Evening, Dec. 2, at 7 1-2 o'clock,

and appropriately notice the CAUSE and the MARTYR, by the free expression of such opinions as may be suggested by the occasion, and the furnishing of MATERIAL AID to the family of JOHN BROWN.

N. B.--Ladies are especially invited.

Joseph Crafts,	Samuel Noyes,	E. B. Blackwell,
Miles Pratt,	Wm. L. Stiles,	Chas. E. Brown,
Wm. H. Ingraham,	Geo. W. Horn,	William Tucker,
Francis Kendall,	N. Henry Crafts,	D. T. Huckins,
John W. Coffin,	Artemas Locke,	A. Lewando,
Edward S. Rowse,	Otis A. Train,	Charles Haley,
C. C. McLauthlin,	George M. Steele,	Horace Clark,
James W. Magee,	George F. Pinkham,	John Dickinson,
George Marsh,	William H. Bustin,	Luther Bent,
Luke Perkins,	James Sharp,	John Tucker,
Bradshaw Whitney,	E. F. Tainter,	C. Wilkins,
Delano March,	Charles H. White,	Jesse A. Locke,
Joseph Coolidge, Jr.,	Royal Gilkey,	C. W. Lenox.

WATERTOWN, Nov. 30, 1859.

Hastings,—Printer,—Waltham.

Notice of public assembly, Nov. 30, 1859.

President Lincoln observed testing of the Rodman Gun at Ft. Monroe, Va.

but he was determined to succeed. He hired Luke Perkins, formerly of the gristmill, as foundry superintendent, and Oliver Shaw as manager; both men had been fellow townsmen of his in Carver, Massachusetts. Col. Thomas Rodman, commander of the Arsenal, discussed with Pratt and Perkins the possibility of molding cannonballs at the foundry. All twenty Pratt workmen were willing to undertake the job, even without the assurance of orders from Washington, and the working force soon rose to one hundred. At about two o'clock in the afternoon molders, stripped to their waists, could be seen transferring molten iron from a blast furnace

into sand molds with long-handled ladles. Occasionally the fiery liquid would burn through their boots. Into the sand molds were poured 275 tons of scrap iron a month, producing small canister shot, solid cannonballs, and shells for guns up to fifteen inches in bore.

The Pratt and Perkins families moved into houses of similar design standing beside each other, at 106 and 112 Mt. Auburn Street, respectively. A few years later Oliver Shaw built a third house at 120 Mt. Auburn Street where he lived until his death in 1894.

WAR IS DECLARED

Anticipating war, one Massachusetts regiment had mobilized the previous January; soon after war broke out, the unit was ready to go into battle. When

they left, cheering crowds gathered at Boston & Albany Railroad stations along their route. The crowd at Newton depot included many Watertown

127

Thomas J. Rodman, Commanding Officer of the Watertown Arsenal from 1859 to 1865.

people, including town officials. On the way home Sam Stearns, a twenty-year-old carpenter, asked Selectman Luke Perkins, "Why can't we raise a company?" Eight or so young companions heard him say, "I'm going to enlist." His fervor infected other Watertown citizens, and they met in a special session the following week at the town hall. Miles Pratt was elected moderator of the meeting and made a stirring speech. Young William Ingraham, the town clerk, recorded the proceedings. Sam Stearns was the first to enlist for three years and was followed by James Harrington and a number of others. Each volunteer received thirty dollars as an enlistment bounty; uniforms were provided from town money and private gifts. Cavalry boots were furnished by A. D. Drew at thirty dollars a pair.

The men were first quartered in tents in a field near the West School. They called it Camp White and marched from it to the Spring Hotel for three bountiful meals a day, provided by the proprietor, Samuel Batchelder, famous for his good food. The enlistees made up Company K, the flag company, of the 16th Massachusetts Infantry Regiment. Volunteers from Watertown entered other regiments and services as well, such as the navy. After the first wave of enthusiasm cooled, many would-be draftees met their obligation by paying for a substitute to serve for them, a controversial but legal practice at the time.

THE TRAVAIL OF COMPANY K

Company K was temporarily transferred to Cambridge before leaving for the South in August under Col. Powell Wyman of Boston and with the local Unitarian pastor, Arthur Fuller, as chaplain. They were stationed in Baltimore until September and prior to the next summer were sent to various posts near the mouth of the James River in Virginia. Many later remembered the attack on the *Merrimac* by the ironclad *Monitor* with its revolving "cheesebox" gun turret. In June they joined the Army of the Potomac under Gen. Joe Hooker in the drive toward the Confederate capital of Richmond. At Glendale they encountered stiff opposition as they attempted to hold the right flank. General Hooker, whose statue on horseback now commands the front of the State House in Boston, later declared, "There is no doubt but at Glendale the 16th Massachusetts saved the army. . . . I can trust them anywhere." Unfortunately, their de-termined resistance cost the life of their commander, Colonel Wyman.

"I was slightly wounded in the left shoulder," recalled Sam Stearns in describing the Battle of Bull Run. The clatter of horses' hooves bringing word of the bloody two-day battle interrupted church services in Watertown on the last day of July. The regiment appealed for dressings for the wounded. The women immediately hurried to the town hall in great excitement and spent the rest of the day making bandages, and medical supplies were soon dispatched with those from four other nearby towns. President Lincoln sent a letter of thanks "for the large amount of hospital stores" in a letter dated September 1862 which concluded with, "have the kindness to convey to the generous donors the assurance of my grateful appreciation of their efforts." The women continued to send packages containing stockings, handkerchiefs, needlebooks, and other small necessities. A chaplain in the battle area said to a dying Watertown soldier, "John, the folks at home have sent you something." "Home?" murmured the man, "then, Chaplain, pin it above my head that when I open my eyes I can see it." The chaplain, Joseph Lovering, later was a minister in Watertown.

After effecting several withdrawing actions in December of 1862, Company K marched the muddy road toward Fredericksburg, Virginia. Before crossing the Potomac River, the Reverend Arthur Fuller resigned as chaplain, shouldered a rifle as a private, and was among the first to be shot on the streets of the city. His body was brought north to be buried in Mt. Auburn Cemetery. In the same December engagement the Reverend Henry Hempstead, who had been released by the Watertown Methodists to serve in the army, died outside the city, having served as chaplain for another Massachusetts regiment. Hempstead was mourned by both his comrades and his parishioners.

On New Year's Day of 1863 four million slaves were declared free by President Lincoln's Emancipation Proclamation (formally issued the previous September). Benjamin Curtis, a strong believer in the U. S. Constitution, felt that by this act the president had arrogated to himself power vested in Congress. When Lincoln's Republican party succeeded the Whigs, Curtis withdrew his allegiance from the new party.

The next summer found Watertown welcoming home some of her men who had served for nine months in the South. They marched from the local depot to the Galen Street home of their captain, Joseph Crafts, their parade ending at the Grove on Whitney Hill with speeches and refreshments. One soldier, Charles Brigham, only briefly out of high

Samuel F. Stearns, Watertown's first volunteer, in 1861.

school, was already listed as "architect." The Otis brothers, Horace and Ward, also served in this regiment; Horace enlisted for additional service and was wounded. It was for the Otis brothers that Otis Street was named.

In July the three-day Battle of Gettysburg took a heavy toll of Sam Stearn's regiment but turned the war in favor of the North. Company K came home a year later. One day while Sam was working in the foundry a selectman came to ask for sixteen volunteers for military service. Fifteen men said they would volunteer if Sam would, and he and his companions enlisted in the Frontier Cavalry.

VICTORY AT LAST!

Grant met Lee to discuss surrender on April 9, 1865, and on April 15 President Lincoln died from an assassin's bullet. Lincoln's policy, "With malice toward none, with charity toward all . . . let us bind up the Nation's wounds," was carried on by Vice-President Andrew Johnson. The task of reconstruction was made more difficult by a hostile secretary of war, Stanton, who refused to quit, and by a hardhearted Congress which overrode the new president's vetoes and enacted harsh and vengeful

legislation for dealing with the South. The lower house of Congress started impeachment proceedings against President Johnson, who was to be tried before the Senate with the chief justice presiding. Both Johnson and his cabinet favored the selection of Benjamin Curtis for the defense. Clear of thought and brief in language, Curtis was easily the foremost legal mind of the country.

The Curtis law practice was thriving, and so, although the president could not afford counsel,

129

1861 engraving in "Harper's Weekly" pictured men and women making war materials at the Arsenal.

Curtis responded at once and left for Washington. On meeting Johnson for the first time he was impressed with the President's sincerity and calm assurance. He sent word to his brother, George, an attorney in New York City, to come to his aid in clarifying one of the charges against Johnson. George did not remain for the trial, which took place in March 1867.

Those assembled in the Senate court were still. Curtis rose—large, effective, yet modest. As he spoke he either placed his fingers lightly on the table in front of him, or joined his hands behind his back. "Mr. Chief Justice," he began, "I am here to speak to the Senate . . . as a court of impeachment . . . Here party spirit . . . can have no fit operation." His argument closed with the challenge that injustice would return to plague its inventors. Johnson was acquitted by one vote.

A boulder was placed in Watertown Square in honor of Benjamin Curtis. A monument was also erected in Saltonstall Park in tribute to Watertown men who had served in the Civil War. It represents an infantryman loading his rifle. Veterans of the war organized the Grand Army of the Republic,

Town Hall Memorial Day decorations featured President Grant.

and the Watertown unit took the name Isaac S. Patten Post. Isaac was a sailor of nineteen who enlisted in the Union army for the last year of the war and died in a Carolina prison. The last GAR member to survive was Alvin Tolman.

TEMPERANCE

During the 1870s the Baptists and the Woman's Christian Temperance Union crusaded for the prohibition of alcohol. So unpopular were the "dries" that on occasion bottles filled with tar were flung through their windows. It was recorded of Sylvester Priest, a partner in Whitney's Paper Mill, that he "came all through those times of Rum unharmed," and in seventy-seven years spent "only ten cents on tobacco." Yet in 1880 the voters voted to put an end to the local traffic in intoxicants. Saloons closed, as did the Spring Hotel.*

The hotel's upper floor was the living quarters of Mrs. Alice Potter Silsbee. Her brother Briggs Potter for many years kept a livery stable on Spring Street for the hire of horse-and-buggy or carry-all outfits. In the Watertown Square area there were a number of blacksmith forges and harness shops servicing four to five hundred horses. Two granite watering troughs for animals were located at highway intersections, one of them in the Square. Ross's shop on Spring Street made carriages to order, including one for Dr. Alfred Hosmer.

THE LIBRARIES

After the Civil War town leaders turned their civic minds to the establishment of a library for high school students. Joseph Bird, Jr., was a singing master and loved both children and books; he "was said to have read every book which came under his

hand and remembered every book he read." Fair haired and ruddy cheeked, he was a good-humored man with a deep bass voice. Bird had voted in favor of merging the old Union Social Library in his father's Bird Tavern with the North District Library to implement Education Commissioner Horace Mann's statewide plan to make libraries available to students. Pupils were permitted

*The traffic in intoxicants did not, however, end, and in fact "blind tigers," as the speakeasies were called, abounded.

131

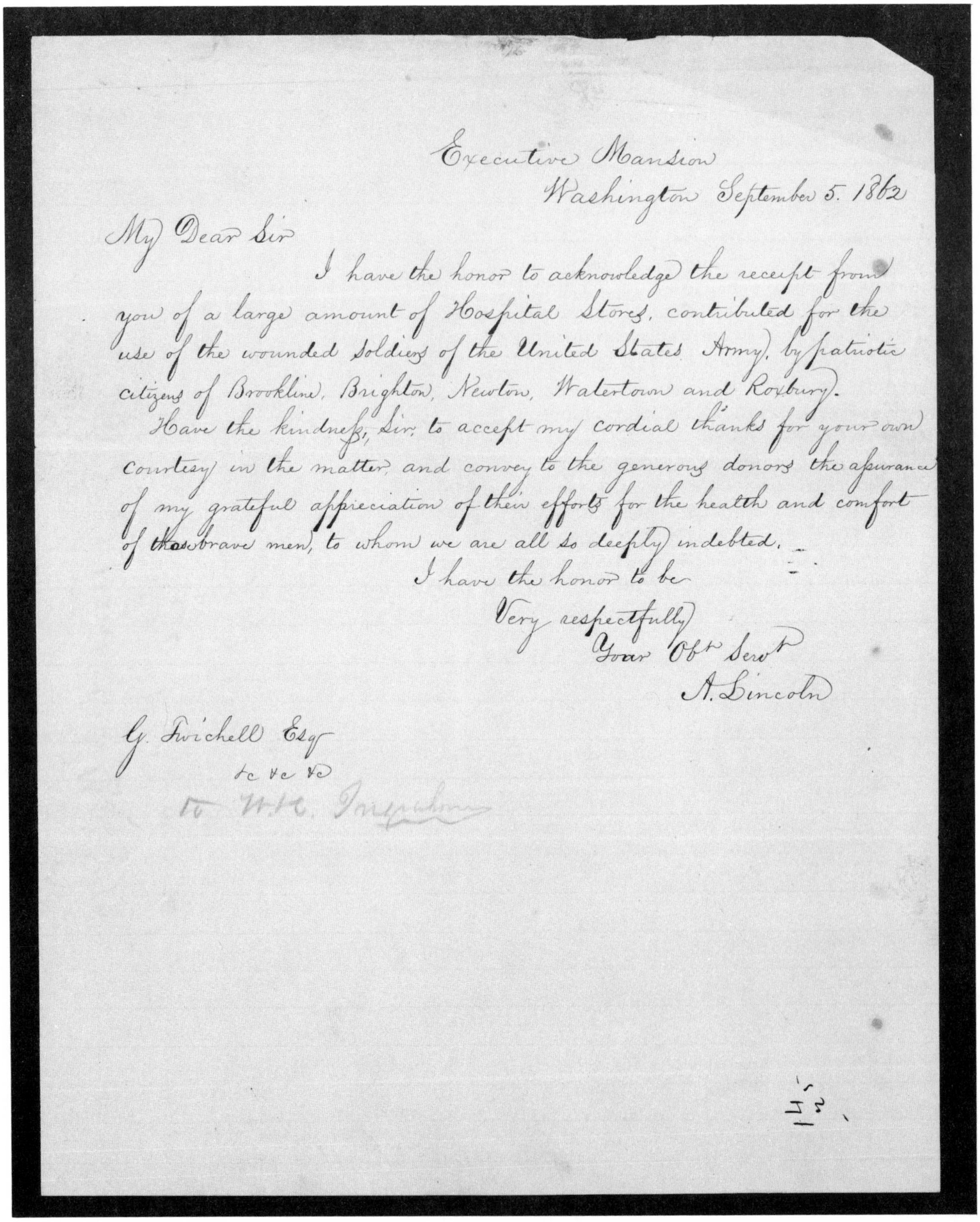

Executive Mansion
Washington September 5. 1862

My Dear Sir

I have the honor to acknowledge the receipt from you of a large amount of Hospital Stores, contributed for the use of the wounded Soldiers of the United States Army, by patriotic citizens of Brookline, Brighton, Newton, Watertown and Roxbury.

Have the kindness, Sir, to accept my cordial thanks for your own courtesy in the matter, and convey to the generous donors the assurance of my grateful appreciation of their efforts for the health and comfort of those brave men, to whom we are all so deeply indebted.

I have the honor to be
Very respectfully
Your Obt Servt
A. Lincoln

G. Twichell Esq
&c &c &c
to W.H. Ingraham

Unauthenticated letter of thanks from President Lincoln to W. H. Ingraham.

to use the books free of charge, but since there was no control over the circulation of books many had been lost by the close of the war. Acting for the school committee, Bird formed the nucleus of a high school library.

The new library proved a success and the pupils came to depend on it. No sooner had this been accomplished than the school committee invited the public to an open hearing to discuss the establishment of a "FREE PUBLIC LIBRARY"—these letters were printed in capitals across the invitation. The meeting convened at the Unitarian Building and appointed a committee to raise the necessary funds. Joseph Bird worked enthusiastically for the library and was joined by two doctors, Alfred Hosmer as chairman, and David T. Huckins, a longtime school committeeman, together with Capt. Joseph Crafts, a teacher and wool manufacturer; John Weiss, minister of the Unitarian church; Miles Pratt, of the Walker and Pratt Foundry; Leonard Whitney, Jr., of the Whitney Paper Mill Company; Solon Whitney, principal of the high school; and Jesse Locke, representative to the legislature (who gave his salary of six hundred dollars to start the fund-raising campaign). They worked hard and raised six thousand dollars to build the new public library.

The money was then presented to the town on condition that the town agree to establish a library by supplying quarters and appropriating a like sum. A committee consisting of the writer Edward Bangs; Henry Chase, the teacher; Alvin Adams, the expressman; and David Flint, the builder; with the Reverend John Weiss as chairman, and Solon Whitney as secretary was directed to organize a library. A summer town meeting in 1868 appropriated $1,000 and elected ten trustees, including Josiah Stickney, Abiel Abbott, and Joshua Coolidge. The committee made careful buying lists and stored books in a first-floor room of the high school building. In March 1869 the Watertown Public Library opened on the first floor of the town hall in a room which had previously been used as a dry-goods store. The opening was not marked by speechmaking but by a day of work during which the trustees filled the shelves with new books, happy in the conviction that they had contributed a valuable asset to the community.

Public appreciation expressed itself in the first year's circulation of ten thousand books. As the

library room became crowded, a second room, a shop where medicine and groceries had been sold, was added. Solon Whitney was librarian in addition to being high school principal. In 1871 when he moved to Cambridge to teach in the Cambridge High School, he retained his library position in Watertown, a job he kept for a half century.

Civil War recruits boarded at the Spring Hotel, built about 1824.

The Town Hall Library

The library soon outgrew the limited space in the town hall. To raise money for a library building, the trustees obtained pledges for twenty thousand dollars which they hoped the town would match. The donors included Seth Bemis, Father Robert Stack, William Ingraham, Sam Noyes, J. K. Stickney, Sam Payson, and Charles Barry. Hollis Hunnewell pledged ten thousand dollars in memory of his father, the Main Street physician, if the gift could be matched by an equal amount. Sam Walker offered four thousand dollars with the proviso that the location for the library be the Main Street land lying in front of his house but divided from it by a belt of trees and the railroad track. (Capt. John Fowle's house had stood on this site before it was moved to 49 Mount Auburn Street, and later also Mrs. Bates' shirt factory.) The trustees raised the amount necessary to match Hunnewell's gift.

133

Solon Whitney, from a portrait by James H. Rattigan.

The New Town Library

In 1884 a library of French Renaissance design was built of brick with red sandstone trim. Pillars supported the beamed ceilings and ornate fireplaces heated the reading room.

The Pratt Room of the library was named for Asa Pratt. His son Charles was born into a large family, the father Asa having operated a furniture workshop for fifty years at the corner of Spring and Summer Streets. Asa was poor, scrupulously honest and compassionate. Charles showed such promise that his sister Ann, out of her bank savings from working as a housemaid at $1.50 a week, gave him $100 to embark on the oil business. Charles Pratt went to Brooklyn, entered into partnership with John D. Rockefeller, and eventually became a multi-millionaire. Pratt founded the Pratt Institute in Brooklyn and to honor his father, he gave to the Watertown Library a trust fund, called the Asa Pratt Fund, of five thousand dollars for the purchase of magazines and newspapers. By his instructions the room later used as a children's room was prepared as a reading room for workingmen and, provided with its own entrance door, was known as the Pratt Room. He gave additional money to furnish it. The room next to the children's room now bearing his name is a later development. Upon Mrs. Barry's death her husband Charles, a trustee, left the library a trust fund of one thousand dollars in her name to be used for the purchase of books.

The public library's excellent relationship with local industries was demonstrated by the fact that in 1898 Solon Whitney reported that, "as in former years we have received from the Union Bag and Paper Company a plentiful supply of excellent covering paper for such of our books as it has been deemed best for sanitary reasons to cover." Whitney was instrumental in raising money and obtaining books and other gifts for the new library.

THE HISTORICAL SOCIETY

At the same table at which had been drafted the invitation to discuss the establishment of a town library a dozen years before, a group of men led by Alfred Hosmer signed a charter forming the Watertown Historical Society. The group included William Ingraham, town clerk; the architect Charles Brigham; Dr. Julian Mead; Solon Whitney, the librarian; Dr. Bennett Davenport of the "Fountain Hill" family; and the Reverend Edward Rand. Dr. Hosmer was elected the first president. Membership quickly grew to fifty, and rather grudgingly admitted women. The object of the Historical Society was to preserve the history of the town and to secure its records against mishap. At their meetings the members presented papers on historical subjects, often expressing the belief that they were entering a Golden Age of achievement. Due to the society's efforts and with one thousand dollars appropriated by the town the handwritten records of town meetings, 1634 to 1680, were edited and printed in a single volume, accompanied by statistics of births, marriages, and deaths, and a listing of early land grants. Solon Whitney gathered the historical papers presented by the members into the book, *Historical Sketches of Watertown,* which included a reproduction of his own portrait painted

Exterior of the Watertown Free Public Library before 1900.

by a prominent artist, James H. Rattigan of Watertown.

Death overtook Mr. Rand before he filled his fifth scrapbook with clippings recording the society's activities. His collection, called the *Rand Scrapbooks* are available in the public library. Under his apple trees on a September afternoon, Rand discussed plans for a Historical Society meeting with Jesse Fewkes. Then he wrote these last words in Scrapbook V,

I'm sorry I'm so crippled, I cannot go to the meeting. It will be fifteen years from the start of this historical enterprise—my first absence from any kind of meeting . . . A blessing on his white hair [Jesse Fewkes'] , his joy, and his fine spirit.

Dr. Hosmer and William Ingraham both died soon after Rand. All three had ensured their own memorials by working to preserve the town's history.

SCHOOLS

Status of the Schools in Mid-1850s

In the middle of the nineteenth century there were three school districts. The Coolidge School served the East End; the Howard Street School in the West End had been replaced in 1857 by a new school nearer Main Street. The West School came to be referred to as old Spring School; one of its best-loved masters was Henry Chase, who had a long tenure.

The Brick School served the middle or double district and soon became inadequate. Next to it, on land later acquired by the Methodist Church, the

first Francis School was constructed; its admirers described it as "one of the finest structures of its kind in the vicinity . . . It will compare with the schoolhouses of Boston and other large cities."

Need for a High School

A new central high school became a priority for Watertown in 1853. Civic leaders, including Nathaniel Whiting, worked vigorously to discontinue the district system, to overcome objections to cost, and in the annual town meeting of 1853 to obtain the vote, not only to organize a three-year

Watertown Historical Society gathering in an earlier day.

high school course, but to build a new school building. The new high school stood on the site of today's Phillips School and became part of it. The fifty-two pupils who started at the Watertown High School on October 17, 1853 had their picture taken on the steps of the Universalist Church with their first headmaster, William Webster. Besides being the only teacher of the first class, Webster was the founder of the Pequossette Lodge of Free Masons in Watertown. After having his salary cut by a penny-wise town, he transferred to the Boston Latin School at midyear. Mr. Chase of the West School replaced Webster for the remainder of the school year.

Even with the addition of new entering classes, the total enrollment of the high school was less than fifty for several years. In 1857 the first group of graduates included six girls and Charles Brigham of the former Coolidge Tavern.

The next winter a fire partially destroyed the building. While repairs were being made classes were held in the former West School. On the old first floor one teacher had charge of five dozen

primary grade children, and the room above them in the old building held the temporary high school. When the high school returned to its restored building a large number of students enrolled. It was reported: "There seems to be a charm about the high school which stimulates each member." The charm was soon interrupted by the Civil War.

The Parker School

When the Universalists vacated their meetinghouse on Galen Street, many town meetings vociferously argued the merits of using it for a south school. In 1868 for a purchase price of thirty-five thousand dollars, plus six thousand dollars for remodeling, its steeple and belfry were removed and the interior fitted out as classrooms, two on each floor. It was named for Theodore Parker who, in his student days, had held a private school on the opposite corner of Water and Galen streets.

In the last year of the Civil War the schoolchildren were vaccinated against smallpox, and not a single case occurred in Watertown. Doctors Morse,

136

Charles Pratt, 1830-1891, founder of Pratt Institute.

Hosmer, Huckins, and Richardson received thirty-five dollars per one hundred children inoculated. Children owned their own schoolbooks and used slates for figuring problems in arithmetic.

The Problem of Absences

The habitual absence of certain children from school troubled the townspeople. One third of the Center School enrollment might be absent on any given day. The problem was relieved somewhat by imposing fines, by appointing truant officers, and by increasing contact between parents and school committee members. A large number of children of recent immigrants went to work instead of entering high school; this situation led to the introduction of evening and summer courses. Greater emphasis was placed on relating lessons to life rather than to memorizing information. Children were taught to lead the horses when ice was being cut; they weeded gardens and picked berries, peas, and other fruits and vegetables for marketing; they were hired to work at the Aetna Mills. War work at the Arsenal drew away older high school boys, who became a disturbing influence with their firing of guns, shouting, setting fires, and using foul language. Headmaster George Dwelley, although popular and capable, found the situation more than a handful.

Dissatisfaction With the Schools

With the temperance and abolitionist controversies abating, considerable discontent over public education surfaced. One point of view believed that

the town is one of the smallest in the area in the State, one of the richest in material wealth, one of the richest too in its historic past, action, energy, and enterprise in the present; let her not falter in this, her most important duty—public schools second to none.

The critics complained, "Graduates can't earn a dollar, write a good letter at fifteen, or read a newspaper well." School committee reports were ridiculed so much in town meeting that Dr. Hosmer and one of the ministers resigned. One speaker quipped:

a pupil may review arithmetic yet be unable to measure a load of wood, or tell how much corn goes into a bushel of meal, or keep books for a grocer who is sharp enough to sell sand for sugar, and clover leaves for tea.

School was deadening, it was argued, when the need was for air and exercise. An educated committeeman, J. J. Sullivan, asserted that teachers did not teach and that pupils studied too many subjects. There were three high school principals in the 1870s, each of whom served one three-year term. One of them did not trouble to appear for an all-teacher testing and left for a position in a Boston high school. The furor abated when responsibility for the school system was placed in the hands of a superintendent. John Prince was engaged for the position with the understanding that he would divide his work week between Waltham and Watertown.

St. Patrick's School

Another aspect of school discontent had long been coming from Catholic taxpayers who agreed with a widespread objection voiced in the *Boston Advertiser:* "Catholics will not be taxed either for educating children of Protestants or for having their own children educated in school under Protestant control." The valuable help of Father Robert Stack was lost from the school committee when he withdrew to establish a parochial institution, St. Patrick's School, in the summer of 1888. He erected a brick schoolhouse and partitioned the old

Watertown High School, circa 1880.

Academy into rooms to accommodate the members of a teaching order of nuns from Kentucky. The Catholic school attracted four hundred children, the loss of which was soon replaced in the public school system by a rapidly growing population.

This priest labored mightily in the parish—his only one—for twenty-one years. He built the rectory on Chestnut Street, intending to use the remaining part of the lot for a larger church, for his membership soon numbered fifteen hundred. He did not live to see this plan carried out, but before his death in 1895 East End Catholics built the Sacred Heart Church, a project which had been dear to his heart. After a tumor operation from which he did not rally, Father Stack died. He is buried in St. Patrick's Cemetery.

Other School Matters

A schoolhouse under construction in Saltonstall Park at the time of his death was named for President Ulysses S. Grant. Children from the crowded West and Center schools were transferred to the Grant School, the last schoolhouse to be constructed of wood. The other schools were officially named the Coolidge, Francis, Parker, Phillips, and Spring in honor of former townsmen.

An ugly incident marred the school administration. A school committee stooped to the unfortunate removal of George Dwelley, first as high school principal and the following year as superintendent. He had served faithfully as principal for twenty-two and one half years and as superintendent for fourteen years. At the same time the committee also removed a capable woman teacher from the high school; however, she was reinstated. Adelaide Coolidge, later joined by James H. Vahey, was the only committee member to protest the removal.

Although the Grant, Bemis, and the parochial schools were absorbing many children, the school committee was faced with the old problem of finding space in the center of town. Its chairman, young Dr. Julian Mead, pressed for a new building on Spring Street near the high school and saw his dream realized from plans drawn by Charles Brigham. The new Francis School was of glazed yellow brick with slate roof and arched entrances. In two years its capacity was strained, and its hall was divided to make another classroom. The growth in school population at the East End was solved by the building of the Hosmer School. The school's name honored two doctors, Hiram and Alfred, the father and cousin of Harriet Hosmer. At opening ceremonies Miss Hosmer addressed the student body, promising to carve a bust of her father for the school. Unfortunately, she did not live long enough to fulfill her promise.

The Challenge of Change

1900/1980

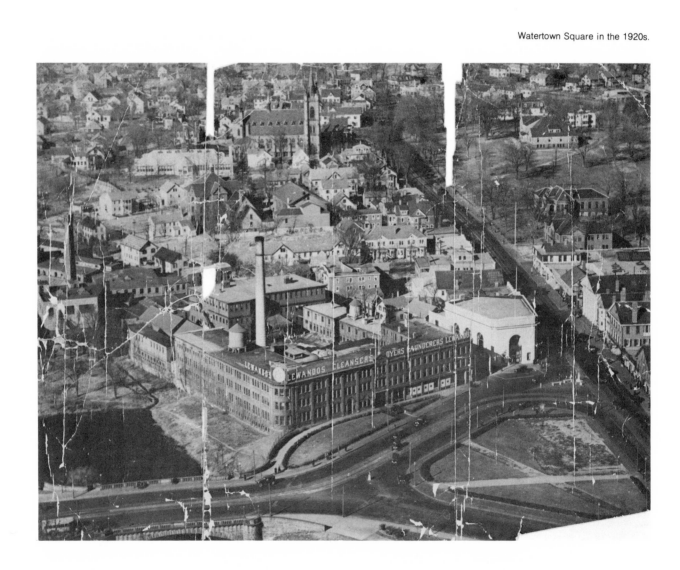

Watertown Square in the 1920s.

14

The Town

TOWN AFFAIRS

HE TOWN noted the centennial of national independence on July 4, 1876 by holding a celebration in the Grove on Whitney Hill. Music was played and a patriotic address was delivered by the Rev. John Lovering. The town's oldest war veteran, Leonard Whitney, Sr., was present. The celebration continued into the evening with fireworks and music.

The drowsy little village of two thousand at the opening of the 1800s gained another thousand citizens by the time of the building of the new high school in 1853, and doubled the figure in the next quarter century, mainly by immigration from Ireland. Boston people were moving to Watertown, attracted by jobs and homes. The Aetna Mills, the stockyards, factories in the Square and on the South Side all attracted workers. The Crawfords were among the newcomers. Calvin Crawford, a "forty-niner" returned from the California gold rush, became superintendent of the Stickney estate and took under his wing a young nephew, Fred E., who graduated from the high school. When the uncle retired to his Lincoln Street home, another Vermont nephew, Fred's brother, succeeded him as caretaker of the Stickney gardens.

In 1901 the belfry and steeple of St. Patrick's new brick edifice appeared on Main Street. At the

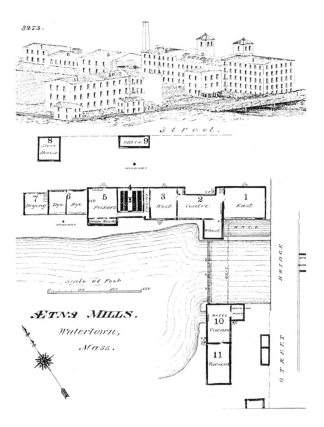

Sketch plan of Aetna Mills.

Advertisement in "The Ideal Watertown," Feb. 23, 1898.

turn of the century Watertown had begun to grow. The population increased, new businesses were established, government provided more services, and the face of the town changed radically.

Problems With Water Supply, Sewers, and Drainage

Hydrant service was bought by contract with the Watertown Water Supply Co., a stock company formed in 1880. Its well at Bemis drew underground spring water. Forty feet deep, it also drew water from the river. The combined water then entered filtering galleries or tanks. From the same source, piped water, not always clear or pure, replaced the need for well-pumps and cisterns in the houses. Dr. Julian Mead, who was relieving Dr. Hosmer with his medical practice, was district health inspector. He was also president of the water company, which paid a dividend of 10 percent to its stock holders.

The town bought these water rights in 1897 for four hundred thousand dollars. Money had to be borrowed, and the loans, as they fell due, were refunded at high interest; this constituted a continuing burden on the town. Furthermore, worn pipes had to be replaced. In 1898 the town made the decision to join the water district under the jurisdiction of the Metropolitan Water Commission. Since reservoir water was purer, it was possible to close the Bemis pumping station.

At the same time sewers were being laid throughout the town. Beginning with an appropriation of $35,000, the work of waste water disposal was extended to all sections, costing a total of $150,000 before the end of the century. It was realized too late that landowners who benefited by this service should have been billed for their share of the expense. However, it was a convenience in comparison with the old outhouses and cesspools; the old Coolidge School privies were removed and replaced by indoor toilets as recently as 1901.

A main pipe collected waste water from the East End, another from the West End, and seven outlets carried the contents to the river and into the Metropolitan Sewer System. The "Met" pipe, following the river underwater, was laid in the 1890s for the benefit of bordering communities and ended their bickering about water. The Watertown sewer pipes were not large enough to carry their load, and their spring caps or underwater valves often opened and spilled refuse into the river.

A separate system was also being laid to drain off surface water. Treadaway Brook and its railroad branch from upper Main Street were walled in and their contents diverted into an outfall drain which flowed into the river at Watertown Square.

Town Improvements

Eight sprinklers were drawn by fire station horses to lay street dust. These cylindrical wooden tanks, which resembled oil trucks, drew water from twenty-nine standpipes. Improved road construction followed the purchase of a stone crusher and a steamroller, and the eventual appointment of a highway superintendent. Streetlights depended on kerosene or gas. The contractor for these, the Newton and Watertown Gas Light Company, did not send its lamplighters around when it expected the moon would shine on the town. The company supplied one hundred arc lights at one hundred dollars each per year for street crossings; these consisted of a pair of cones which carried a bright light between their points. Later incandescent bulbs were installed throughout the town.

Candles and kerosene lamps in the homes gave way first to gaslight and later to electricity. Some buildings were fitted with both kinds of lighting. In 1892 a modern sewer system was begun. A health department report in 1894 listed a total of one hundred bathtubs made of zinc or copper, but there were few telephones. Fifty new dwellings were reported erected in one year. Builders and real estate developers were very active, opening the Paige estate on Galen Street, in addition to Russell Avenue, Whiting Park, and Otis Street. An increase in land valuation followed. Sale of lumber was brisk for Sylvester Priest, later for Gilkey and Stone in the Watertown Lumber Company, and then for Chester Sprague, all doing business at the corner of Irving and Arsenal streets.

NEW CHURCH BUILDINGS

The Good Shepherd parish (Episcopal) of which the Reverend Edward Rand was the minister was the first to build a stone church, following the Anglican country style. Within a decade, three more handsome stone churches rose on Mt. Auburn Street—Sacred Heart in 1893, fulfilling a dream of Father R.P. Stack; a Methodist church in 1894 and a Baptist church in 1900. The first (1847) Francis School and its grounds were bought and added to the Methodist premises by Frederick Whitney, who also presented the church with a carillon for its tower.

RIVER IMPROVEMENT

Launching of the S.S. Watertown on the Charles River in 1890.

The Charles River had attracted settlers with its plentiful fish; its falls had provided power for its mills; its stream had furnished a route for transportation of persons and goods. Lewandos and other industries found it a handy place to dump their effluent, sewage overflowed into it and the filth killed off the fish, but boys and girls still waded barefoot through the muddy stream where the bed was shallow.

Because only small freighters could navigate the tidal river, public opinion favored dredging it. In 1890 Solon Whitney wrote, "A little dredging would make the whole River navigable to the Bridge and be of great value to the Town. It is hoped that a new era in navigating the River has begun." This dredging never took place, even though the federal government had promised twenty thousand dollars for this purpose, provided that two bridges over the Charles be built to permit the passage of larger vessels. The S.S. *Watertown* built by Boston wine merchant John Cassidy was launched, the first steamer to ply the river. (Cassidy lived at 227 North Beacon Street.) The launching took place near Cassidy Brook, where there were a wharf and a shop. Over five thousand spectators came from Watertown and surrounding towns; they banqueted and listened to speeches and band music. The four-hundred-ton vessel had a double hull and was driven by twin screws. For its trips to and from the harbor, the drawbridge at North Beacon Street was lifted in order for the loaded ship to pass. The Honorable George Dale later recalled being aboard when a shipment of cattle was being carried on the lower deck; although it was July Fourth, snow filled the air. The steamer

143

The Crawford range, as advertised in 1898.

was often in trouble and ended its service when it burned at Deer Island in Boston Harbor in 1893.

Those who dreamed of beautifying the riverbanks had their supporters. Charles Davenport spent years attempting to persuade civic groups of the merits of beautification. In 1900 the federal government had engaged in dredging operations from the Charlestown Navy Yard well into the Boston harbor, and from 1901 to 1903 the Metropolitan Park Commission (MPC) conducted a two-year study of the Charles River Parkway and the Charles River Dam. Jeremiah J. Sullivan submitted to the town the results of an investigation of land claims along the riverbank. Through action of the federal government tidewater was acquired by the MPC, as

were thirty miles of riverbank and ten miles of oceanfront land.

A boulevard one mile in length and twenty-six feet wide running from the Arsenal to the Galen Street Bridge was completed under the direction of John Starr, a local engineer. He dug river gravel for fill, built fifty catch basins, and provided space for the planting of trees. Tides continued to ebb and flow on the river until 1903 when work started on the viaduct dam. In his declining years Mr. Davenport had reason to hope that his dreams for the riverfront would be fulfilled.

For the next seven years the viaduct dam was under construction, providing locks to carry small craft to and from the tidewater. The dam was built at the location of the Craigie Bridge, a crossing much used by city traffic and later the route of trains to Lechmere Station in Cambridge. The cost of the new bridge over the Charles River Dam was borne by the cities of Boston and Cambridge. After its completion, upstream the Charles River was kept at seven and one half feet above harbor level and the tides and mudflats disappeared, although the water was still too polluted for bathing. Yachts, cabin cruisers, racing shells, and ice skaters appeared on the river, and automobile traffic flowed on the state road on the river's north bank.

Local planning was needed to deal with the need to provide public services before beautification of the river could be completed. The town's businesses were expanding, and its population was being increased by the arrival of Italians, Greeks, and Armenians, the latter fleeing from Turkish oppression. Many Armenians found jobs at the Hood Rubber Company and they soon numbered one fifth of the town's population. A settlement center called Abraham Lincoln House was established under the direction of Jennie Kinsman.

LAND IMPROVEMENT

Houses were built for the employees of the Walker and Pratt foundry between the Hood factory and the stockyards. Arthur Walker of Malden joined the firm at a time when foreign as well as home markets called for Pratt furnaces and Crawford stoves. Superintendent Bartlett Shaw succeeded his uncle Oliver, and Harvey Lucas and Homer Perkins were also associated with him. A new brick Walker and Pratt foundry was con-

structed in a parklike setting near the Union Market depot on Dexter Avenue between Cypress Street and the railroad tracks. The process of stovemaking moved on one floor from the pattern shop to the shipping room near the railroad, in assembly-line fashion. The factory held open house for 150 stove dealers on "Crawford Day," when, as bands played, two steam engines pulled out of the station drawing thirty-four cars loaded with twenty-one hundred stoves.

In other parts of town tracts of land were divided into house lots. The Watertown Land Company, whose principals were the Otis brothers, Samuel Gleason, and Chester Sprague, laid out Whiting Park, the Otis Street district, and the Paige estate. Taking advantage of the new river view and boulevard, one hundred house lots were put up for

sale by Cornelius O'Connell and E. L. Stone. O'Connell picked a choice site for his own new mansion and had streets surveyed and named for his children. A new board of survey restricted the type of dwelling, prohibiting three-decker houses, such as the one Mrs. Alice Silsbee, a school committee member, had already erected on Riverside Street. Watertown was among the first towns in Massachusetts to adopt a zoning ordinance.

WATER FOR THE GROWING TOWN

The water department began laying water pipes in the 1880s and installing water meters in 1905. New rules were initiated to regulate the cost and use of water. In 1892 the highway department began installing sewers for the new homes and also provided surface drainage for streets. Wilbur

Learned, the town engineer, supervised the building of streets, sidewalks, curbs, sewers, and drains. Although crushed stone and Tarvia began to be used in road building, it was still necessary for sprinklers to lay the dust as late as 1910.

PUBLIC UTILITIES KEEP STEP

Electricity came to the town early in the century, furnishing power for trolleys, factories, and incandescent lights for homes and streets. In 1906 a ten-year contract was signed with the Newton and Watertown Gas Light Company, whose superintendent was Waldo Learned, brother of the town

engineer. The next year, however, the town transferred its business to the Boston Edison Company and thereafter had all-night street lighting. Electric wires were laid underground as the streets were widened or repaired, and Watertown became one of the best-lit towns in the state.

THE NEW HOSPITAL

In 1902 "the pesthouse," as the hospital was called, was built on land behind the almshouse, just before an outbreak of smallpox. It provided a men's and a women's ward and an attendant's room. Tuberculosis caused more deaths in 1908 than any other disease. The health officer published this caution: "Patients should not spit on the floor, carpet, wall, stove, or anywhere, but into a special cup. Male patients should not wear beards." Dr. Mead and J. J. Sullivan established a health department in 1886. The District Nursing Associa-

tion was organized in 1903, and the Watertown Home for Old Folks took over the Oliver Shaw house on Mt. Auburn Street in 1912. Cook's Pond was considered malarial and was filled by the town. The slaughtering of cattle could be done only in the presence of an inspector, who also supervised tuberculin testing. New sanitary codes meant that few of the small milk dealers could compete with the large milk companies, and most either went out of business or merged.

CHANGE IS SEEN ON ALL SIDES

William Maguire became town clerk following Fred Critchett, who had served in that capacity for nineteen years; the office of tree warden was created; and John O'Hearn was made the first fire

chief. O'Hearn moved his department from the town hall annex into the new fire and police headquarters on Main Street; the East End station was added later. Daniel Cooney became police chief in

Glen House, from a color lithograph published by C. H. Baker of Boston.

1901 and remained in the department for twenty-seven years. A group of public-spirited men formed a board of trade to attract new business and to improve transportation and communication services.

By the late 1890s garden estates were being divided into house lots. Oakley became one of the first golf courses in the country. Its western end was purchased by Gilbert Payson, whose family had made its fortune from New Hampshire textile mills. He moved the Otis-Pratt barn nearer to his stone mansion, and both buildings later became part of Mount Trinity Academy. The spacious wooden house on the former Adams (and later Warner) estate east of Oakley was operated as a drinking and gambling club for wealthy Bostonians. The Winsor clubhouse, consisting of a dancehall, stage, and rooms for bowling and pool, was built in 1905 and provided a place for the production of popular theatricals. South of Oakley, the Stearns property was divided. Cushing Gardens became Payson Park after The Bellmont burned and was abandoned by its owner, Col. Everett Benton. The Stickney heirs sold out to Perkins School for the Blind, which had been located previously in South Boston. The Lovell market gardens of Orchard Street, however, continued to flourish.

Wealthy families who summered in Watertown lost their privacy when trolleys replaced horse cars. Watertown first refused to permit these new vehicles on Mt. Auburn Street but reversed this position in 1893. A few years later the Boston Elevated Street Railway bought the Brigham property south of the Galen Street Bridge on which the Coolidge's Tavern had stood. A brick-and-wood carbarn was built to house 250 cars.

Hackett Bros. on the Delta in Watertown Square before 1905.

Square. Many times each day men and women, boys and girls are spilled from their wheels on account of their tires catching in the tracks." Trolley traffic necessitated the widening of Mt. Auburn, Arsenal, Main, and Galen streets, and a single track to Boston was laid on North Beacon Street, so that riders could choose among several routes to Boston. All lines originated in Watertown Square, and at that time the fare was five cents.

The clock located in the tower of the Unitarian church was maintained at town expense. Once a week fireman John Holt mounted the narrow stairs of the church tower to wind the old timepiece. In those days Watertown Square hummed with traffic and industry.

For many years the Otis brothers had carried on a dry goods business in the Square succeeding Jesse Wheeler. During the twenties Otis Hawes purchased the Otis block. The Butler drug store changed hands and W. T. Grant opened a branch store.

The following warning was printed in the town's weekly newspaper: "Bicyclists! Wheelers! Do not ride between car tracks which pass through the

PREPARATION FOR THE NEW BRIDGE

Main and Mt. Auburn streets converged in Beacon Square. At that time there was a clutter of factories, shops, and stables between the Square and the river. In 1905 the Metropolitan Park Commission demolished several buildings, leaving part of the stove foundry, the Barnard block, and the mill. The old mill had been grinding western corn until 1900. The appearance of the Square changed as it opened up on the river side.

The New Bridge

Two years of planning under the chairmanship of J. Hathaway Coon preceded the construction of the new bridge. The old narrow Galen Bridge joined Main Street at an awkward right angle. The Great Bridge of 1719 (sometimes called Nonantum Bridge) for many years had been the only bridge spanning the Charles between the Boylston Street "Great Bridge" (in Cambridge) and Watertown.

In 1905 the worn planking was ripped up, ending nearly two hundred years of heavy service and many disputes over the responsibility for repairs. A temporary structure was erected by a local builder named Murdough. The new bridge was designed

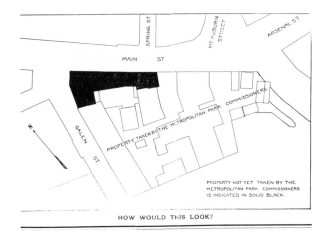

Map from *Ideal Watertown*, February, 1898.

by Wilbur Learned, the town engineer, and it combined strength, utility, and beauty.

The new structure was a broad, wide arch of concrete with a ninety-foot span. T. Stuart and Son of Newton, the contractors, poured the cement, reinforcing it with corrugated bars one inch thick. The bridge was faced with granite blocks cut in Deer Isle, Maine. The roadbed was eighty feet

147

The WCTU Fountain, reproduced from a published photo with the caption "No Art Commission Would Pass This Funereal Memorial Fountain."

wide, spreading out at both ends to provide access for vehicles. Mt. Auburn Street was extended to meet it, and Galen Street was also widened on its eastern end. Balustrades along the sides bore these inscriptions:

This River called the Massachusetts by Captain John Smith A.D. 1614 was named the Charles by Prince Charles A bridge crossed near here as early as A.D. 1641. Here by the mill, bridges were built A.D. 1667 and 1719.

Striking Irish workers stopped construction but were soon replaced by others who were willing to work eight-hour days at two dollars a day. Frosts delayed the completion until the spring of 1908. The MPC dredged a channel five feet deep between this point and the next bridge downstream, widening the river by fifty feet. Willow trees lined the south side of the Charles, where another river road was in the planning stage. The commission constructed a bandstand, and summer concerts were held on the lawn opposite Irving Street. The Barnard block in the Square was bought and razed by the town. On Galen Street, near the bridge, the Women's Christian Temperance Union installed a

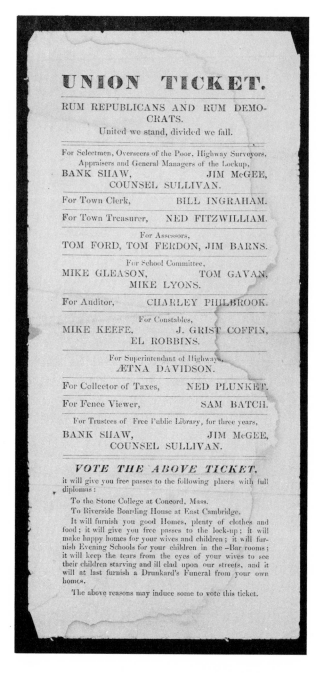

"Union Ticket" handbill.

drinking fountain and a horse trough.

Engineer Learned's overloaded street department was now reorganized. After completing the bridge, Learned was reassigned as engineer for inside work. The street, sewer, and drainage projects were entrusted to Bartley Maloney, a capable boss. His first six months of service gained him

148

extravagant praise: "More work has been done during the past year than in any other in the existence of the Town," which should have meant no discredit to the efforts of the town engineer Learned. When the dredging of the river made it necessary to lower the sewer at the bridge Maloney used canvas connecting pipes lined with tar and cement which conveyed sewage across the river without interrupting its flow.

Three years later both Maloney and Learned were removed by the selectmen and the department was once again combined under a superintendent. A dissenting selectman contended, "Both the engineer and the superintendent of streets deserved better from the Town they had served so

well. I believe the best results have come from the separation of the offices. The former Engineer had given the best years of a long, honorable, and useful life to this Town (though of the opposite political persuasion). Aside from his past services, he has a knowledge of local conditions which it would take a new man years to acquire. I believe he was entitled to something better from the Town than summary dismissal for no cause given." Following the election the new board reversed the decision, and both Learned and Maloney were reinstated. Learned was a modest man whose illustrative charts in the town annual reports of the period show the quality of his painstaking work.

THE WHITNEY FAMILY

Arthur Whitney, a selectman, served as a member of the Galen and Bridge committee. He was a son of Leonard Whitney, who had established the Whitney Paper Mill (later Hollingsworth and Whitney). An event of the 1905 social season in Watertown was the twentieth wedding anniversary celebration of Arthur and Minetta Osgood Whitney. In the Napoleon room of the Whitney mansion on Main Street the couple received five hundred guests; as anniversary gifts Mrs. Whitney was given a necklace of three hundred diamonds and an opera carriage by her husband.

Mrs. Whitney was a celebrated hostess and often opened her house for civic activities. The Whitney house was decorated with the treasures which the family had brought home from trips abroad; in the Chinese room, for example, were tapestries and a Buddhist shrine. Their wealth did not, however, protect them from tragedy. Shortly after the anniversary party their daughter Isabel was burned to

death in a fire caused by a curling iron. Harold Whitney, Isabel's brother, enlisted in the army during World War I and was stationed on Nantucket Island. Maj. Charles Whitney, Arthur's brother, succeeded his father at the papermill; Frederick devoted his energies to his interests in art and music. Frederick, who had lived in Italy for some time, had also been the organist of the Methodist church and became its benefactor, buying an additional plot of land which extended the church property to Summer Street and endowing the church with stained-glass windows, furnishings, and a new organ. The church, renamed St. John's, was rebuilt of stone and was associated with the Whitney family from its founding. The Whitney farm was inhabited by family members throughout eight generations beginning with John Whitney, who had first settled on the site on Lexington Street.

THE STONE FAMILY

The Stone family is one of the earliest Watertown families with descendants still living in the area. Helen Stone (now Mrs. William W. Norcross) lives in the Coolidge Village apartments in Watertown, and Beatrice and Frances P. Stone live just over the line in Belmont. They are the tenth-generation descendants of Deacon Simon Stone

who brought his wife and five children to America from Great Bromley, England, in 1635 and settled in Watertown.

The Stone family lived in East Watertown on land known as "the Stone Woods," or "Sweet Auburn," consisting of many acres of farmland and woods used for raising produce which was sent

149

daily to the Boston market. The property remained in the possession of each succeeding generation of the Stone family until it was sold to the Mt. Auburn Cemetery Corporation in 1912.

Members of the Stone family have been active in town affairs in Watertown for many years. After graduating from Harvard College in 1894 and Harvard Law School in 1896, Walter Coolidge Stone, the father of Beatrice and Frances, served as a member of the Board of Health from 1897 to 1900. He served as a Selectman from 1907 to 1911, as Chairman in 1908, and occupied the office of town counsel for several years. He practiced law in Watertown and Boston for fifty-five years, was a town meeting member all his adult life, and was very proud of his almost perfect attendance. He was president and director for over nineteen years of the Watertown Home for Old Folks (now known as the Marshall House), and his interest in genealogy led him to the post of secretary of the Water-

town Historical Society where he was well-known for his work on local history. He was an active member of the First Baptist Church, where he served as its moderator for several years. He resided in Watertown until his death in 1950 and is buried in the family lot in Mt. Auburn Cemetery only two hundred yards from where he was born.

Edwin Lincoln Stone, the father of Helen Stone Norcross, and his older son, Ronald Mason Stone, were active in the real estate and insurance business and in civic and church affairs in Watertown. Both served for many years on the Board of Assessors. Helen Stone Norcross was secretary to the Selectmen in Watertown for several years.

Each generation of the Stone family demonstrated a tenacious devotion to family, church, and town. For ten generations the Stones worked hard to shape the culture and the religious life of Watertown.

ANOTHER DISTINGUISHED COOLIDGE

Rosamond Coolidge, who lived in the family home at 206 Belmont Street, became a distinguished painter. Born in Watertown in 1884, she was the daughter of Joshua Coolidge the library trustee. Rosamond studied at the Massachusetts College of Art and the School of the Museum of Fine Arts, and during her youth was active in local theatricals. She became a member of a number of artists' groups and received an award from the

Copley Society and a gold medal from an exhibition sponsored by the Jordan Marsh Company. Well-known for her portraits and still lifes, she painted Robert Frost for Curry College in Milton, Samuel Eliot for Boston's Arlington Street Church, and in Watertown her portrait of Sir Richard Saltonstall hangs in the First Parish Church and her portrait of Convers Francis in the Phillips School.

TOWN FINANCES AND POLITICS

For a number of years there had been a growing awareness that the town's finances suffered from a lack of planning. Spending was approved at town meetings each year and reflected a piecemeal approach to solving the town's problems. By 1908 the town debt had mounted to eight hundred thousand dollars, the legal limit. Yet the town needed money for new schools and to pay MPC assessments. On the other hand, the tax base was being broadened by an increase in house building and by industrial and business growth. The MPC contributed ten thousand dollars to a fund which paid for the new road over the Galen Street Bridge; and Mt. Auburn Cemetery, which had purchased

the Stone estate, paid twenty thousand dollars to the town in lieu of taxes.

P. Sarsfield Cunniff, a school committeeman for several years, had taken a special interest in financial matters. A lawyer and politician, he ran for, and was elected to, the office of selectman. During his term of office a finance committee was formed, its members appointed by the moderator. The committee was responsible for examining all departmental requests and money articles submitted to town meeting and for making recommendations relating to expenditures.

In order to put the town's financial affairs in order, Cunniff appealed to each department to request only the amount of money it needed. He installed a new bookkeeping system and was determined to collect unpaid taxes, with the result that delinquent taxpayers paid their back taxes to avoid embarrassment. The introduction of these needed reforms improved the town's financial standing and enabled Sarsfield Cunniff to write in the annual report of 1912, "We were the first to discover the mote in our own eyes, and set out to remove it." Cunniff was reelected five times.

"I AM NOT AFRAID OF TURMOIL"

For Mr. Cunniff, however, a new challenge was to bring about his political downfall. Watertown was a dry town, and anyone who wanted a legal alcoholic drink had to go across the river to neighboring Brighton, part of the city of Boston, to get it. Acting on a complaint that liquor was being sold illegally in Watertown Square, Sarsfield Cunniff instigated several predawn police raids on four local drugstores one Sunday morning and two proprietors were brought into court. The Oakley clubhouse was raided, as was its neighboring Commonwealth Motor and Driving Club. After the patrol wagon made two trips to cart the liquor and gambling equipment away from the Commonwealth Club, its charter was revoked and the club was closed.

The demise of the Commonwealth Club was a severe blow to its members. The club, which inhabited the former Ralph Warner mansion at the corner of Belmont and School streets, was a famous showplace in its day, with mahogany paneling, and hand-carved furniture, as well as Italian paintings decorating its ceilings. It also boasted a picture of a nude over the bar. Later in the winter of 1911 the greater part of the building burned in a spectacular fire. Equipment to help fight the blaze was summoned from neighboring Belmont, Waltham, and Newton. The latter provided no help, however, since as the Newton firetruck approached the Galen Street Bridge the front axle broke, and after it had been repaired the shaft cracked and all three horses ran away, leaving the truck and men stranded.

The liquor interests now banded together with the drinkers to retaliate against Sarsfield Cunniff by attempting to defeat him in his reelection campaign. His supporters were perhaps overconfident; in any case, he came in third in the number of votes cast, which insured his perpetuation in office but reduced his effectiveness. Cunniff had showed his mettle; as he wrote,

I like harmony, but I am not afraid of turmoil. . . . If you draw the shades and close the doors when you attend to the public business, the public can only conjecture what you are up to, and its conjecture is not apt to be complimentary. . . . The white light of publicity is a cure for many ills.

In 1912 resentment against him for the liquor and gambling raids had faded and Cunniff was reelected. For the next seven years he served on the finance committee and devoted the rest of his time to the private practice of law. However, this was to be his last term as selectman.

THE "EL" COMES TO TOWN

The railroad provided excellent service from Boston to Watertown and the west for many years; Watertown then had two freight yards and six local stations. In the peak year of 1900 thirty-two passenger trains ran on weekdays and fifteen on Sundays.

A major change occurred in 1912 with the extension of the subway of the Boston Elevated Street Railway from Park Street Station to Harvard Square. On an early morning in March of 1912, the first train with a hundred passengers pulled out of the Harvard Square station bound for Park Street, to the cheers of a large crowd of spectators. Mt. Auburn Street was widened, a new roadbed for heavier rails was laid of crushed rock, and tracks were laid for heavier trolleys. Factory workers, business persons, and commuters were glad to see the extension of the street railway to Watertown, and it was in large part due to improved transportation that Watertown, now an even more popular place to live, became the hub of the transportation network west of Boston.

151

The hoped-for improvement of Watertown Square and the beautification of the riverbank came to fruition in May 1927 when the Delta, as it was called, was dedicated. On condition that no structure would be erected on it other than a flagpole, the MDC transferred the deed of the Delta to the town of Watertown. G. Fred Robinson asked for assurance that no trees along the north bank would be disturbed, and the town contributed thirty-five thousand dollars to the state's projected construction of Nonantum Road on the south bank on condition that nothing would be done to alter the river's width. This caused a temporary delay, since the MDC had plans that required either the filling of a portion of the riverbank or the taking of land. Finally, however, the matter was resolved to the satisfaction of all. The river was narrowed (but not at the expense of G. Fred's trees), and the ugly old chimney stacks of the gas works were removed. Traffic lights were installed, and the flag was run up the new flagpole in the center of the Delta with appropriate ceremonies.

15

Watertown in the Twentieth Century

EARNING A LIVING

The Hood Miracle

IGHTY YEARS before the founding of the Hood Rubber Company in Watertown, Thomas Hancock had formed the first rubber. Discovered in South America, rubber was formed by Amazonian Indians who dipped wooden shoe-lasts into fluid latex, thus producing "gum shoes." The process of vulcanization was accidentally discovered by Charles Goodyear in 1839 when he spilled molten rubber on his kitchen stove.

A miracle in manufacturing, the Hood Rubber Company got its start at the East End of Watertown. Frederic and Arthur Hood had been employed under their father's management in branch plants of the U.S. Rubber Company at Chelsea and Franklin, Massachusetts. When the plants closed in 1896, the Hood brothers with ten other young stockholders formed the Hood Rubber Company. For its location they considered Hyde Park with its Neponset River, but were persuaded to locate the new company in Watertown by a group of prominent men who had organized under the name of the Young Men's Assembly. Meeting monthly in the former Masonic room of the Otis Block, the Assembly functioned as a combined Chamber of Commerce and Rotary Club; during the 1890s and for a quarter of a century its members worked hard to attract industry to the

town. Their members included Henry Derby, Bartlett M. Shaw, Sam Gleason, Dr. Julian Mead, Herbert Davidson (first president of Library Bureau), and Chester Sprague. It was Sprague who succeeded in presenting the arguments that won over the Hood Brothers; he pointed out the proximity of Watertown to the port of Boston, the railroad which skirted the proposed factory site and would transport laborers and materials, and the abundant supply of underground water for the production of rubber.

Alfred Glidden, who served in a number of managerial capacities at the Hood Rubber Company, joined the Hood Brothers as one of the original stockholders when he was only twenty-two years old, and became an outstanding townsman. He was born in Franklin, Massachusetts, and came to Watertown as one of the company's original stockholders and founders. Glidden held more than fifty patents in the processing and production of rubber, and served the community as town meeting member, building committee member, as director of the Union Market National Bank and as corporator of the Savings Bank.

For many years the Hood Rubber Company was an important employer in Watertown. During its early years the company hired many immigrant Armenians and was mainly responsible for the de-

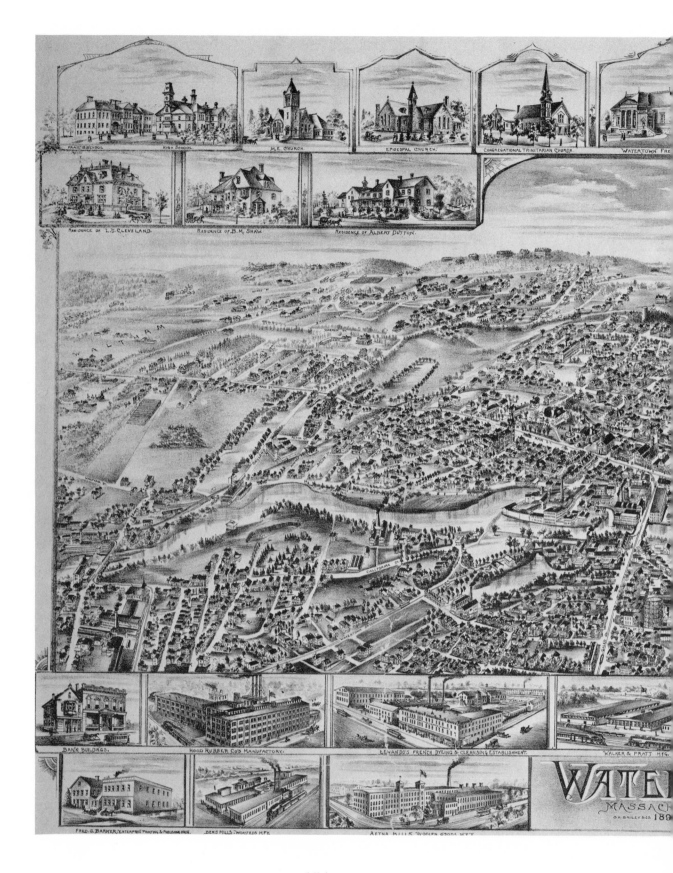

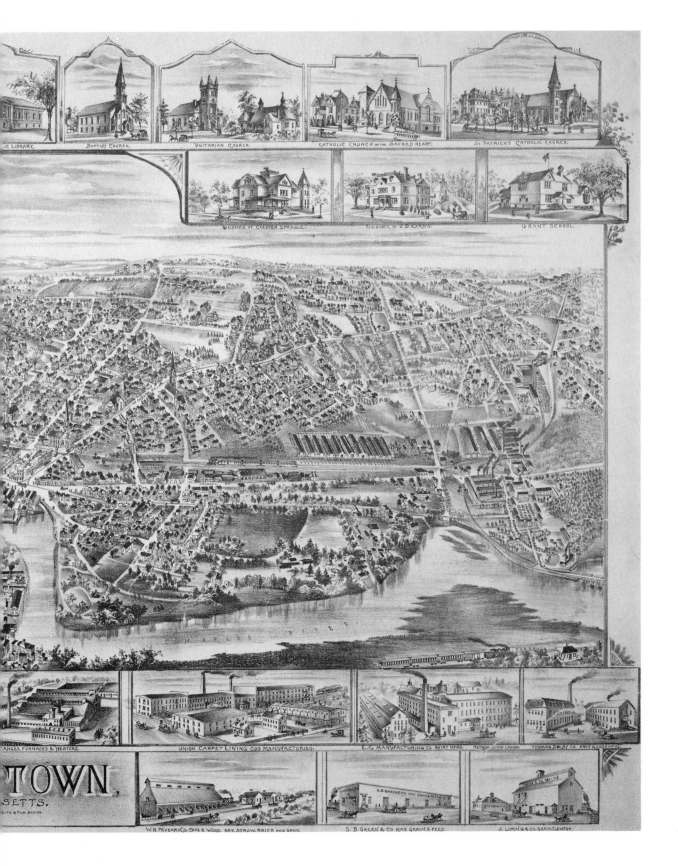

IC LIBRARY.   BAPTIST CHURCH.   UNITARIAN CHURCH.   CATHOLIC CHURCH OF THE SACRED HEART.   ST PATRICK'S CATHOLIC CHURCH.

RESIDENCE OF CHESTER SPRAGUE.   RESIDENCE OF J. S. EVANS.   GRANT SCHOOL.

CHARLES RIVER.

ANGES FURNACES & HEATERS.   UNION CARPET LINING COS MANUFACTORIES.   E. G. MANUFACTURING CO. SHIRT MFRS.   METROP. LINEN LAUNDRY.   THOMAS DALBY CO. KNIT GOODS MFRS.

TOWN,
SETTS.
LITH. & PUB. BOSTON.

W. H. PEVEAR & CO. COAL & WOOD. HAY, STRAW, BRICK AND SAND.   S. B. GREEN & CO. HAY, GRAIN & FEED.   J. LORING & CO. GRAIN ELEVATOR.

velopment of East Watertown into an Armenian neighborhood.

By 1920 the Hood Rubber Company was employing ten thousand men and women. In 1929 the company was purchased by the B. F. Goodrich Company of Akron, Ohio, and from that time on, by agreement, the Hood plant ceased its production of rubber tires and B. F. Goodrich no longer produced rubber footwear. For many years Hood produced rubber gloves, floor tile, battery boxes, and a variety of hard rubber and plastic-coated products. The company was a pioneer in employee relations, having established a company policy of service to its employees and to the community. In 1912 the company helped establish the settlement house, Abraham Lincoln House in East Water-

Hood Rubber Company plant in July 1919 employed 8,700.

town, and encouraged employees to attend Americanization classes. Employee turnover was low, for Hood was considered an excellent and enlightened employer. During the twenties, however, when the company had to contend with what Superintendent Glidden called "fang and claw competition," labor troubles materialized for the first time at Hood.

The Second World War brought defense contracts to the B. F. Goodrich Company. The Watertown plant manufactured bullet-proof fuel cells, battery "jars," de-icers for aircraft, plastic helmet liners and special "sub-zero pacs" (aviation boots for wear in the Arctic). The company was awarded the Army-Navy "E."

During the fifties and sixties, imports of rubber and canvas footwear from Japan, Czechoslovakia, Korea, and Taiwan vastly undersold American products. Duties on their manufactures were so low as to present insurmountable obstacles to B. F. Goodrich, U.S. Rubber and other American companies.

Labor and management worked to keep the Hood Rubber Company in Watertown. Representatives of both labor and management went to Washington and fought for a trade readjustment allowance (under the Tariff Act of 1955) which would enable the company to continue in business in New England. This was successful in enabling the workers to receive the allowances, but B. F. Goodrich, unable to sustain the squeeze between competition and the demand for higher wages, moved its business to the more favorable climate of the South and eventually closed. The loss of this employer was a severe blow to the Watertown economy, which for many years had depended on the rubber company for as much as 10 percent of its tax revenues.

Labor troubles during the turn of the century period were not confined to the rubber industry. In 1913, resisting the imposition of pay cuts, the weavers struck at the Aetna Mill, asking restoration to fifteen dollars a week. In 1916 the first strike in eighteen years occurred at the Walker and Pratt stove foundry, due to the demand of the workmen for $2.50 a day. A strike in 1916 at Lewandos, which had also maintained paternalistic employment policies, astonished the management which had discharged two employees for union activity. Before returning to work the employees demanded a 10 percent increase in wages. At that time men received fifteen dollars a week and women eight.

Developments at the Watertown Arsenal

Until the Civil War, the Arsenal had been used for the manufacture of cartridges and wooden-wheeled gun mounts, as well as for the storage of military supplies. During the Civil War the commandant, Captain Thomas Rodman, established the first foundry and the laboratory for testing the strength of materials. The Emery tester was invented and installed at the Arsenal to test strength of metals and resulted in many improvements to the steel industry. Steel replaced wood and iron in the construction of gun carriages. A railroad spur

156

led onto the grounds of the Arsenal where a fifteen-ton open-hearth furnace was located.

During the immediate pre-World War I period the Arsenal supported a work force of sixteen hundred men who worked three shifts producing shells and sea coast carriages. Charles Wheeler was commandant from 1908 to 1917. During World War II the Arsenal manufactured anti-aircraft guns, howitzers, and trench mortar tubes. In cooperation with MIT, a two-year ordnance school was established at the Arsenal which graduated a number of experts in the field. At various points in its history, abandonment of the Arsenal was contemplated by the federal government, but those plans were changed by a new outbreak of war. In 1966, however, the government ceased many of its operations there except for the Army Materials and Mechanics Research Center, and in 1968 sold fifty-five acres to the town for five and a half million dollars.

The Wool Industry

The Aetna Mills, successors to the Bemis textile factory on Pleasant Street, wove fine woolen worsted fabrics during the early years of the twentieth century. With a working force of 350 and 200 looms, the company was doing such good business in 1919 that two new buildings were erected. Ten years later, however, losses of one and a half million dollars necessitated consolidation of the company's activities in Fitchburg. The Watertown plant was auctioned and remained idle for three years until 1934 when the John T. Lodge Company established its wool reprocessing company in the old Aetna plant. Here woolen materials from all over the world were reclaimed for reuse in the manufacture of woolen coating and suiting materials.

In the vicinity of the Bemis factory three manufacturers continued to produce rubber, plastics, and adhesives. Bemis Associates was established by Harry True in 1910 to manufacture thermoplastic adhesives from gutta-percha and balata and from synthetic resins. Founded in Boston in 1911 as a distributor of automotive fabrics, Haartz-Mason Coated Fabrics manufactured lifesaving equipment from nylon and synthetics for the navy and the air force and continued to produce coated fabrics for the automotive, shoe, sporting goods, baby carriage, luggage, garment, and novelty trades, besides a line of friction and electrical tapes.

The H. M. Sawyer Company of Cambridge purchased the Brunsene Company of New Jersey in 1916 and in 1917 moved its facility to the old Bemis shoddy mill on Stanley Avenue. Managed for many generations by the same family, the Sawyer Company manufactured oiled slickers for fishermen and then developed processes to coat ducks, drills, nylons, and glass cloths, and painted fabrics for use in the awning and outdoor furniture trade.

Changes in the Town Economy

In 1918 the old Coolidge Tavern, the scene of many historic events, had been demolished by the Boston Elevated Railway to make room for its car-

Flying boots developed by Hood and supplied to the Army and Navy Air Corps in World War II.

barns and for the trolley tracks leading from Newton Corner; this measure was dictated by the death of two workmen who had been pinned between the tavern wall and a trolley. Across Galen Street, E. M. Loew's rebuilt the thirty-year-old Strand Theatre at a cost of $40,000 and re-named it the Watertown Square Theatre. David Bachrach started his portrait photography business in Maryland and soon established photographic studios in major cities; the Bachrach photographic laboratory occupied the Stanley Steamer plant where for many years David's son Louis Fabian personally supervised production; his sons Fabian and Bradford eventually took over the business from their father. The

Warren Soap Works, which had been a feature of the South Side for many years, went out of business following a fire.

Lewandos and Lewis-Shepard

The Lewandos cleaning business expanded greatly after 1900. Deliveries were made all over the eastern seaboard by horse and wagon, Railway Express, parcel post, and later by company trucks. During the 1930s the company thrived, and the main building was replaced by a new four-story structure. The company discontinued its dye business and initiated rug cleaning and fur storage operations. Ernest E. Edgar came to work in the management of Lewandos in 1935 and became vice-president of the firm. By the 1950s there were fifty-five Lewandos stores. When John H. Harwood died in 1954, Edgar bought the business from his estate. He built three additional plants in Needham, Concord, and Brookline, installing self-service dry cleaning and washing machines but the laundry and dry cleaning industry continued to change and business diminished because of the advent of wash-and-wear and polyester fabrics.

At one time the largest cleaning-and-dyeing business in the United States, the location of the Watertown store right in the Square, clogged with traffic and with newly-installed meters, made parking difficult for Lewandos' customers. In 1969 Edgar was forced to close the Watertown plant and move Lewandos' headquarters to Needham, ending 150 years of the firm's presence in Watertown.

In the stockyards area during the 1920s several industries replaced the old cattle trade. The Lewis-Shepard Company was built on the location of the old Stockyards Hotel. For years the company built jacklifts, skid platforms, and stackers for the moving and storage of goods. During World War II the company prospered, at one time employing 650 workers. Founded by Arthur Lewis and Frederick Shepard, the company stayed in the hands of their sons until 1973, when it was purchased by the Hyster Corporation.

United-American Soda Fountain Company

The familiar drugstore soda fountain had its origin in New York, when in 1832 John Matthews mixed carbon dioxide with water and flavorings to

158

Woodland Dairy on parade, 1930.

produce "soda." Matthews's dispenser resembled an urn, and this eventually became the modern soda fountain. In 1926 the American Soda Fountain Company built a plant on land adjacent to the Lewis-Shepard Company and in 1932 combined with the United Soda Fountain Company. United-American manufactured equipment for Howard Johnson restaurants, H. P. Hood Ice Cream Company, Schrafft's, and many corner drugstores.

The Underwood Company

The Underwood Company, manufacturers of deviled ham, traced their process back to the discovery by a French scientist of a process for sterilizing food. William Underwood was an apprentice in a London pickling plant where fruits and vegetables were blended with spices. He emigrated to Boston in 1819 and formed his own company where he processed fruit and shipped it in glass jars.

Underwood experimented with the preservation of many foods and invented the tin can. The business continued under the control of the Un-

derwood family, and one of William Underwood's grandsons developed the process of canning foods under pressure. During the Civil War the company provided spiced ham in tins for the Union army. In 1907 the Underwoods built the Watertown plant next to the soda fountain company on Arsenal Street.

Several Generations of Stuarts

Timothy Stuart established a small business in 1901 to build cranes, eventually passing it on to his son Frank and to his grandson Raymond T. Stuart. The company located west of the stockyards at 70 Phillips Street because of its proximity to the railroad line. The Stuart company's cranes were used to build bridges, trestles, and viaducts, among them the Boston University Bridge; the Queen City Bridge at Manchester, New Hampshire; and the elevated railroad trestle at Lynn Square. The company manufactured crawler cranes, platform trucks, and tractors for sand and snow removal.

159

Suit Manufacturing

Minas S. Kondazian, an enterprising Armenian immigrant, built a brick factory in 1924 on Coolidge Hill for the manufacture of suits, having expanded from modest beginnings in 1903, to a business employing a work force of three hundred.

Kondazian manufactured men's clothing until the 1950s, when the business changed, limiting its operation to retail sales. In 1963 it was purchased by the Eastern Coat Company which took over both its customer list and the building.

Hay and Peabody Burial Vaults

Cement burial vaults were constructed by the Hay and Peabody Company on Arlington Street from 1926 until the company moved to Belmont in 1952. The company manufactured eighteen different sizes of vaults which were impervious to moisture and the normal pressure of earth.

Of Shirts and Paint

Charles Leavitt devoted his lifetime to the manufacture of custom shirts. He came to Watertown in 1905 from Maine to work for Simons, Hatch and Whitten on Spring Street, where he worked for sixteen years as the superintendent. For many years Leavitt produced shirts for Filene's and other stores in New England, output during the 1950s reaching 1,200 dozen shirts a month. In 1932 Leavitt purchased the company in partnership with George Wellman, but after Wellman became town clerk, Leavitt became the sole proprietor.

Waterproof Paint and Varnish Company

A paint factory was located on Spring Street as early as 1890 and subsequently became the Waterproof Paint and Varnish Company, relocating on Fayette Street. When the factory burned in 1920, the manager, J. J. Meehan, moved the company to 446 Arsenal Street. Thirty-five workers produced half a million dollars' worth of paint for the New England market and during the war years contracted with the U. S. Navy for 125,000 gallons of paint.

The Andrews Brothers and Charles Woodland's Dairy

When the Andrews brothers milk business on Franklin Street closed, the leading Watertown milk dealer became Charles Woodland. Woodland purchased the premises of Charles W. Pierce in 1919 and later built a milk plant on Waverley Avenue. From a single route furnishing two hundred quarts a day, Woodland increased his fleet of trucks to fifty-five, covering forty routes in sixteen communities and delivering as many as nineteen thousand quarts of milk a day. The familiar bulb-necked bottle (to hold the cream as it rose to the top) was his trademark; Woodland Dairy also manufactured ice cream. The business passed to the second generation of Charles Woodland's family and by 1966 the business had ceased operation. The dairy buildings were razed, the land was sold to the town, and Woodland Towers Housing for the Elderly was built on the site.

Western Electric

The Western Electric Company was founded in 1882 to manufacture electric apparatus for sale to the Bell Telephone and Telegraph Company, the world's largest communications system. In 1931 the Western Electric Company purchased the Coolidge farm on Mt. Auburn Street, promising the town of Watertown that it would erect a structure suitable to its environs on Mt. Auburn Street in the East End. The Coolidge farmhouse was moved to Grove Street and became the home of the Watertown Elks Lodge. Constructed of reinforced concrete with limestone trim, the building maintains well-kept grounds and employs factory workers who manufacture telephone parts and relays as well as repairmen who maintain telephone instruments.

WORLD WAR I

With the entry of the United States into World War I, Watertown residents buried their differences. About a thousand young men and women from Watertown were involved in the conflict, and their names are cast in bronze on a tablet in the town hall. Lt. Edward Hayden wrote letters from

160

the battlefield in France which were published in the local newspaper, the *Watertown Enterprise*. John R. O'Brien, a local war hero who had won the Croix de Guerre for bravery in battle, was portrayed on a poster advertising Liberty bonds. At the L. C. Chase Company on Pleasant Street, a "dime dance" raised money for bonds. A newspaper advertisement appealed to the public to "buy Liberty bonds. Set your teeth, clinch your hands, and hang on, oh, hang on." The drive was such a success that the U. S. Navy christened the first Liberty ship built at the Boston Naval Shipyard the *S.S. Watertown.*

Residents of the town backed the war effort in various ways. Some planted potatoes or raised pigs or poultry. Others got together in school buildings during the summer to can vegetables, and many gave up sugar and white flour. Streetlights were extinguished after midnight. Boys and girls worked on farms, rolled bandages, and did volunteer work for the Red Cross.

Soldiers assigned to the Arsenal were quartered in Watertown during the war. The Arsenal gates were closed to the public, and special protection was provided to guard the Arsenal against subversive acts. With the advent of refrigeration, the Union Market Stockyards were no longer needed for the temporary storage of beef cattle and were now used to quarter horses and mules on their way from Canada to France by way of Boston. In spite of the resistance of the town to this practice on the grounds that it was unsanitary, the railroad company unloaded horses in the dead of night, thus avoiding detection. The Board of Health was unsuccessful in stopping it even though local residents complained vociferously about the supposed danger, noise, and health menace of keeping horses in the area, as well as about the rude, boisterous behavior of the cowboys.

In the autumn of 1918 the opening of school was delayed for four weeks because of an outbreak of influenza, which afflicted 250 people. Manpower was so desperately needed during the epidemic that the town furnished men to help the local coal company make deliveries to people in need.

When word reached Watertown that the armistice had been signed, townspeople gathered at Saltonstall Park for a celebration. A flag, bearing 1,023 stars, was unfurled in front of the town hall. In May 1922 a great parade was held, and Victory Field was dedicated to the dead of World War I with these words: "Through desperate war on war, men fought for us on flood and fiery field; Live worthy of their deeds and sacrifice."

THE TOWN TURNS TO CIVIC CONCERNS
IN THE AFTERMATH OF THE WAR

During the immediate postwar period Watertown saw rapid business and population growth. From 1920 to 1930 the town increased in population from twenty-one thousand to nearly thirty-five thousand. The Stearns potato farm; the Locke and Lovell market gardens; and parts of the former Adams and Coolidge estates, famous for their apples, pears, and asparagus, were subdivided into 520 house lots. Streets were paved, wires were laid underground, and a uniform house numbering system was adopted.

Much had been done to streamline town government, but to many people the town meeting form of government now seemed awkward and cumbersome. Authority rested in the thirty-eight hundred registered voters acting at the annual town meeting. Special interests often packed the hall only to vote on the specific article in which they were involved. Under the leadership of Charles Abbott, legislation was filed to permit the town to institute representative town meeting; the bill was enacted into law in 1920.

Hope soon faded, however, that representative town meeting would furnish the solution to all the town's governmental problems, among which were insufficient control over the departments by the selectmen, extravagant spending, poorly qualified officeholders, an interfering finance committee, and an inadequate town hall. Some citizens argued for a change to the city form of government; others favored becoming a part of Boston, as Brighton had done. Finally it was decided that the town should retain the town form of government at least through the celebration of its tercentenary in 1930. During this period George Dale, an executive of the Hood Rubber Company, who had served on

President and Mrs. Calvin Coolidge at the Arlington Street Cemetery, June 27, 1925.

the 1926 committee to study the town government, had challenged Sarsfield Cunniff for office in the General Court. He won but subsequently lost to Cunniff in the next election. Dale, however, served several additional terms in the state legislature, and in 1928 Sarsfield Cunniff was named to the Waltham district court by Governor Alvan T. Fuller.

In 1925 the town was embarrassed by an unannounced visit by President and Mrs. Calvin Coolidge to the cemetery on Arlington Street where Joseph Coolidge was buried. The Coolidges climbed over the low stone wall and walked through the long grass to the plots where John and Mary Coolidge, the ancestors of the President, were buried. Afterward the town tidied up the cemetery and installed an iron fence and a new entrance gate.

The Historical Society held meetings at which papers were read on local history; some of these papers were collected into a book by G. Fred Robinson, *Watertown's Military History.* The society also restored a number of headstones in the old cemetery, collected the town records into volumes, and purchased and remodeled the Edmund Fowle

house on Marshall Street.

Watertown's central location provided a convenient place for Thomas J. McCue to establish his road-building business. McCue built the Newburyport Turnpike and repaved Arsenal and North Beacon streets. McCue's house was located across the street from the Vose Piano Company on North Beacon Street; the piano factory erected an attractive building surrounded by well-kept lawns and flowerbeds, the property being absorbed later by the Arsenal.

In 1930 Watertown celebrated its three hundredth birthday with pageants, parades, church services, a special convening of the Watertown legislature, the writing of a tercentenary history, and a memorial monument. Fred Crawford was chairman of the celebration, and the history, *Great Little Watertown,* was written by G. Fred Robinson with the collaboration of his daughter Ruth Robinson Wheeler. G. Fred, who had been active in town affairs for many years, raised thirty thousand dollars for the·creation of the Founders Monument, depicting Sir Richard Saltonstall in colonial dress and decorated with bas-reliefs of Clap's Landing

162

and the antitax protest. Designed by Henry Hudson Kitson, the sculpture stands on the bank of the Charles River near the intersection of Charles River Road and Riverside Street.

SCHOOLS IN THE TWENTIETH CENTURY

After the dismissal of George Dwelley as headmaster of the high school, Frank Whitney was appointed to replace him. During Dwelley's nineteen-year tenure, school population increased so much that serious thought had to be given to the construction of a high school building. The town was already using the Francis and Hosmer schools and the one-room Lowell School at the corner of Orchard Street and Waverley Avenue. A new school was built in 1907 on Waverley Avenue following a plan drawn by Curtis Bixby and was named after Dr. Marshall Spring; it replaced the old West School on Howard Street.

The high school was quartered in the Phillips building but was strained to capacity. In 1908 a town-appointed building committee was unable to solve the problem and was reduced to wishing for a fairy godmother. Perhaps such a creature heard their wish, for in 1909 Henry C. Derby, a meat distributor, offered the town forty thousand dollars for construction of a new school. Eugene Foss, later governor of Massachusetts, offered three and a half acres of land valued at fifteen thousand dollars near the Hosmer School; this property had been part of the estate of Alvin Adams, founder of the Adams Express Company. Charles Brigham offered to donate plans for building a high school after the design of a school in Fairhaven.

Charles Brigham had a distinguished career both as a townsman and as an architect. Born in Watertown in 1841, he served as a soldier in the Civil War. After the war he became an architect. With John Hubbard Sturgis he formed the partnership which produced the designs for many famous buildings, including the Museum of Fine Arts in Copley Square and the Church of the Advent on Brimmer Street in Boston, as well as many fine mansions in the Back Bay during the eighties. He is also credited with the design of the extension to the State House in Boston, the addition to the Maine State Capitol, the Christian Science Mother Church, the Foxboro State Hospital, and several buildings in Fairhaven. A resident of Garfield Street in Watertown, Brigham served the town as

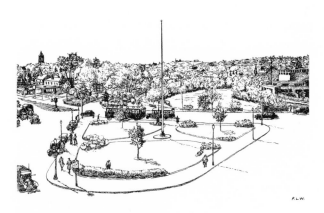

Sketch of Watertown Square in 1935.

selectman, school committee member, water commissioner, and as a trustee of the public library. He was a founder and first president of the Watertown Cooperative Bank and a director of the Union Market National Bank. Brigham gave the town the plans for the high school (which later became the East Junior High), and never billed the town for any of his professional services, including the design of the town seal, which shows the first settlers exchanging a loaf of bread for a fish with the Pequossette Indians.

Grateful for Brigham's offer of the high school plans, the town appropriated one hundred thousand dollars, and construction was begun according to his design. In 1914 the first class, consisting of 219 pupils, moved into the new building, a castle-like medieval design with four towers flanked by medieval battlements. Said a town official, "Our high school, both in architectural beauty and in the completeness of its equipment, is probably unsurpassed by any high school of its size in Massachusetts."

On the South Side, Derby again made a contribution, this time of twenty-one thousand dollars, with which the town built the Theodore Parker School in 1914. Charles Gray was the architect. In 1915 the Coolidge School was built in the East End

163

according to the design of Charles Hoyt. In 1925 the old Coolidge School, which had continued in use after the construction of the new school, was sold, and the newer Coolidge School was given an addition that doubled its size.

In 1917 the school committee decided to force the resignation of Wilfred Price, the superintendent, but Price refused, insisting on his right to tenure. The committee reversed itself, and the superintendent stayed on and was granted yearly pay increases until he retired in 1937, by which time his salary had risen to forty-five hundred dollars.

During Price's tenure the educational system underwent a change, and the junior high school system was introduced. In 1922 the West Junior High School was ready, but an addition was needed by 1927. East junior high students were located in the lower floors of the high school until the completion of the new high school on Columbia Street in 1925, at which time the Brigham building was converted into the East Junior High School.

A. Houston Burr, architect of the new high school on Columbia Street, called it the finest high school in the world. It cost $730,000 and was built on land purchased from the Russell family. The building included an auditorium, a gymnasum, and training facilities in both household and industrial arts.

The new Lowell School was constructed in 1927 to replace the smaller school which had been built in 1883. It was erected on land which Maria White Lowell had received as part of her dowry when she married James Russell Lowell and which the family had later donated to the town. The old building was used later as the North Branch Library.

Watertown High School, 1914, now East Junior High School.

THE DEPRESSION YEARS

The Great Depression had its effect on students as well as adults: fewer entered college; many wanted to leave school to work; and absenteeism was high. Schools were crowded, but the town could not afford to construct new schools. In 1934 the town borrowed $135,000 from the federal government to build an addition to the high school.

THE PERKINS SCHOOL FOR THE BLIND

The Perkins School for the Blind moved to Watertown from its former location in South Boston in 1912. Edward E. Allen, its director, after accepting an invitation to visit his friend Fred Crawford at the Stickney estate, purchased the land on the understanding that the thirty-four acres would be kept intact. The school had been founded by John Fisher and had become famous under the leadership of Samuel Gridley Howe.

The tower of Perkins's main building has a carillon whose peals may be heard for miles around.

The Massachusetts Asylum for the Blind was incorporated in 1829, "to educate sightless persons." It was founded by Dr. John Fisher with the help of William H. Prescott, the blind historian, and Thomas Handasyd Perkins, a wealthy merchant in the China trade. In 1830 the corporation elected its first officers and twelve trustees, one of whom was Horace Mann. One day when walking down Boston's Boylston Street, Fisher met Dr. Samuel Gridley Howe, a physician who had come home from fighting in the Greek war for independence from Turkey.

"Howe!" he exclaimed. "The very man we have been looking for!"

Howe, a close friend of Horace Mann's, became the first director, and he worked hard to increase the availability of embossed books for the blind. In 1837 Laura Bridgman, the first deaf-blind pupil ever to be successfully educated, became Dr. Howe's personal pupil.

The school occupied the home of Perkins on Pearl Street in Boston, and when the old Mt. Washington house in South Boston came on the market, Mr. Perkins generously allowed his Pearl Street estate to be sold; the school was then changed to bear his name. Howe served as director until 1876 and was succeeded by his son-in-law, Michael Anagnos, during whose administration Anne Sullivan, a recent graduate, was sent to Alabama to work with Helen Keller. Anne and Helen spent the years 1889 to 1893 at Perkins at Anagnos' invitation.

Dr. Edward E. Allen was responsible not only for the move to Watertown but also for many other firsts in the education of the blind. He insisted on the retention of the Stickney estate intact because he was convinced that physical activity was essential to the education of blind children and that the grounds would provide the needed space. This conviction led him, in 1908, to appoint the first trained physiotherapist in any school for the blind. He carried to fruition the cottage plan inaugurated by Dr. Howe; he appointed a home visitor to maintain close contacts with students' families; he engaged a psychologist to prepare the first psychological tests for blind children, the Simons-Binet Intelligence Tests, which successfully demonstrated for the first time that blind people do not differ in intelligence from sighted persons. In 1920, in cooperation with Harvard University, he established the first graduate-level teacher-training program for teachers of the blind. In 1924 he appointed the first full-time speech therapist in a school for the blind—all these efforts being in line with his objective of enabling blind persons to take their place in the mainstream of society.

Dr. Allen was succeeded by Dr. Gabriel Farrell, an Episcopal minister, who organized the work for the deaf-blind into a special department where the vibration technique was used to teach such children to speak. Dr. Farrell established a magazine, *The Lantern,* in 1931 to publicize the work of the school. The fifth director was Dr. Edward J.

Tom Gavin and Charles Brigham talk it over.

Waterhouse, who in 1951 was finally able to close the sheltered workshop which had been started by Howe in 1837. The workshop was now superfluous, both because any remaining needs were fulfilled by the state, and because the majority of blind persons now found it possible to undertake training and obtain employment in normal surroundings. Perkins became the home of the Regional Library for the Blind and Handicapped and also of the Howe Press, publisher of materials for the visually impaired.

The hoped-for diminution of a need for a special school for blind children was not, however, to be realized so soon. In 1946 the first child whose blindness was caused by retrolental fibroplasia was enrolled, and in 1968 a day program was initiated to accommodate deaf-blind pupils, victims of the 1963-64 maternal rubella epidemic.

Benjamin F. Smith became director in August 1971 after thirty-two years' experience at Perkins.

165

Perkins School for the Blind.

He was the first visually handicapped person to head the school. Recent changes have included special programs to accommodate the increasing number of multi-impaired students and a career education program. Legislation enacted by Massachusetts in 1974 mandating education for every child regardless of handicap, has provided the choice of educational placement of children in private schools such as Perkins if other options are not practicable. Perkins has been able to provide programs for a broad range of multi-impaired students as well as for the visually impaired.

Charles C. Woodcock became the director of Perkins on July 1, 1977, after serving at similar schools in Oregon and Iowa. Throughout its history, Perkins has called upon experts in blind education from across the United States and around the world to widen its horizons and enrich its perspective. Its emphasis on self-reliance and its attitude of responsibility and receptiveness to new ideas has earned the respect of leaders in education throughout the world.

> Mr. Anagnos is away and I am unable to get a printed ticket; but I have written two for you which will do just as well.
>
> Lovingly yours
> Helen Keller
>
> Please excuse this hastily written note.

THE LIBRARY GROWS

Solon Whitney was librarian for forty-nine years; after his death in 1917, Lydia Masters, his former assistant, was appointed librarian. Miss Masters was a descendant of John Masters, a Watertown freeman of 1631, and her maternal grandfather was Joseph Bird, who had been actively involved in the formation of the Union Social Library in the old Bird Tavern. Miss Masters's dream had been to expand the branch system so that all persons would have easy access to a neighborhood branch library regardless of age.

The payment in lieu of taxes which the proprietors of the Mt. Auburn Cemetery had made to the town when they acquired the Stone estate had been allowed to accumulate for ten years until it amounted to thirty thousand dollars. The resourceful chairman of the finance committee, Charles F. Sanborn, suggested that the money be used to build a branch library on Mt. Auburn Street on land that had been donated by former Governor Foss, part of the land remaining when Fossland had been divided into house lots. In 1927 the East Branch Library was opened and at first the main floor was used for both adults and children. Later a children's room with a separate entrance was provided in the basement. In 1930 the West Branch was opened in the Browne School building. The Lowell School had been located at the corner of Orchard Street and Waverley Avenue but had been replaced by a new building. After being used by the public library for several years, the building was enlarged and given a new brick facing in 1941 with thirty thousand dollars which the town received from auctioning the old town hall property in 1932. At the Main Library, Miss Masters refurbished the lower floor for a children's room, and there the books were placed on open shelves. A larger circulation desk was installed on the upper level in front of the stacks. During this period Ruth Furber, a trustee of the Watertown Public Library, served as a member of the Massachusetts Board of Library Commissioners from 1933 to 1938.

Lydia Masters retired in 1946, completing nearly a half century of service to the town. Under her management the library had expanded its ser-

167

The storefront library on Mt. Auburn Street preceded the present East Branch building.

vice to adults and children through three branches as well as the Main Library. Miss Masters served two consecutive terms as president of the Massachusetts Library Association, from 1936 to 1938. In 1947 she was succeeded as librarian by Helen Hutchinson, who initiated a popular local radio show called "Leaders Are Readers." Miss Hutchinson left to accept a post as director of personnel at the Enoch Pratt Library in Baltimore. Catherine Yerxa, who had served as East Branch librarian,

left her position as director of the Bureau of Library Extension in the Massachusetts Department of Education to return to Watertown as librarian in 1949. During her administration an addition was built onto the Main Library in 1956, the phonograph record collection was established, and the Friends of the Library was organized. Miss Yerxa served as president of the Massachusetts Library Association in 1951-52. She retired from the library in 1963.

A NEW TOWN HALL

By the time of the tercentenary the old town hall was totally inadequate. Space was badly needed for town offices and for the safekeeping of records. Various locations were considered until, by act of the legislature, permission was finally granted to build the new town hall on a corner of Saltonstall Park beside the public library. F. C. Sturgis was the architect of the new town hall, or administration

building, as it was called. The building had four stories, with the fourth set back in a kind of penthouse. The roof was surmounted by a cupola, and the front was decorated with Corinthian columns, busts of Washington and Lincoln being set into recessed niches in the facade. In the lobby two maps showed Watertown, respectively, as a small

168

colonial town and in its later appearance as an industrial center. The second-floor hearing room was decorated with handsome wainscoting and chandeliers. The cost of the building was $230,000.

OTHER TOWN MATTERS

Between 1900 and 1920 the tax rate fluctuated between twenty and thirty dollars per thousand dollars of valuation; during the 1920s the rate rose until in 1932 it stood at thirty-two dollars. From 1919 to 1939 the town debt rose to over one million dollars. Political controversy centered on taxes, and party platforms promised economies. The years of the Great Depression did the job the politicians could not, but at the cost of much hardship. Town departments economized; sidewalk repairs had to wait; town employees took a 10 percent pay cut; and street laborers went on a four-and-one-half day week to spread the work, at which they earned fifty cents an hour. Property tax payments were often in arrears. Half of the arrests made by the police were for drunkenness, and the circulation of books from the public library reached its highest point.

Federal funds authorized by the Public Works Administration furnished five million dollars to employ workers. Projects completed included grading playgrounds, Ridgelawn Cemetery, and the town farm; filling Cook's Pond for a playground for the Parker School; and making repairs in the schools. Some PWA workers built an addition to the stack wing of the Main Library while others prepared two more volumes of the town records for printing. Money was raised by members of the police and fire departments for the relief of the poor, and the welfare department provided food, housing, and fuel in the form of coal, for which it charged only $2.50 a ton.

The town no longer owned horses and needed a garage in which to house its vehicles. A town barn was built on filled-in, rat-infested land near Victory Field. A police headquarters was constructed to the

Original North Branch Library building, built in 1882 as the Lowell School.

rear of the main fire station on Main Street. The discovery of quicksand on the site of the police station was dealt with by mixing it with other materials to make a strong foundation. Railroad Brook, which ran under ground level, required repeated pumping.

Many physical changes were made in Watertown during the 1930s and 1940s. The post office had been quartered in the Eagles' Lodge on Mt. Auburn Street; in 1942 it moved to a new building on Main Street. It was built on the site of the Jacob Caldwell house which had been located there since early in the 1700s. The American Legion acquired the old Phillips Church parsonage at 215 Mt. Auburn Street. The Phillips Church built a new edifice in 1937 during the pastorate of the Reverend Edward Camp. In 1940 the Knights of Columbus placed a stone marker on the Delta in honor of Christopher Columbus.

THE SECOND WORLD WAR

The involvement of the United States in the Second World War brought an abrupt end to unemployment in Watertown. Over four thousand men and women served in the armed forces, including 10 percent of the employees of the town.

The Watertown Arsenal and other local industries employed an additional ten thousand workers from outside the town. The federal government purchased the property at the end of School Street and converted the old Vose Piano Company fac-

169

tory into a large brick building to house a weather study laboratory. Students at the high school were permitted to do part-time war work in factories.

Two ex-army officers took charge of the training of students in a junior reserve officers' training corps.

AFTER THE WAR

G. Frederick Robinson, 1860-1949.

After the war, in 1954, four bronze tablets listing the names of the men and women who had served in World War II were installed flanking the World War I memorial in the Administration Building. The memorial cost $9,500 and listed the names of 123 who had been killed in action. To meet the needs of the students who had left school to go to war, the town instituted a veterans' high school in the Phillips School and graduated sixty-six students.

A veterans' officer was employed to help returning service men find jobs and places to live. Fuel was short and construction work was hard to find because of the scarcity of materials. The American Legion offered their headquarters for the use of four families, and the town garage and the Grant School accommodated a dozen more. A veterans' housing development consisting of 168 units was built just west of Lexington Street. In 1949 the Housing Authority was organized to build and administer housing for veterans; another colony of sixty units was constructed off Nichols Avenue in the East End.

A survey of the schools had recommended that teachers' salaries be based on educational attainments and a new pay scale was instituted in 1945; equal pay for both sexes was voted into effect the following year.

George Frederick Robinson, ex-selectman, conservationist, and historian of the town died in 1949 in his ninetieth year. For sixty-five years G. Fred had been a town meeting member, working for the beautification of the river banks, the dedication of the Founders' Monument, and the recording of town history, and persistently objecting to a billboard advertising an alcoholic beverage which dominated the Square.

During the post-war period the population stabilized at about 37,500, and it was considered that the town had reached its capacity. The East End had changed from being predominantly Irish with the infusion of Armenians and Greeks, who built a number of churches and established businesses. Three schools and an addition to the library were built in the fifties. The Cunniff School was named for Judge Cunniff, who died in 1953; the Phillips School was extended on the site of the old Francis School; and an addition was built onto the East Junior High School. Congestion in the Square prompted the acquisition of space for parking from the Boston and Maine Railroad, since the tracks had been torn up and the station was no longer needed.

In town affairs, the high school and the Phillips Church celebrated their one hundredth birthdays. In 1954 the town approved the formation of a recreation commission and a director of recreation was hired. Plans were made for anti-pollution measures to be taken so that the river would be fit for bathing. With the advent of the Korean Conflict, civil defense was reactivated under the direction of

John Corbett, who organized wardens and prepared for air raids. Once again local businesses received orders for war materials.

The complexities of keeping roads, sidewalks and sewers under repair, and the removal of trash and snow devolved upon the highway department, the largest department under the control of the selectmen. A town incinerator was built in East Watertown for the disposal of trash and garbage. Its use was discontinued in January, 1975.

In 1939 the town, as part of the MDC, received its first water from the Quabbin Reservoir. During the 1940s and 1950s many changes took place in the personnel of town government. A third fire station was built on Orchard Street in the northern part of town, which had seen the development of planned housing at Fairfield Gardens. The office of the purchasing agent was created to concentrate the buying power of the town in the hands of one individual.

NEWSPAPERS

As Watertown's population increased and diversified the need for town-wide communication developed. Social gatherings, notices of meetings and participants, town government proceedings, church news and advertisements for markets, products and services filled the pages of the earliest local papers. Several newspapers began publishing in the mid-nineteenth century and recorded the activities of the growing town: the *Mount Auburn Memorial* (1870-1875), the Watertown *Press* (1870-1875), the *Pequossette* (1873-1878) and the Watertown *Observer* (1878-1879).

The Watertown Enterprise

In 1879 the Watertown *Enterprise*, a weekly newspaper that served Watertown until 1947, began publication. Its founder and first publisher was the realtor Samuel S. Gleason who lived at the corner of Church and Oliver Streets and whose daughter's name was given to Marion Road. The newspaper was first printed on Spring Street opposite Fayette Street by Fred G. Barker, but the first issues had their cover pages printed out of town. Other publishers of the *Enterprise* during its sixty-eight year history were Fred G. Barker, George Stratton and William Canady. In his opening editorial Sam Gleason extolled the virtues of Watertown, compared it to its neighbors, found them wanting, and vowed to help make Watertown into an eminent and progressive town.

The *Enterprise* enjoyed seasons of invigorating influence over the townspeople, chronicling such events as the efforts of the South Side to join Newton, the naming of the new school buildings and the details of the various labor strikes in Watertown industries. In 1902 a rival newspaper was started in

Offices of "The Watertown Enterprise" in 1893.

Watertown called the *Tribune*. The *Enterprise* bought it out in 1903 and from 1903-1947 the paper was known as the Watertown *Tribune Enterprise*. In December 1947 it ceased publication.

The Watertown Sun

The Watertown *Sun* this year is fifty-nine years old, and like any long-time resident of the town, has been molded by the decades, the people and events which have both delighted and dismayed the community through most of this century.

The *Sun*, founded in August of 1921 by newspaperman Avery Brown of Belmont, has gone through a number of transformations—as well as owners—in the intervening years. It is now published by the Herald Publishing Company, owned by the Martin family of Belmont which purchased the paper in 1954. But we should back up a number of years to understand what Avery Brown invisioned and what he set out to do.

From the turn of the century, Watertown had been served by the *Tribune-Enterprise*, published at 4 Church Street. That weekly was the intrepid child borne of a merger in 1903 of two competing papers, and featured social events, community activities, and the predictable comings and goings of any small town: "Sister Bridget of St. Patrick's convent arrived today from Kentucky. Sister Bridget was accompanied by a number of new teachers."

It was notable, however, that such local news appeared on page one; for years, due to printing and mechanical limitations, the front pages of a number of such weeklies were composed and printed in New York and featured exotic news of faraway lands: "A Prussian Dragoon's Excuse for Carving a Civilian," or tales of torture from Morocco.

New publisher-editor Brown would focus strictly on the local scene, and saw his newspaper as an integral part of community progress. He described the paper as "a community newspaper," and wrote: "We are here to build a bigger, better and happier Watertown through the encouragement of the true community spirit." There were 21,000 people in town, and from his office at 60 Main Street, the premises of the Watertown Savings Bank, he wanted to reach as many of them as he could. Brown's first issue brought home in a graphic manner the horror and misery of World War I: "Perkins Students Hear French Hero of Great War," the headline read. Guy Envin in saving his comrades had been blinded by enemy fire, and was in Watertown to visit students of the Perkins School for the Blind, with whom he had so suddenly developed a tragic kinship. That story played off lighter though no less newsworthy events, such as the arrival of celebrities of the time.

The following headline tells of both the visit to Watertown by a renowned thespian, and the determination of a *Sun* reporter: "Noted Actor E.H. Sothern Gives Local Interview" (and as a subhead) "World Famous Actor Breaks Rule of 'No Interviews' When Questions Presented By The Watertown *Sun* Arouse His Interest In His Art and His Plans." Brown's newspaper featured a sports section, and local readers were able to learn just how

manager Wilbert Robinson of the Brooklyn Dodgers felt on the advisability of using pinch hitters. The community's often tumultuous political trials and tribulations must have stung Brown at some point, for he soon found himself defending the impartiality of his newspaper. "We are independent . . . not a political paper," he wrote, as if to beat back those who accused him, and thwart others who sought to use his pages for political gain.

In the year 1925, a young man by the name of George B. Wellman joined the staff of the *Sun* as associate editor and sports editor. He was to remain with the paper until 1935, when he left to accept a "temporary appointment" as town clerk. The next year, he was elected to a full term in that office, and he was to remain in that position until his death in February of 1974. Like many businesses which were weathering the Depression, Brown's journalistic effort was not turning an acceptable profit, and in effect, he lost the *Sun* to Cyrus Eaton, who owned the shop which printed the paper. Frank Lightbody, who is now active with the Watertown Historical Society, was a newspaperman of regional experience at the time, and became editor in 1942.

Later the newspaper passed into the hands of W. G. Van Keuren, a local manufacturer who published the paper until he in turn sold it to Sam Bass Warner, Jr. a journalism professor at Boston University. Warner ran the weekly with his brother Lyle during the late 1940s and early 1950s. A talented and widely-known reporter and editor by the name of Fred Greene joined the paper when the Warners owned it. Greene was a veteran of the Boston newspapers, and had covered many of the important stories of the day, but was more than content to nestle into Watertown with his popular column, "With Creel and Bag." In March of 1953 Bob Ford, ambitious young reporter from the Waltham *News Tribune,* came to take charge of the *Sun.* The same Bob Ford is now editor of the rival Watertown *Press.*

Speaking of competitors, John and Peter Martin of Belmont began the Watertown *Herald* in 1938, and competed head-to-head with the *Sun* for years. Eventually Warner let it be known he wished to sell the *Sun* which was at that time located in the old Wright House on Mt. Auburn Street where "Dunkin' Donuts" now stands. In early 1954, the Martins heard that the paper was for sale. When he found out the asking price, John Martin wrote out a check for the sum on the spot. On March 11, 1954, Martin became publisher and his brother Peter became managing editor of the Watertown *Sun-Herald.* Ford was editor, Robert B. Kennedy was advertising manager and Helen J. Lang was assistant editor. Ford left a year and a half later to help found the *Press,* and former editor Fred Greene returned to the helm, where he remained until 1960. Upon Greene's retirement, Bob Mead, a young man who had been trained as a reporter on the *Sun's* sister paper, the Belmont *Herald,* became editor. Mead later left to assume the editor's desk at the *Herald,* and the *Sun* went through a number of editors and writers until Dave Gardner came to the paper in 1969. Gardner's unique style and wit, reflected in his "Man About Watertown" column, was popular reading, and his twenty-five years in the business gave him insight into human nature as well as the nature of the town.

In September of 1974 Steve McFadden, fresh from Boston University, was hired as a *Sun* reporter. His dogged determination to get the story and his pointed writing style soon made him a favorite of some and anathema to others. When he assumed the editorship in the following year his columns and editorials on issues of the day left no doubt in anyone's mind where he stood. During this period writer Mary Reilly, born and bred in Watertown, joined the paper, and her feature stories, thoughtful, heartfelt and well-written, are an asset to the *Sun.*

In February 1977 Michael O'Connor was hired as editor to replace McFadden who had decided to focus his considerable talents on freelance writing. Issues including development of the Arsenal property, housing, public safety, and municipal reform have occupied the newspaper in recent years, as town officials and the citizenry seek equitable and workable solutions to these problems. The Watertown *Sun* continues not only to record these challenges, but also to foster debate by which the town may benefit, now and in the future.

The Watertown Press

The Watertown *Press* was established as a new weekly newspaper in Watertown in the fall of 1955. The first issue of the paper (with six pages) published on November 17, 1955, carried news items including a report on the twenty-seventh polio case

of the year and progress on the addition to the Main Library. The advertisements included such bargains as five pounds of hamburger for one dollar.

The newspaper was founded by three men: William P. Dole, publisher of two long-established weekly newspapers, the Cambridge *Chronicle-Sun* and the Somerville *Journal-Press,* and the son of newspaper publisher William A. Dole, Jr.; Robert M. Ford, who had served for several years as editor of the Watertown *Sun* weekly newspaper; and Robert B. Kennedy of Watertown, an advertising representative for a number of weekly newspapers in Watertown for fifteen years. At the time both weekly newspapers in the town were owned by the same publisher, and the trio felt a competing editorial voice was needed. Dole and Ford were still with the paper twenty-five years later. Mr. Kennedy retired due to illness.

The Watertown *Press* was among the first weekly newspapers to provide consistent coverage and detailed reporting of town meetings and of governmental bodies, aided by a new state law on open meetings which forced public agencies with rare, specific exceptions, to conduct their business in public session.

In the mid-1960s the *Press* campaigned and editorialized to end a widespread practice of nepotism and political patronage in the town's school system, and aided the successful effort of a reform coalition to gain control of the School Committee. The reform group established qualifications and criteria for the appointment of principals, directors, and administrators; began recruiting for teachers outside Watertown, and appointed an out-of-state superintendent, Dr. Raymond Delaney, whose innovations continue to have a progressive effect on the system. For its efforts, the *Press* was awarded the 1965 Community Service award of the New England Press Association, whose membership includes most of the small daily and weekly newspapers in the five-state area.

On July 29, 1965, the *Press* published its first editorial in opposition to continued U. S. military involvement in Vietnam and continued until U.S. troops were finally withdrawn, to support Congressional and Presidential candidates committed to ending the war.

In the 1970s the newspaper supported the efforts of town officials and residents considering community uses for part of the Watertown Arsenal redevelopment site, an effort which culminated in the creation of Arsenal Park. The paper was less successful, in the same period, in urging construction of a new high school. In the mid-1970s, the *Press* supported the candidacies of a reform group which gained control of the Watertown Housing Authority, with the newly-elected members establishing procedures to guarantee impartial placement in public housing and successfully seeking federal and state funds and programs to provide

housing and housing aid for low-income persons. The *Press* was among the first weekly newspapers in the Boston Metropolitan area to endorse candidates for public office in its community.

In January, 1980, as it entered its 25th year, the *Press* removed all advertisements from its front page to improve the appearance of the newspaper. The offices of the *Press* were for many years located in the historic Captain Fowle House at 49 Mt. Auburn Street (until the building was razed), and have always been in the Watertown square area.

16

Watertown's Newcomers

HE SEVENTEENTH CENTURY village of Watertown with its population of 160 families had grown to a population of two thousand by the early 1800s. As a farming community close to Boston, possessed of the waterpower necessary for manufacturing and situated on the crossroads leading to and from Boston and the western settlements, Watertown was particularly well suited to develop as a modern country town.

THE IRISH

In January of 1847 the first ships began arriving from Ireland with the news that a terrible famine was taking place in that country. Hardship was not a new experience to the Irishman and woman of the 19th century, yet the staple of their diet, the potato, had been hit by a blight. With food shortages and lack of proper nourishment came many diseases. The people of Ireland had no hope in the future as each year brought another failed crop; children died and villages disappeared. Sad to say, the hardships endured by the people could have been greatly eased. During the most trying years of the famine food was constantly being exported from the Irish market to the Continent, while little or none was retained for the native Irish who needed the foodstuffs. As the situation in Ireland grew more severe, the thoughts of the people turned towards escape from hunger. America, the far-off land of opportunity, offered a ray of hope to a desperate people.

The Irish who first came to American shores shared harrowing experiences aboard ship.

Greedy ship owners crowded their passengers in unsafe and decrepit vessels. They charged exorbitant rates for passage and starved the ignorant immigrants on the six to eight week journey to the United States. An even greater problem for the poor immigrant was the danger of the dreaded "ship fever." A people already weakened by years of starvation were easy prey to disease due to poor ventilation and inadequate quantities of food and water on board the ships and the crowding that existed in the filthy holds.

Between the years 1850 and 1860 approximately 1,500,000 people left Ireland. Few wished to leave their green homeland, but the knowledge that death and disease were their daily companions forced them to undertake the terrible hardships involved in leaving friend and family to travel to the new world—the "new island"—as they called it.

What did our forebears find upon their arrival? Crowded ports filled with fellow immigrants attempting to find their way through the paper work and pass the physical examinations. The first need

Irish boarding house group in the 1890s.

of each new arrival was to secure housing and above all to find some form of employment. As the waves of immigration increased, the sympathy that was originally shown by native Americans began to diminish. They looked upon the Irish as a threat to their established way of life, because Irish workers were willing to accept the most menial work in order to establish a foothold in the new country.

The search for employment brought the first Irish to Watertown. In the nineteenth century Watertown was a small but growing industrial town. Its proximity to Boston and Cambridge and the Charles River made it the ideal location for manufacturing. Some of the institutions that offered the new immigrant employment were the Walker and Pratt Manufacturing Company, the Aetna Mills, the Watertown Industrial Fiber Company, the Porter Needle Company, the Empire Laundry Machine Company, the Watertown Dye House, the Metropolitan Laundry, Lewando's French Dyeing and Cleansing Establishment and the Newton-Watertown Gas Light Company. For the male immigrant ample opportunity existed for

work, but women faced a greater difficulty, often finding life in the mills or as domestics their only opportunity for self-support. As the years passed more employment became available when the Hood Rubber Company and the Watertown Arsenal began production. Here many an Irishman found his chance for financial security.

As more Irish moved to the town, their natural tendency was to share the music, songs and stories of their native land. Perhaps the most unifying force in the Irish community was their Catholic faith, which had sustained them through the dark years of oppression at home and had given them succor during the time of the famine and the dangerous crossings to America. Wherever he went, the Irishman brought his faith with him. In Watertown the strength of the Irish community led to the formation of the Saint Patrick and Saint Theresa parishes. The people of Ireland welcomed the religious freedom offered in the United States; they, accustomed to a strong church-state relationship, found strength in the separation that existed between these bodies in their new country.

176

Being deprived for generations at home of a political voice, the Irish-American seized upon the opportunity in America to show his concern and gratitude for what his new country had to offer. Immigrants soon recognized the importance of political power as a means of assimilation and acceptance into American society. The Democratic Party attracted large numbers of Irish immigrants due to its reputation as the party of the working man. The Irish took advantage of the opportunity and began to gain politically and socially within the Watertown community. Employment with the town as laborer, office worker, policeman or fireman were the desired occupations for the Irish-Americans. As is evidenced today, the Irish community in Watertown has continued to maintain its interest in the political affairs of the town. During each election campaign one cannot help but notice the number of Irish surnames that appear on a local ballot.

The most important Irish organization that exists in Watertown is the Ancient Order of Hibernians. This organization began in Watertown in the 1890s as an offshoot of the original brotherhood in Ireland that aided Catholics in their pursuit of religious freedom. The Hibernians in Watertown came to the aid of their countrymen by providing monetary and physical support to needy members of the community, and offered in addition a social and religious flavor to early Irish-American community life. As government took over the responsibility for the physical needs of its citizenry the Hibernians became a more socially motivated organization. They offered a center for the growth of Irish culture in America and have sponsored numerous programs to aid local charities. Currently the Ancient Order of Hibernians maintains a clubhouse and hall on Watertown Street. Perhaps the most famous member of the Watertown Club was President John F. Kennedy, the first Irish Catholic President of the United States, who became a member early in his political career.

Over the past one hundred and eighty years the Irish community has made its mark on the history of Watertown. Many have intermarried with other Americans, especially those of Italian origin. Numerous Irish have given their lives in the service of the country that opened its arms to their ancestors. Local businesses operated by Irish-American men and women daily offer a variety of services to the citizens of Watertown. Town employees of Irish extraction continue to show the concern that the principles which drew our ancestors to these shores will continue to be safeguarded and that the Irish community in Watertown will at all times be represented.

THE CANADIANS

Although Europe and Asia were the chief sources of immigration to modern Watertown, additional currents from within the Western Hemisphere joined the flow in the twentieth century.

Today in Watertown the largest group of immigrants consists of Canadians, either by birth or parentage, mainly from the Maritime Provinces.

Canadians began moving to Watertown about one hundred years ago. They were tradesmen, carpenters, and skilled workmen who became part of the middle-class exodus from rural Canada to New England, and then from the cities to the suburbs. Many Canadians settled in Watertown because of its quiet residential character.

In 1937 the Canadian American Club was formed as a social center, and in June 1969 a building on Arlington Street was purchased as a permanent home for the organization.

WATERTOWN'S ITALIAN-AMERICAN COMMUNITY

The Immigrants

The great wave of immigration from Italy to America occurred between 1875 and 1921. Ninety percent of the Italian immigrants were from the area of Italy referred to as the Mezzogiorno ("The Land Time Forgot"). It is an area that includes the provinces south and east of Rome: Abruzzi, Campania, Apulia, Lucania, Calabria, and Sicily. In ancient times Roman emperors, senators, and rich merchants owned large estates in these provinces. They frequently visited their beautiful estates in order to escape the heat, noise, crowds, and the responsibilities of Rome. As the centuries passed,

177

however, the new rulers of Italy abandoned the southern and eastern provinces and concentrated their efforts in developing areas north of Rome. As a result, the North became the rich, industrial section of the country, while the southern and eastern provinces became poor and desolate. The people in these provinces worked exhausted farms that produced meager crops. Unemployment was extremely high in the southern and eastern cities. Those that did find work were paid wages that were far below those of workers in the North. In the 1870s many of these poor people began to receive letters from relatives and friends who had migrated to America. All the letters had the same theme: for a man who was willing to work hard, America offered the opportunity to make a better life for himself and his family. America became the magnet that attracted the people of the Mezzogiorno.

A large percentage of the Italian immigrants who settled in the Boston area formed close-knit communities in the eastern, northern, and western sections of the city. As was the case with most immigrants, there was a natural tendency to live among people of their own ethnic group. The tendency was even greater among Italian immigrants. Unlike the Irish immigrants who had preceded them, they did not speak the language of their new homeland. Their physical characteristics and customs were strange to Bostonians. By forming their own mini-communities within the larger Boston community, they were able to help each other solve the daily problems that had to be faced in the strange new country.

The average Italian immigrant had a very strong work ethic. He was willing to work long hours and seldom complained about poor working conditions. The fact that he was willing to work for less money than the average laborer or factory worker earned caused him to become a threat to other first-and second-generation Americans. They did not understand that these newly arrived Americans had left a country where there was no opportunity to work in order to provide their families with the necessities of life. To many Italian immigrants, to have a job was a luxury they had never enjoyed. Work meant money, and money was to them the key that would give their children a chance to improve their situation in life. As time passed, the children of these immigrants became active in the effort to improve working conditions.

The chance to work and earn a good living attracted the Italian-American to Watertown. Until recently, although geographically small, Watertown was considered to be the most highly industrialized town in the country. The Hood Rubber Company, located in the East End, attracted a large number of Italian immigrants from the various sections of Boston. The availability of work in Watertown led to a constant exchange of letters between Watertown families and their relatives and friends in Italy. As a result of these letters, Italian immigrants began to come directly to Watertown.

The end of World War I witnessed a new trend among first- and second-generation Italian-Americans. Sons and daughters of the original immigrants were tired of living in the crowded "Little Italy" of Boston. They began to move to the suburbs where there was more open space and the opportunity to raise their families in a wholesome environment. By the 1960s Watertown's Italian-American community represented the second-largest ethnic group in the town.

Politics and the New Americans

The Italian immigrant distrusted politicians and individuals who held positions of authority. He had been exploited for centuries in his native land, both by rich landlords and by the Italian government. It was difficult for him to understand the American obsession with politics. When his children indicated an interest in politics, he discouraged them. Italian parents reminded their children that hard work, not politics, was the key to success.

The second generation of Italian-Americans shed the Old World attitude toward politics and demanded a voice in the management of town affairs. It was obvious to them that if they were going to influence town affairs they would have to enter the political arena, but this was easier said than done.

Watertown Republican and Democratic party leaders resisted the attempts of the young Italian-Americans to join their ranks. At first they viewed the Italian-American community as a source of votes rather than as a people who could provide the town with able political leaders.

The Republican party was the first to give in to the attempts of young Italian-Americans to enter politics. To the Italian-American, the Republican party was the party of Lincoln, the party that had

Festa at the Sons of Italy in 1975.

saved the United States from the disaster of permanent division and that had eliminated slavery. The Republicans had built up American industry and had opened new avenues for the employment of labor. On the other hand, the Democratic party had upheld and defended slavery. The leaders of the southern rebellion had been Democrats, and many Italians believed that every traitor to the nation, from Aaron Burr to Jefferson Davis, had belonged to the Democratic party. The Democratic party was also the party of the Irish, the chief rivals of the Italian-Americans in America. Young, ambitious Italian-Americans flocked to the Republican party, and the first town officeholders of Italian descent were Republicans.

The Great Depression of the 1930s caused a dramatic change in the attitude of Italian-Americans toward the Republican party. They felt that the party had let them down; the Republicans had cheated them of their jobs and brought hardship to their families. The Democratic party with its new president, Franklin Roosevelt, offered hope for the future. Previously undeclared Watertown

Italian-Americans registered as members of the Democratic party.

Local Democratic party leaders were slow in accepting the young Italian-Americans who aspired to hold public office. This resistance, along with a habit of nonparticipation in party caucuses, made it virtually impossible for an Italian-American to be nominated as the party's candidate for political office. However, the 1960s saw a change in the party's attitude. The Republican party had successfully sponsored several candidates of Italian descent for town office. Democratic leaders realized that they could no longer ignore the fact that one fourth of the town's population was of Italian descent. If they were to continue to control the town government, they would have to support Italian-American candidates. By the mid-1960s several Italian-Americans had been elected to town office.

The real break occurred in the 1970s. In the late 1960s, the town had voted to eliminate partisan elections. Candidates were forced to run as individuals rather than as members of a political party. Party discipline was eliminated, and office seekers

179

were elected on the basis of their particular appeal to the voters rather than on that of party affiliation.

Today Watertown's Italian-American community has become a political force in the town, with a sizable representation on all town committees and boards.

Italian-American Organizations and Ethnic Pride

One of the first things Italian immigrants did once they settled in America was to form social or mutual benefit societies. The main objective of the original organizations was to assist immigrants in adjusting to their new country. They provided food, shelter, and financial aid to their members in time of need. An immigrant joined the organization that represented the town or province he had migrated from in Italy. Once the children and grandchildren became financially secure, the original purpose of these clubs and societies changed. They became social in nature, concentrating on perpetuating Old World traditions.

It became common practice for the various organizations to sponsor festivals in honor of their patron saints. Old World music, dances, and foods reminded them of the old country. Although religious in nature, the *festas* served to keep Old World traditions alive. Even today suburban

Italian-Americans and their children flock to the North End of Boston to enjoy the various *festas* held during the summer.

Watertown has several Italian-American clubs and societies. Each in its own way is doing what it can to develop ethnic pride among young persons of Italian descent. The largest of these organizations is the Watertown Sons of Italy Lodge Piave Fiume. Unlike other Italian-American organizations, its membership is not based on what part of Italy a person's descendants had come from, and all Americans of Italian descent are eligible for membership. Men and women of other ethnic backgrounds who marry a person of Italian descent may also join the Sons of Italy.

Today, the Watertown Sons of Italy has a modern home on Pleasant Street. The lodge's home has become a major Watertown cultural center. An annual "Festa Italiana" is held every June in the lodge's parking lot. In 1979 an estimated twenty-five thousand people attended the *festa*. Italian movies and language and culinary art lessons are held in the lodge home on a regular basis. All programs are open to the citizens of Watertown and surrounding communities.

The Italian-American community of Watertown is proud of its contribution to the political, cultural, and social life of the town and looks to the future with confidence.

THE ARMENIANS

The Armenians are an ancient people whose history extends more than five hundred years before Christ. Their ancestral homeland, centered around the biblical Mount Ararat, is on the southern shore of the Caucasus Mountains between the Mediterranean, Black, and Caspian seas.

Armenians did not immigrate to the United States in significant numbers until the last quarter of the nineteenth century. The first Armenian church in America was consecrated on January 18, 1891, in Worcester, Massachusetts. During the 1890s hundreds of Armenians came to America, many of them locating in Massachusetts, where they found employment in factories. These immigrants came to America either for economic reasons—to earn enough money to return to their towns and villages to purchase land—or to seek higher education. Another major factor in this

immigration was the escalating Ottoman oppression of Christian minorities that made life increasingly difficult for the Armenian people in their own homeland. Most of these early Armenian newcomers were men, either bachelors or those who temporarily left their wives and children behind with the intention of returning with money earned in the land of opportunity.

In 1896 several Armenian bachelors living in Brighton obtained employment at the Hood Rubber Company, which had just begun operating in Watertown. Near the Hood Rubber Company there was a small community of no more than ten houses and a market which stood on the corner of Crawford Street and Coolidge Hill Road. In 1898 the family of Kevork Nakashian came to live in one of these houses. Nakashian converted the lower floor of his home into living quarters for twenty

These two young women were photographed in Turkish Armenia just before emigrating to the United States in 1880.

without fringe benefits. There were instances of labor strife when native employees, feeling threatened by the influx of aliens, demanded the expulsion of all foreign-born workers. Strikes were threatened and lockouts took place, but the Hood Rubber Company remained firm in its hiring policies, providing Armenians with an opportunity for gainful employment. By 1902 there were perhaps four hundred Armenians working for the Hood Rubber Company. A number of Armenians were also employed in other Watertown factories, such as the Walker and Pratt Stove Company (the maker of Crawford stoves).

At this time the majority of Armenians residing in Watertown were single men, either bachelors or with wife and family in the old country. There were only about ten families, and among the first of these was that of Dr. Hovnan Jellalian, an author and lecturer and a leader in the community.

On July 4-5, 1902, the Constitutive Assembly of the Armenian Church of America took place in Worcester, Massachusetts. Even though there was no Armenian church in Watertown, the community was represented by Ohan Shamgochian, one of the twenty-five delegates who signed the original constitution of the Armenian Church of America. By 1906 the town of Watertown, recognizing the need to teach English and citizenship to new Americans, initiated evening courses for the many Armenians then residing in the town. Over ninety students enrolled with two teachers, one being Aram Tellalian. In 1912 the Federation of Churches received a gift of an old house from Hood Rubber on Arlington Street and organized it as the Abraham Lincoln House, using it as a center for Americanization classes.

Up to this time, most of the Armenians moving into Watertown had come from the city of Kharpert and its villages, as well as from other communities of the upper Euphrates river basin in Anatolia. With increasing political oppression and religious persecution in the Ottoman Empire, more Armenians began to immigrate to America from all parts of Armenia. The Adana Massacre of 1909 was a prime factor in causing many Armenians from Cilicia to come to America. Cilician Armenians from Marash, Adana, and Aintab began to locate in Watertown, and their children and grandchildren form an important segment of the present Watertown community. As more Armenians from various areas of the Old World

Armenian boarders, employees of Hood Rubber. Another twenty Armenian men who commuted from Brighton and Cambridge also worked at Hood Rubber.

Mr. Nakashian's daughter Prapeon came to America in 1897 at the age of nine and attended the old four-room Coolidge School on School Lane, on what is now Western Electric property. She was probably the first Armenian student in Watertown schools. After a few years in Watertown, Prapeon Nakashian moved to St. Paul, Minnesota, eventually returning to Watertown in 1921 as the wife of Dr. Nishan Hampson, one of the founders of St. James Armenian Church. Mrs. Hampson remained a resident of Watertown until her death on November 22, 1979, at the age of ninety-one.

In these formative years the Hood Rubber Company remained the prime employer of Armenian immigrants, who were willing to work long hours for wages of eight to twelve dollars a week began to settle in America, it was natural for these new immigrants, nostalgic for their distant homes and families, to seek out others from their native villages and thus many compatriotic societies were formed to provide financial assistance, in particular to build schools and aid orphans, in the birthplaces of these new Americans. Also, the Armenians in America, in response to the decaying political situation in Turkey and under the influence of American democratic ideals, began to organize into political groups. Exposed to the concepts of freedom, justice, and equality under the law, these immigrants, for the most part from poor peasant stock, dreamed of freedom for their oppressed families in the Old World. The two major organizations active in Watertown at this time were the Social Democratic Hunchakian party and the Armenian Revolutionary Federation. These groups were instrumental in keeping the community cohesive, providing them with education, instilling in them a deep sense of responsibility to the Armenian cause, enabling them to work and sacrifice for their fellow Armenians, and giving them an opportunity for social contact and recreation. Although they were newcomers to a totally alien environment, the Armenians quickly earned the respect of the community as a law-abiding, hardworking, conscientious people.

World War I and subsequent events had cataclysmic significance for Armenians both in their homeland and throughout the world. Ottoman Turkey with its repressive policies had become the hated oppressors of the Armenian people. With the alliance of the Ottoman Empire with the Central Powers of Germany and Austria-Hungary, the Armenians enthusiastically backed the Triple Entente of Great Britain, France, and Russia in the hope of securing Armenia's independence. Armenians, including a number from Watertown, joined volunteer battalions that fought against the Turks either on the Caucasian or the Palestine front. When the United States entered the war in 1917 on the side of the Allies, many Armenians, including at least forty-five from Watertown, served in the U.S. Armed Forces.

Utilizing the occasion, the Ottoman Turkish government initiated its plan to end the "Armenian question" by deporting its Armenian subjects from their ancestral homelands into the Syrian Desert. Starting on April 24, 1915, this project was put into

effect, resulting in the eventual destruction of more than one and a half million Armenians and the removal of the entire Armenian population from their lands in eastern Anatolia.

In that part of the Armenian homeland under Russian rule, an independent Armenian Republic came into being in 1918. Caught between the revolutionary fervor of Soviet communism and a resurgent Turkish nationalism and beset by insoluble problems posed by thousands of starving refugees and internal dissension, the new republic proved to be unviable and collapsed in 1920. It was absorbed into the new communist state, becoming one of the constituent republics of the Soviet Union.

War, genocide, revolution, and famine had profound effects on the Armenians of Watertown. The war effort had expanded industries in Watertown, providing new employment opportunities. Local Armenians under the banner of various political groups or welfare associations such as the Armenian General Benevolent Union and the Armenian Relief Society raised funds to aid Armenian refugees throughout the Near East. Armenian immigration to the United States multiplied. In 1916 there were an estimated eight hundred Armenians living in Watertown; by 1930 there were over thirty-five hundred.

With the collapse of all hope of ever returning to their native land, many of the men tried to find their families, their wives, and their children to bring them to America. In many cases the search was fruitless, as their families had been scattered or killed in the devastation of Armenia from 1915 to 1922. Many Armenian bachelors and widowers who wished to marry and have families traveled to Syria, Greece, or France and returned with wives; other secured their brides through intermediaries. The prime concern of these new families was simply the security of having employment and the prospect of owning a home.

During the 1920s as the Armenian community grew in Watertown, most could be found in the East End in an area east of Walnut Street, west of Grove Street, and south of Mt. Auburn Street. The greatest concentration was on Dexter and Nichols avenues. The dream of every Armenian was to have his own business, and during this decade many opened tailor, shoemaking, and barbershop establishments. In 1925, Armenians owned at least fifteen markets in Watertown. One of these was the

Star Market at Watertown Square owned by Stephen P. Mugar. This Star Market was the first of many Star Markets now found throughout New England, while Stephen P. Mugar, who came to America as a child from Kharpert, became a noted philanthropist and benefactor to many institutions of higher education in the Greater Boston area. In 1924 Minas S. Kondazian built a factory on Coolidge Hill Road, where men's clothing was manufactured and shipped to all parts of the country. This factory still stands and is the home of the Eastern Coat Company, a men's clothing store owned by the Airasian family. The town has named the street immediately below the factory for Minas Kondazian.

The Armenian political organizations— Armenian Revolutionary Federation, Armenian Democratic Liberal party, Social Democratic Hunchakian party, and Armenian Progressive League—had their own centers or clubs which served for meetings and public functions as well as places for the men to gather in their leisure time. The compatriotic associations and benevolent societies continued their activities in behalf of the Armenian refugees. On Sunday afternoons these groups frequently held socials in various halls or outdoor picnics, usually on land made available by Hood Rubber or at Waverley Oaks. The gatherings were frequented by entire families, from infants to grandparents, who passed the afternoon dancing to Armenian folk music, eating traditional foods, reminiscing about the old country, exchanging information about long-lost relatives, and greeting newcomers to America.

Until World War I the Armenian community in Watertown had been basically transient, made up of few families and, as has been noted, of many males who hoped to return to their homeland. In the 1920s the character of the community changed. Now there were families and children. The Armenians were here to stay, and the East End became "Little Armenia." The community became concerned with its own perpetuation—with handing on its heritage and identity to its American-born progeny. So long as a child remained within its family environment, he could speak only Armenian, but once the child entered the Hosmer or Coolidge school he learned to speak English and made American friends. In short, the children were assimilating, becoming less and less adept at speaking Armenian, knowing even less about the history of their ancestors.

In 1923 Mrs. Gulenia Nazar, a noted Armenian educator and author who had been teaching Armenian in Boston, opened an Armenian school in Watertown. This school, which taught Armenian-American children their ancestral language and culture after public school hours, met in various places in the East End. It started in a neighborhood bakery, for a time was located in the East End fire station, and continued in various vacant stores or in rooms rented from one of the Armenian clubs. In 1930 the school had 150 students. By 1931 the sponsorship of this school was assumed by St. James Armenian Church and became known as the Sahag Mesrob Armenian School, which has continued its task of teaching Armenian language and culture to the present time.

Although the great majority of Watertown Armenians belonged to the Armenian Apostolic church, there was no formal parish organization of the Armenian church in Watertown until 1924. Since 1906 the Armenian Evangelical (Protestant) church had maintained a mission in Watertown, supported by the mission board of the Congregational church. Occasional Armenian Apostolic church services were held at the Episcopal Church of the Good Shepherd on the corner of Mt. Auburn Street and Russell Avenue. These services were arranged by a church committee functioning under the supervision of the pastor and parish council of the Armenian church of Boston. In 1924, after a number of public meetings at the Coolidge School that produced public support for an Armenian church in Watertown, a committee headed by Haigaz Akillian was formed to raise funds to purchase a site for a church building. In 1927 the empty lot next to the East Branch Library was purchased for $5,880. The Armenian Apostolic church of Watertown was incorporated on March 14, 1927, by Garabed S. Garabedian, Donabed Boghosian, Harry M. Chopourian, Garabed Zarkarian, Kevork Der Boghosian, Garabed H. Caragulian, Leo Kricorian, Richard Juskalian, Mihran Ounjian, and Ohan Shamgochian. Under the spiritual guidance of the Very Reverend Shahe Kasparian, pastor of the Holy Trinity Armenian Church of Boston, the raising of funds for construction of the new church went

183

forward slowly but surely. On August 29, 1931, the formal ground-breaking ceremony took place, while the cornerstone of the new edifice was blessed on May 22, 1932, by Archbishop Leon Tourian, primate of the Armenian Church of America.

Building continued during almost impossible circumstances of the Great Depression; funds were raised day to day to meet the cost. Much of the work was done by unemployed parishioners who volunteered their services. Various contractors and builders were hired for specific aspects of the construction as money to pay them became available. The first divine liturgy was celebrated on June 4, 1933, in the still unfinished edifice. Services, weddings, funerals, and baptisms took place, although the building was still under construction. Finally on October 31, 1937, the completed church was formally consecrated and dedicated to St. James of Nisibis, with Archbishop Karekin Hovsepian, who was later to become the Catholicos of Cilicia, presiding at the impressive ceremonies.

Since its inception, the St. James Armenian Church has been at the heart of the Watertown Armenian community. With its various auxiliary organizations for men, women, couples, youth, and children, it has grown in activities and membership and is presently the largest Armenian church in New England. It has expanded its facilities and in 1967 opened the St. James Church Cultural and Youth Center, which serves not only the Armenian community but all of Watertown as well with its cultural, youth, educational, and social service programs.

In addition to St. James, two other churches are active in Watertown—the Armenian Memorial Church (Congregational), dedicated in 1950, on the corner of Bigelow Avenue and Merrifield Street, and St. Stephen's Armenian Apostolic Church, consecrated in 1957, between Elton and Bigelow avenues. A number of Watertown Armenians also attend the Holy Trinity Armenian Apostolic Church, the Roman Catholic Holy Cross Armenian Church, both in Cambridge, or the First Armenian Church (Congregational) in Belmont.

The depression years brought much economic hardship, especially to immigrant families with growing children, whose breadwinners' income depended on factory work. Frequently it was necessary for both spouses to seek work in order to make ends meet. This was a deviation from the traditional norm, where the man was the wage earner and the woman took care of the home and family, but this was America. These years also found the Armenian community divided by internal political dissension. This division was a reflection of political polarizations in the world and in America, of the frustrations of a people that had felt itself betrayed and forgotten by its ostensible friends, and of the varying and conflicting attitudes toward the new reality of the Soviet Armenian Republic. Reaching an intense and bitter peak by the mid-1930s, this strife has waned over the years, and at the present time cooperation and unity among the various elements within the community is being realized.

World War II broke out just as the first generation of Armenians born in this country were coming of age. Thirteen Watertown residents of Armenian descent died in the war. During the late 1940s and through the 1950s a slow change took place in the community. Many of the returning veterans, armed with higher education made possible through veterans' benefits, found better jobs and entered the professions, thus realizing the American dream. They married and moved to one-family houses in Belmont, Arlington, Waltham, and Lexington. At the same time, Armenians who had lived in Dorchester, the South End, South Boston, Chelsea, and other parts of Boston now moved up the social ladder by settling in Watertown.

The size of the Armenian community in Watertown remained fairly constant, at perhaps four to five thousand. Gradually the immigrants' children began to assume positions of responsibility within the various community groups. English began to replace Armenian as the language most frequently used at meetings, in stores, and even within the family.

In 1965 the immigration policy of the United States was liberalized. No longer limited by restrictive national quotas, large numbers of Armenians from the Near East, the Balkans, and other countries migrated to the United States. The changing climate of a post-Stalin Soviet Union enabled a certain number of people each year to leave Soviet Armenia, and most of these Armenians eventually settled in America. The Lebanese conflict that has festered since 1975 and the recent upheavals in

Iran caused Armenians from the large communities of those countries to seek refuge in this country.

Today there are at least six thousand persons of Armenian origin in Watertown, including those who were born in the ancient Armenian lands: their American-born children and grandchildren; and the newer immigrants from Soviet Armenia, Iran, Lebanon, Turkey, Syria, Egypt, Greece, Bulgaria, Romania, France, and other countries. Watertown is the social and market center for Armenians of eastern Massachusetts. In the vicinity of Coolidge Square in East Watertown there are a number of Armenian markets, bakeries, and other business establishments. Residents of Watertown have become familiar with Armenian breads, pastries, and foods such as paklava and especially lahmajoun. In addition to the St. James Center, another beautiful edifice, the Armenian Cultural and Educational Center, is being built on the corner of Elton and Nichols avenues across the street from the site of the now demolished B. F. Goodrich plant (formerly Hood Rubber). There are also centers and clubs of the Armenian Revolutionary Federation and the Armenian Democratic Liberal Organization, which has published the *Baikar,* an Armenian-language daily, and the Armenian *Mirror-Spectator,* an English-language weekly, in Watertown since 1962. The Armenian General Benevolent Union has its New England center in Watertown.

Watertown can boast of the only Armenian bilingual educational program in the country; it is supported by federal funds. Armenian is taught as a foreign language on both the senior and the junior high school levels. Not only do the local Armenian churches have Armenian-language schools to teach language, history, and culture on weekday afternoons and Saturday mornings, but the Armenian Roman Catholic Mekhitarist Fathers and the Immaculate Conception Sisters also provide such instruction. In 1970 the Armenian General Benevolent Union opened a full-time school that now goes through the sixth grade and is located in the former Sacred Heart School on Belmont Street.

There are now few Armenian laborers; most Armenian-Americans are gainfully employed in businesses, trades, the arts, or the professions. The Armenians traditionally have a strong work ethic; they are success-oriented and are upwardly mobile. They are proud of their heritage and of maintaining their good name while being productive citizens of the town. Holding elective positions have been Charles Ohanian as state representative; Edward Seferian as selectman; Robert Hagopian as town treasurer; and G. John Gregory, Vahan Khachadoorian, and Robert Jamgochian as school committee members.

With numerous religious, political, charitable, veterans, youth, and other groups, the Armenians in Watertown form a dynamic community engaged in a plethora of activities. The Armenians are a homogeneous people with a passionate identification with their own unique heritage and history. At the same time, a healthy diversity of attitudes reflects their different religious commitments, political attitudes, generational conflicts, places of origin, and levels of accommodation to the American ethos. The homogeneity insures the continued existence of this people, while the diversity insures that being an Armenian will never be dull. Having a history now of eighty years and more, the "Little Armenia" in eastern Watertown—probably the longest continuing concentration of large numbers of Armenians in one locale in America—is not only alive and healthy but also vibrant with the promise of future growth and development.

THE JEWS

In 1900 Jacob Neiberg, who had migrated from Russia to Newton, married Rebecca Needel of Boston's South End. The newlyweds moved into a house at 9 Mt. Auburn Street, and as far as it is known, became the first Jewish residents of Watertown.

For Orthodox Jews, living "in the country" was a hardship. Stores carrying kosher foods were nonexistent, and in order to be able to observe the Jewish dietary laws the Neibergs and other Jewish families who followed them had to travel to Boston every week to purchase kosher food. Then, too, Orthodox Jewish law prohibits riding on the Sabbath and holy days, and no synagogue existed in or near Watertown. Hence, in the first year of their marriage the Neibergs held in their home High

Holiday services for themselves and several other families from the Nonantum section of Newton. Later the Neibergs and seven other families organized and built Congregation Agudas Achim on Adams Street in Nonantum. The descendants of these families still use this synagogue on special occasions, even though most of them now live in other towns. Dr. Sam Perlmutter remembers attending holiday services in a room rented for the occasion at the old movie theater on Galen Street.

Although other Jewish families settled in Watertown after the arrival of the Neibergs, the group remained quite small. They were made to feel welcome in all parts of town both as residents and as business people.

Jacob Neiberg and Benjamin Katz of Myrtle Street were engaged in the junk business and their horses and wagons were a familiar sight on the streets of the town. Morris Cohen of Capitol Street owned a tailor shop and later a haberdashery on the corner of Cross and Main streets. The Shick family founded the Watertown Dairy farm on property they bought from the Stone family on Grove Street and delivered milk to households in Boston's West End and in Dorchester by horse and wagon. Although the dairy was later moved to a larger farm in Sudbury, the family still lives in the Grove Street house. The Rosoff pickle business was founded on Boylston Street early in the 1920s.

Harry Perlmutter had a shoe store on Main Street; his son Samuel practices medicine in Watertown.

The children of these Jewish families attended Watertown public schools. Myer Neiberg was a sports star, a five-letter man for Watertown High School in 1920. In his memory his son established a scholarship fund at Watertown High School.

In 1924 Emma Neiberg Taylor and the Rosoff family of the East End founded a Jewish Community Center, primarily social and cultural in function, where the town's Jewish families might congregate. The first meetings were held in the East End fire station. Later they moved to Payson Hall in Cushing Square and then to a wooden house at the corner of Lexington and Belmont streets. There Sunday school, Hebrew school, and eventually religious services were held. As the Jewish population grew, the Belmont-Watertown Community Center was formed and evolved into the Beth-El Temple Center on Concord Avenue in Belmont.

During the 1960s and 1970s, increased social and economic mobility, the breakup of existing social and residential patterns, and the advent of multiple-unit dwellings in Watertown brought an increasing number of Jewish families to Watertown. Today the new settlers and the descendants of the earliest Jewish families live in Watertown in harmony with their neighbors.

THE GROWTH AND DEVELOPMENT
OF THE GREEK COMMUNITY OF WATERTOWN

The "Glories of Greece" preceded the earliest Greek immigrants to America. The Greek community of Watertown traces its beginnings to the arrival of three families in 1913. The infant community grew to approximately thirty families by 1923. This small group of immigrants had a dream and a burning desire to pass their heritage on to their children. They organized themselves into the Greek Society of Watertown and elected Anthony Pappas as the society's first president. Space was rented on Crawford Street which was to become a headquarters and a springboard for future growth. From this modest center an ethnic community developed which gave substance to the children that would be inspired by the combined traditions of Greece and America.

New and larger quarters on Arlington Street were built in the early 1930s and became the Greek Cultural Center of Watertown. Basileos Avtges was elected president of the board of trustees, and Anthony Pappas became head of the Greek School Committee. Simple day-to-day laborers met with a few professionals to discuss common problems and goals as well as to enjoy the fruits of social and cultural activities.

After attending classes in Watertown's public schools, Greek-American children voluntarily attended the Greek School at the Cultural Center to learn the Greek language and to engage in enriching cultural and social activities.

The new center was also used as a church by itinerant Greek Orthodox priests, with Iovianos

The late Archbishop Michael during Pontifical Liturgy at the Bigelow Avenue Church in 1956.

Male trustees represented the Greek community while women organized and directed the ladies' society, performing social and charitable services. The major responsibilities of leadership of Taxiarchae fell on the shoulders of the versatile and talented Reverend Efstratios Righellis. Under his leadership during years of outstanding service the Greek community strengthened its position.

By the early 1950s the Greek community built a new church and community center on Bigelow Avenue which added a distinguished building to Watertown's roster of churches. The new church, with its masterpieces of iconography and a functional community center, enjoys the dynamic leadership of Reverend Emmanuel Metaxas, who in over twenty-five years of service has earned the respect of many Greeks and non-Greeks in the community. In combining the values of Hellenism and Greek Orthodoxy, Watertown's Greeks exemplified the strong and colorful Greek-American family.

Children reared in this family setting became restaurateurs, merchants, teachers, doctors, lawyers, and scientists. Greeks served Watertown and the nation in war and peace. The prospects of the Greek community continue undiminished. The new Greek immigrant has brought us new defenders of the democratic way of life. Like his predecessor, the new Greek emulates the early struggling Greek immigrant in pursuing success by means of hard work.

Michael Anagnostopoulos (or Anagnos), the second director of the Perkins School for the Blind, was a Greek. Like him, the famous as well as ordinary Greek-American citizens of the little Greek Community called Taxiarchae have given and continue to give Watertown the zest on which America thrives.

Lavrakas the first to celebrate the Greek Orthodox liturgy. In a drawing of lots, not too differently than the manner done in ancient Greece, "Taxiarchae" (meaning "Archangel") won as the permanent name of the church.

Organization and development continued to progress with more and more immigrants and migrants joining the Greek Orthodox community of Watertown. It became difficult to separate church and community, since all members of the Greek community related to Taxiarchae.

17

Epilogue

HE Hodges *History* ends (1955) on a somewhat cautious note, observing that the town seems to have paused in its growth following the end of the Korean War and expressing hope for, rather than confidence in, the future. The town was actually approaching a period of decline. Population grew slowly and peaked at forty thousand in 1965. According to the state census of 1975, the town's population had declined to thirty-six thousand, equal to its population in 1935.

Between 1961 and 1971 there was a sharp drop in employment and payrolls. The loss in payrolls occurred in manufacturing establishments, the backbone of the Watertown economy, where two out of every three jobs were lost. By contrast, employment in non-manufacturing enterprises increased by half. In 1977 total employment was unchanged from 1971, but the total payroll, swelled by inflation, had again reached the 1961 level ($148,000,000). There was a slight increase in the number of business establishments. The decline had apparently ceased. As of this writing, later figures are not available, but the redevelopment of the old industrial districts is expected to bring about general improvement.

There was an average emigration rate of 350 per year between 1950 and 1960 and of 500 per year between 1960 and 1970.

The loss of industry during the 1960s was in large part the result of the termination of a signifi-cant part of the Arsenal's operations in 1964 and the closing of B. F. Goodrich (formerly the Hood Rubber Company) in 1969 and of the Lewis-Shepard Company in 1973. The Underwood and United Soda Fountain companies also ceased their Watertown operations during this period, and East Watertown became an area of abandoned factories.

The Arsenal retained about half of its property on which a materials laboratory was located, and offered the eastern portion for sale. In an attempt to control the future of this large tract, the town bought the property for $5.5 million. It was expected that the town would act only as a broker, selling the land promptly to a developer. However, fifteen years of quarreling among Town boards followed before a plan was approved and a developer chosen in 1979. It appears that the property will be developed, although some problems remain. A portion of the land will be retained by the town, part to be developed as a park, the remainder to be used in other ways.

When the Goodrich property on Arsenal Street opposite the Arsenal came on the market, the company's management proposed that the town acquire the land and combine it with that of the Arsenal in developing one great project which would entail roofing over Arsenal Street. Fortunately, this idea did not find favor, and private buyers were permitted to acquire the land. Most of it has since been put to new uses. The old factory buildings have been torn down, and although it is not a beauty spot, today this part of town is more attractive than it has been since the brooks and groves of "Hog's Back" gave way to factory buildings nearly a hundred years ago.

Much of the Goodrich property was converted for use as a shopping center, and the new center has brought to Watertown stores of a type it has not had before, attracting business from the old shopping areas in Watertown and Coolidge squares. Another large portion has been bought by the Boston Edison Company for use as a base for its service operations. Several manufacturers have purchased the remaining portions, and as of 1980 construction of buildings was underway. Nearby an incinerator was built on the old dump, but was soon abandoned as a nuisance. The dump is no longer used, and rubbish is hauled out of town for disposal. The area is still derelict, a sad contrast to the time when an attractive lake stood here, overlooked by the resplendent Glen House, a sporting house of some notoriety in the 1880s.

The old stockyard area, abandoned by Lewis-Shepard, United Soda Fountain, and Underwood, also found new owners. A building of the New England Telephone Company now occupies the site of the Union Market House, and a fencing academy has opened in the old haybarn, taking advantage of the open space provided by the large loft. Other industrial firms have moved into the old buildings and are sources of jobs as well as tax revenue for the town.

A new industrial area has developed west of Watertown Square, between Pleasant Street and the river. "Dirty Green" had been long occupied by Haartz-Mason, but the new development extends to the Waltham line, overleaping the old Aetna Mills. A town-built and town-operated skating rink opened on Pleasant Street in 1972 on the site of the old town wells, and in 1974 the Sons of Italy built a commodious clubhouse nearby.

Miss Hodges noted the many small companies making tools and other industrial products. There are still many companies of this type in Watertown, and both of the town's largest employers, Barry-Wright and Unitrode, are manufacturers of parts related to the electronics industry.

On Main Street the old stores with family names have given way to banks; and even here there have been changes: the old names, Watertown Coopera-

tive Bank and Union Market National Bank, vanished as these institutions were absorbed by giants owned and managed by strangers to Watertown. Only the Watertown Savings Bank, Watertown's first bank, retains its local identity.

Watertown's new generation of employers—public utilities, technology-oriented industries, and banks—offers a more stable economy than did consumer-oriented industries such as the rubber factory, and it appears that the long decline may be over. A rejuvenated chamber of commerce is actively working to bring about a reversal of the decline of the 1960s.

Other changes in the appearance of the town were also taking place. A change in zoning laws permitted the construction of high-rise apartment buildings, which subsequently appeared on Mt. Auburn Street, Bigelow Avenue, and Galen Street. The old Woodland Dairy was replaced in 1970 by Woodland Towers, a town-owned high-rise apartment for the elderly. In East Watertown the Coolidge Theatre was replaced by a fast-food establishment, since boarded up. As of now, except for the school halls, Watertown has no theater or public meeting place.

An old landmark disappeared in 1975 when the Unitarian church, built in the 1830s to replace the meetinghouse, was torn down. Its congregation was no longer able to maintain the large building and now uses a smaller one nearby, built many years ago as a social club. The site of the oldest church in town, the First Parish Church, organized in 1630, is now occupied by a bank, a symbol perhaps of the triumph of the material over the spiritual which is characteristic of the times.

An addition to the library on Main Street was opened in 1956. Miss Yerxa retired as library director in 1963 and was succeeded by Joseph Hopkins, who served until 1970. During the decade of the 1960s, perhaps the most significant development in connection with the library was the town's adoption of collective bargaining, which resulted in a new relationship between the library's trustees and its staff. In 1971 Sigrid Reddy was appointed to succeed Mr. Hopkins as director. Her incumbency has been characterized by an expansion of community programs.

The Watertown Boys Club was opened in 1971 on Whites Avenue. The land, the former site of the Grant School, was leased by the town at nominal

189

cost. The new building houses a gymnasium, a swimming pool, a child-care center, gamerooms, and shops, and the club is supported by a group of citizens, generously assisted by Watertown business and industry, without tax support. Its membership is open to children of both sexes. Except for churches, it is the only such privately supported facility in Watertown.

In the elementary schools the decreasing population ended the pressure to construct new schools, and in fact a surplus of classroom space developed. Proposals to eliminate schools have been furiously opposed by those living near them, but the Parker School was finally discontinued as an elementary school in 1979.

Agitation for a new high school building continued throughout the 1970s. Several costly proposals for a new building were rejected at a town meeting. An addition to the old building was finally approved, and its construction was begun in 1979.

Not only did the population decline somewhat during the years 1955 to 1980, but there were also changes in its composition, and these were reflected in the political life of the town. Notable were the upheavals in Lebanon that resulted in a renewal of Armenian immigration and the Italians succeeding the Irish as the dominant political power.

In the 1960s a new town meeting act reduced the number of representatives per precinct and eliminated a number of ex officio memberships. Town elections had become very one-sided as a result of the dominance of the Democrats. In an effort to obtain wider participation in town affairs, elections were made nonpartisan in 1964. Candidates were no longer selected in primary elections by registered members of the national political parties, and the field of candidates was reduced to twice the number to be elected for each office in a preliminary election.

In 1968 the voters approved a legislative act which established a board of public works. This had the effect of combining the functions of the highway, water, engineering, park, tree and moth, and cemetery departments into a single department. The inspectors of buildings, wires, plumbing, and gas were also placed in this department, as was the sealer of weights and measures. The selectmen,

now constituting the board of public works, became responsible for all of these activities. The act eliminated a number of town officers, both elected and appointed. The position of town treasurer was combined with that of collector in 1979 upon the death of John Kennedy, who had been collector for forty years.

As was indicated in regard to the library, collective bargaining for town employees was adopted in 1965; some years later compulsory arbitration was introduced to settle disputes involving the police and fire departments.

These changes together with other town bylaws and acts of the state legislature, greatly eroded the power of the town meeting, so that in the 1970s it wielded less power than it had in the days of George III. This resulted in a general decline of interest in the town meeting and a lack of candidates for town meeting membership. A growing disenchantment with the working of the town form of government led to the election of a charter commission in 1979. The commission worked intensively in 1979 and on January 14, 1980, offered a preliminary draft of a new charter for consideration at a public hearing.

The charter proposed a city form of government, although for sentimental reasons the municipality would still be known as the "Town of Watertown." The legislative body would be a town council, with a president whose functions would be primarily ceremonial. Members to this council would be elected to office. School committee members and trustees of the free public library would be the only other elected officers. All administrative officers and several boards would be appointed; the selectmen and the town meeting would be eliminated. Strong administrative authority would rest in a town manager, appointed by the town council. He would appoint several boards and officers formerly elected. Overall, the number of elected officers would be reduced from forty-two to twenty-two.

The charter in final form is to be offered to the town in May 1980. If adopted, it will go into effect on July 1, 1981, and Watertown will enter the balance of its fourth century with a greatly altered governmental structure.

Addendum

18

Business in Watertown in 1980

INCE ITS FOUNDING in 1630 Watertown has been a center of trade and commerce. Following the tradition established when the town's first settlers built America's first gristmill, Watertown retains the features which attracted business throughout its history: proximity to the port of Boston, convenience to public transportation, and accessibility from railroads and highways. The number of banks, industries, and commercial establishments reflects the favorable business climate of the town. This section includes biographies of a number of typical Watertown enterprises which contributed information for this book.

Arax Market
603 Mt. Auburn Street

Vahan Setian and his brother Varougan and sister Elizabeth came from Lebanon, and Elizabeth's husband Hagop Basmagian from Syria during the 1975 war in Lebanon. They had been in the clothing import business, but in 1975 purchased the Arax Market in the East End. They import fresh fruit, spices, cheeses, olives, and grains from the Middle East—Syria, Turkey, Egypt, Lebanon, Greece—and food products from European countries as well. Their stuffed grape leaves, made by Elizabeth, won the *Boston Magazine* prize for the best in the Boston area. Elizabeth also makes tabbouleh,

baba ganouj, moussaka, basterma, and soujouk, and the store offers its customers hot pickles, pomegranate juice, rosewater and other flower waters, rose syrup, grape molasses from Syria, and carob beans, as well as many different varieties of coffee in the bean. Pastries and breads available at Arax Market include lokoum, baklava, spinach pie, zhahtar bread, Syrian bread, cheese bread, and finger bread. Shoppers come to Arax Market from all over New England and even from New York and Philadelphia because of the wide selection of Middle Eastern products available.

The owners are Varougan Setian and Hagop Basmagian. The store is open daily Monday through Saturday from 8:00 A.M. to 8:00 P.M. and on Sundays from 11:00 A.M. to 3:00 P.M.

Ark-Les Corporation
52 Water Street

Founded in 1937 by Malcolm MacNeil, Ark-Les manufactures electrical switches and electrical terminals for automobiles and appliances. It employs 375.

Associated Radio Company
92 Main Street

The Associated Radio Company was purchased in 1947 by William Feinberg, the present owner.

The establishment was located originally at 98 Main Street before moving to the corner location at 92 in 1966. The business was originally founded as a radio service organization; with the advent of television it was expanded to include radio and television sales and service. The radius of home service and sales has expanded to include most towns surrounding Watertown. The company has now acquired the authorized dealership for Quasar Television sales and is also an authorized Quasar factory service organization. All other makes are also serviced.

Doing business for thirty-two years in Watertown has brought a large clientele to the Associated Radio, many, even now, being original customers. The company also enjoys the privilege of doing business with many established organizations in the area.

Atlantic Battery Company, Inc.
80-86 Elm Street

Atlantic Battery Company, founded in 1934 by the late Augustus J. Migell, is celebrating forty-five years in business, twenty-eight of which have been spent in Watertown. The oldest remaining originally-owned battery company in New England, and the only one manufacturing batteries today right from pig lead, the company is run by the founder's son, Bruce A. Migell. Atlantic Battery manufactures all its own lead parts, plates and components from scratch, including steel trays for industrial batteries weighing from 500 to 3,000 pounds to be used in fork lift trucks.

Originally on Northampton Street, Boston, the plant was moved to Prentiss Street, Roxbury Crossing in the early 1940s, and to Watertown in 1951. Of the thirty-five employees, several have long experience in this and other companies, and two have been with the company since Prentiss Street days.

Atlantic Battery supplies heavy duty, custom-built batteries to hospital emergency vehicles and emergency power equipment, and to most schools and colleges in this area. The MBTA and the Philadelphia Transit Authority as well as various agencies of the Federal government are also supplied by Atlantic Battery Company.

Like its founder, the current president is active in industrial, business and civic circles. Mr. Migell is incoming president of the Watertown Rotary Club, trustee and corporator of Watertown Savings Bank, and former advisory director of Shawmut Community Bank, Watertown. He is president of North Medford Track Club, and a member of Watertown Chorale. He is also past president and director of the Association of Fleet Maintenance Supervisors, past president of International Management Society, Boston Chapter Inc., and past treasurer and secretary of Independent Battery Manufacturers Association, President of Molds Corporation and past director of World Battery Corporation.

Bacon Industries, Incorporated
192 Pleasant Street

Bacon Industries, Inc., founded by Frederick S. Bacon in 1955, and presently owned by Richard S. Cass, is a manufacturer of high technology epoxy and urethane adhesives, potting compounds and specialty elastomers. The company succeeds Frederick S. Bacon Laboratories which was established at the same address in 1939. The company has grown from its original sole proprietorship to twenty-three employees in Watertown and twelve employees in a second manufacturing operation in Southern California. The company sells its products to electronics and instrument manufacturers throughout the United States, Europe and Asia. Its products were utilized in our manned space program and are presently used in aircraft, missiles, computers, and varied electronic devices. Close proximity to the Boston "Golden Circle" of electronic companies and to the excellent shipping facilities at Logan Airport make Watertown an ideal location.

Barker Steel Company, Inc.
42 School Street

The Barker Steel Company, Inc., was founded in 1922 by Harold L. Barker. In 1938 Barker opened an office and plant at the present location. In 1943 he was joined by his son-in-law Robert P. Brack, and in 1960 by his grandson Robert B. Brack, chief executive officer since 1971.

Barker Steel details and fabricates reinforcing bars for the construction industry serving the New England area. In 1974 Barker acquired Pioneer Valley Steel Company and built a plant in South Deerfield, Massachusetts, to service Western Massachusetts, Vermont, and parts of New Hampshire. In 1979 Barker acquired Northern Steel, Inc. in Medford, Massachusetts. Barker has employed Watertown residents through the years and enjoys its relationship with the community.

Barry Wright Corporation
680 Pleasant Street

Barry Wright Corporation manufactures and markets products, systems, and services in two major lines of business: products for general industrial applications, including aerospace; and products, systems and supplies for organizing, filing, accessing, and protecting all types of computer and other information media. The company has been a part of the Watertown community since 1950, when one of its predecessor companies, Barry Controls Incorporated (now a Division of Barry Wright's Industrial and Aero Products Group), moved from Cambridge to a building on Pleasant Street. That facility, which has since been expanded several times, now houses the corporate headquarters of Barry Wright Corporation, the management of its Industrial and Aero Products Group, and Barry Controls' Eastern Operation with its design, development, manufacturing and test facilities. A satellite plant to this operation is located on Bridge Street. The company employs approximately four hundred people at its Watertown facilities.

Barry Wright Corporation was formed in 1960 when Barry Controls Incorporated of Watertown and Wright Line, Inc., of Worcester, Mass., were merged. Barry Controls had its origins in 1943 when Mr. Ervin Pietz and two other individuals formed a partnership to manufacture and market a product developed by Pietz, a special shock and vibration mount designed to protect naval electronic equipment from the effects of gunfire. Barry Controls now manufactures and markets a variety of engineered products to control the effects of dynamic forces and motions, such as engine vibration isolators for jet aircraft, cab mounts to reduce operator fatigue in industrial and military vehicles, and isolators to protect computers from vibration. In addition to its Watertown facilities, Barry Controls operates plants in Woburn, Massachusetts, and Burbank, California. It serves foreign markets through a joint venture in Germany and foreign licensees in other countries.

Ervin Pietz, Chairman of the Board.

Barry Controls became the nucleus of the company's Industrial and Aero Products Group, which includes, in addition to Barry, the Vlier Engineering Division, of Burbank, California, a manufacturer of products for holding, positioning and locating parts during manufacture and for reducing "in plant" noise and vibration; and Zero-Max Industries, of Minneapolis, Minnesota, and Orange, Connecticut, a manufacturer of mechanical and electronic speed control devices for electric motors.

Barry Wright Corporation's other predecessor company, Wright Line, Inc., was also founded by a man with an idea. In 1934, Mr. E. Stanley Wright and an associate began manufacture in Wright's cellar of filing guides for use with IBM tabulating cards. Wright Line Inc., a wholly-owned subsidiary of Barry Wright Corporation, has now become a leading manufacturer of accessory products that provides solutions to the problems encountered in organizing, filing, accessing, and protecting all types of computer and other information media. Its headquarters and principal manufacturing facilities are located in Worcester, with sales and warehousing subsidiaries in Canada and West Germany.

Barry Wright Corporation is a New York Stock Exchange-listed company with 1979 sales of approximately $100 million. Ervin Pietz, the founder of Barry Controls, is Chairman of the Board, President, and Chief Executive Officer.

195

BayBank Middlesex
7 New England Park
Burlington, Massachusetts 01803

BayBank Middlesex was chartered by the Commonwealth of Massachusetts and is a member of the Federal Deposit Insurance Corporation. The new institution is the fifth largest commercial bank in the commonwealth of Massachusetts and the largest outside of Suffolk County. BayBank Middlesex has the most extensive branch network in the state with sixty-three offices serving the thirty-one communities in Middlesex County. Total assets of the merged bank are in excess of a billion dollars.

BayBank Middlesex was formed by the merger of BayBank Middlesex, N.A. and BayBank Newton-Waltham Trust Company. The newly formed financial organization continues to be a member of BayBanks, Inc. The merger, completed in November 1979, was the largest bank merger in the history of New England.

BayBank Middlesex, N.A. has roots that date back to 1853, when it was established as the Lechmere Bank of Cambridge. In 1864 its national charter was authorized and its name changed to Lechmere National Bank. The year 1903 marked the bank's consolidation with Cambridge National Bank. This was the first of many such subsequent consolidations in the bank's long history.

The bank has undergone many name changes in its 126 years of existence to accommodate its broadening market area. In 1936 its name was changed to Middlesex County National Bank; it became Middlesex Bank, N.A. in 1968, and BayBank Middlesex, N.A. in 1976. As of June, 1979 BayBank Middlesex, N.A. operated thirty-three branch offices in nineteen communities of Middlesex County with reported assets of $476 million.

BayBank Newton-Waltham Trust Company began in 1894, when it was granted a charter under the name of the Newton Centre Trust Company. In 1906 total resources surpassed a million dollars. In 1908 it consolidated with the Newton National Bank, changing its name to the Newton Trust Company.

The institution merged in 1945 with the Waltham National Bank, at which time the name Newton-Waltham Bank and Trust Company was adopted. It subsequently joined forces with the Union Market National Bank of Watertown in 1976 and in 1979 merged with its affiliate, BayBank Middlesex, N.A. As of June, 1979, BayBank Newton-Waltham Trust Company operated thirty branch offices in twelve communities of Middlesex County. At that time reported assets equalled $505.9 million.

Joseph P. Healey is chairman of the board of the merged BayBank Middlesex; Giles E. Mosher, Jr. is president. The bank's headquarters are located at 7 New England Executive Park, Burlington, in the attractive eleven-story office tower adjacent to the Burlington Mall and Route 128. The Watertown Square office is located at 39 Main Street, with branch banks at Coolidge Square (631 Mt. Auburn Street), the Warrendale office at 734 Main Street, and the Watertown Mall branch at 550 Arsenal Street. The bank employs forty-eight persons in its four Watertown agencies.

Bon Ton Rug Cleansers, Incorporated
81-85 Coolidge Hill Road

Bon Ton Rug Cleansers, Inc. was founded in 1901 as the H. M. Dohanian Rug Company by Hagop M. Dohanian. It moved to its present site on Coolidge Hill Road, Watertown in 1926 in a new building specially designed for the cleaning of rugs. Bon Ton was incorporated in 1926. It has seen two expansion programs in that time; in 1938 a second floor was added doubling the size of the building, and in 1941 an office area was added to the building. Bon Ton is primarily a service company specializing in the cleaning and restoration of rugs and carpets, although it also has a modest selling department dealing in most types of rugs. Bon Ton services the entire metropolitan Boston area and is recognized as one of the leaders in its industry not only in this area but throughout the country. Bon Ton is presently operated by Armen Dohanian, Sr. and Armen Dohanian, Jr., son and grandson of the founder. Even though they are not residents of the town of Watertown, the Dohanians have always supported many of the town activities and firmly believe in the future of Watertown.

Boston Edison Company
108-118 Arsenal Street

Boston Edison Company was no stranger to Watertown when it broke ground in September 1979 for its new Materials Management Center off Arsenal Street; the association between the electric company and the town goes back to 1905. That was the year when Boston Edison contracted for the electric rights of the Newton and Watertown Gas Light Company, and electric service has been provided for the three-quarters of a century since then.

In the early years of electrical service, Watertown considered itself to be one of the best lighted communities in the state, boasting of "all night" street lighting. Today there are 2,125 street lights in the town illuminating the way for Boston Edison's 14,685 customers.

Over the years as streets were widened and repaired, electrical distribution went underground. Now, in 1980, there are 10.1 miles of cable in conduits inter-connected with 27.3 miles of overhead wires bringing electricity to residential, commercial, and industrial customers.

In 1931 Watertown was the top ranking town in American industry, producing more than $50 million of goods that year, more than any other community of its size in the country. Boston Edison made a substantial contribution to this record in that Watertown's industrial development can be directly traced to greater and greater use of electricity.

The development of Boston Edison parallels Watertown's growth. Station 124 at 18 Spring Street, which went on line in May 1923, was the oldest Edison facility in Watertown, and stood back-to-back with the old railroad depot. In 1948 Edison purchased a 14,000 square-foot parcel on Arlington Street and opened Station 285 in February 1950.

Rapid growth continued in the town and a third station, 336 on Howard Street, opened in October 1955. On January 11, 1968, Boston Edison purchased the land and buildings of the Watertown Lumber Company from Vernon M. Mattson, its proprietor for forty years. The location at 108-118 Arsenal Street became Boston Edison Station 467 and began operation in February 1970.

It should be no surprise, then, that Boston Edison continues to feel at home in Watertown, even setting up headquarters in the highway department building during emergencies. When the Materials Management Center opens in 1980, the three-building complex will provide central warehousing and servicing facilities for Edison's electrical power network at the location originally occupied by the B.F. Goodrich plant and across the street from the former Watertown Arsenal. Interestingly, B.F. Goodrich and the Arsenal have been Boston Edison's two largest Watertown customers.

Not only is there a long association between Watertown and Boston Edison but also between Edison employees and the community. The company's chairman of the board and chief executive officer is Thomas J. Galligan, Jr., a former town meeting member and finance committee chairman. Retired assistant vice president Oscar B. Benson not only is a life-long Watertown resident, but the first Boston Edison fifty-year employee to retire.

Boston Edison salutes the Town of Watertown on its 350th anniversary, anticipating that the firm and established relationship between the company and the community will continue.

Boston Gas Company
525 Pleasant Street

Boston Gas, founded in 1822, is a public utility serving nearly one-half million customers in seventy-four communities in eastern Massachusetts, including Watertown and the city of Boston.

The Newton-Watertown Gas Light Company, established in 1854, was one of many gas companies formed in the middle 1800s in Massachusetts. Many of these companies, including Newton-Watertown, merged with the larger Boston Consolidated Gas Company (now Boston Gas) from 1905 through 1921. For many years the gas company operated from a location on Water Street, serving Watertown and several surrounding communities. Later, Boston Gas occupied facilities on Taylor and Arsenal Streets and, eventually, on Irving Street where the company's western distribution (i.e., "street") operations were headquartered. In 1964 the Irving Street location was vacated and personnel were reassigned to another company location in Jamaica Plain.

In 1973 Boston Gas returned to Watertown with the opening of a combined meter reading, cus-

197

tomer service, and distribution training center at 525 Pleasant Street. From this site Boston Gas today serves approximately 10,000 customers in Watertown as well as customers in the nearby communities of Newton, Waltham, Wellesley, Brighton, and Allston.

Cass The Florist, Incorporated
531 Mt. Auburn Street

Mary and Edward Cass started their business on Commonwealth Avenue in Boston, and moved their flower shop to 567 Mt. Auburn Street in Watertown in 1945. Now operated by Mary and her daughter Faith, Edward having died, the shop moved to its present location at 531 late in 1979 when the Casses bought the building. The family name was originally Casabian, and Faith Cass Patriquin, Mrs. Cass's daughter, was born in Melrose. Faith and her husband have four children.

Faith Cass, with 1978 award from the Massachusetts Horticultural Society.

The company specializes in authentic European and Japanese flower arrangements, having been among the first to make them commercially avail-

able. Faith has taught general courses in flower arrangement for the Cambridge Center for Adult Education for eighteen years, and also teaches a course in professional flower-shop work for the Massachusetts Horticultural Society at the shop in Watertown.

Cass the Florist has won major awards from the Massachusetts Horticultural Society and has been an America's Cup Winner in the contest sponsored by FTD. Their entries have been a regular feature of the Massachusetts Horticultural Society's annual Spring Flower Show, the Chrysanthemum Show, the Camellia Show, and the Christmas Show. Faith says Cass the Florist has done work for the local TV stations, Channel 4, 5, and 7, and for the White House, Colonial Williamsburg, and the New England Orchid Society. She has lectured and designed arrangements for the Museum of Fine Arts, for "The Vale" in Waltham, for "Beechwood," the Astor mansion, and other famous mansions in Newport, Rhode Island. She numbers among her customers Sharon King and Sonya Hamlin of local TV fame. The shop is well-known for its unique and artistic flower arrangements. It is open from 9 to 5 Monday through Saturday, and is closed on Sunday.

Century 21 West Realty
413 Mt. Auburn Street

West Realty was founded by Charles Agrillo and Dominic Savarese in 1972 and joined forces with Century 21 in 1977. According to Connie DelRose, in each of the past several years Century 21 West Realty has relocated over a hundred families.

The company is expanding with a branch in Waltham at 76A Weston Street, and a Rental Division developed and run by Frances Savarese and Elaine Agrillo with assistants Irene Mondello and Vinnie Auditore. The company also offers investment property to prospective buyers. Recently the block of stores at 413 Mt. Auburn was remodeled by Dom Savarese and was considered so handsome that the Watertown Chamber of Commerce chose it as one of three finalists in their 1979 Business Revitalization Award Program.

Century 21 West Realty is open from 9:00 A.M. to 8:00 P.M. Monday through Friday, from 9:00 A.M. to 5:00 P.M. on Saturday and Sunday and is staffed by twelve employees.

Coolidge Bank and Trust Company
65 Main Street

The Coolidge Bank & Trust Company was founded in December 1960 by a group of thirty-seven investors, with Milton Adess as the first president. Their aim was "to bring to the Boston area the sort of banking institution that would give its customers service they could find nowhere else."

The first office was in Coolidge Square at 585 Mt. Auburn Street and was the main office until 1971 when a new building was constructed at 65 Main Street. There are presently nine branches in Watertown, Cambridge, Bedford, Lexington, Everett, and Arlington. The bank employs 300 persons, 176 of whom work at the main office.

The Coolidge Bank and Trust Company was the first to offer service-charge-free checking and twenty-four hour "Cool Cash" machines to its customers in addition to checking, savings, money market certificates, loans, Master Charge and American Express accounts.

Coolidge Hardware, Incorporated
662 Mt. Auburn Street

Coolidge Hardware was founded by Milton Adess and his father and was purchased in 1973 by Natale Mancusco. Coolidge now employs ten persons. The company is located in Coolidge Square on the site of the former Joseph Coolidge farm in East Watertown, and deals in the usual hardware, wallpaper, and paint supplies as well as industrial hardware. Customers come from all over Greater Boston for hardware supplies and OxLine and Dutch Boy paints. Coolidge Hardware services many local industries and the school and other town departments in Watertown.

Coombs Motor Company
66 Galen Street

In December 1931 The Coombs Motor Company was established as a Ford dealership located at 49 North Beacon Street, Watertown. At the beginning of the second World War, the business moved to Marriott's Garage at 130 Galen Street, Watertown. Mr. Marriott had his Stanley Steamers in the front of the garage and Coombs had the few cars they had left to sell in the rear (the Ford Company had suspended production for the duration of the war).

Coombs also ran a machine shop and did subcontracting for Raytheon and other companies which were doing machine work for the government. At the conclusion of the war in 1946 the company built their present building at 66 Galen Street, Watertown, where they now operate a salesroom, service department, and body shop.

Damco Incorporated
5 Bridge Street

Watertown through its Chamber of Commerce has been supportive of new businesses locating within the community and has encouraged existing businesses to expand, while maintaining a strong suburban atmosphere for the people who reside in the town.

Ten years ago, Damco's founder and President George E. Danis moved his company to an old mill building located on 5 Bridge Street, Watertown. Damco, a manufacturer of precision sheet metal, services the electronic industry and other equipment manufacturers with an excellence in quality and price. With Danis' perseverance and guidance the original group of employees has grown to over one hundred and is still increasing at a steady rate. In April of 1975 Danis began a second company called Fastener Supply Corporation, a distributor of nuts, bolts, screws, and other related items. Danis has said that the growth rate of F.S.C. (which has almost doubled since 1978) has evolved from the administrative efforts of the company's Vice-President John Gianakouras and his support staff. Damco and F.S.C. are proud to have become a contributing part of Watertown's past, present, and future growth.

Demos Restaurant
64 Mt. Auburn Street

John G. Demos and his wife Helen are the owners (and the chefs) of Demos' Restaurant. John opened his first restaurant on March 14, 1960, in the North Station area of Boston, and his first customer is still a regular visitor to the Watertown restaurant. Demos' specializes in shish-kebab, lamb dishes, and other Greek specialties, as well as American food and features an international menu. John says that the customers enjoy the quick and efficient service provided. Customers order their meals at the counter, and dishes are brought to each customer's table by a waiter. John and Helen bought the present building in 1971 when they moved the operation to Watertown. They employ about ten people, and attract customers from all over Greater Boston. About a third of the people who visit the restaurant in the evenings are patrons from Demos' old days in Boston. The restaurant is open from 11:00 A.M. to 9:00 P.M. Monday through Saturday and closed on Sunday.

Doble Engineering Company
85 Walnut Street

The Doble Engineering Company was founded in 1920 by Dr. Frank Currier Doble (1886-1969) and has been located since that time during various periods in Boston, Medford, Belmont, and Watertown, Massachusetts. Officers of the company are John P. Petrou, president, Anthony L. Rickley, senior vice president, and Jerry A. Jodice, vice president. The company employs 150 persons.

Since 1920 the Doble Company has specialized in the development of test equipment and techniques for the detection of operating failure hazards in transmission line insulators and electric-power insulation. The Doble Company has also developed and is providing equipment for timing and monitoring the operation of high-voltage and extra-high-voltage circuit breakers of all ratings, and test equipment specially designed for power-system simulation and relay testing.

Doble test equipment is currently in use on systems operating approximately 80% of the total electric energy generated on the North American continent, and on numerous large power systems on other continents.

The Doble Company has occupied its present facility at 85 Walnut Street in Watertown since December 1975, when it acquired the property formerly occupied by the William Underwood Company. The Watertown location was selected because of its nearness to the former Belmont site and accordingly convenience for employees, availability of technical labor force, nearness to Boston, and excel-

lent opportunity for growth offered by the new location.

Eastern Coat Manufacturing Company
76 Coolidge Hill Road

The Eastern Coat Company was founded in 1937 by Peter and John Airasian, brothers who came to this country in 1912 around the time of the Turkish genocide of the Armenians. After spending their early working years learning the clothing business as employees of other manufacturers, they founded their own firm.

Manufacturers of boys' topcoats, trenchcoats and sportcoats, Eastern Coat supplied clothing to retail outlets all over the country, their largest accounts being Sears Roebuck and J.C. Penney.

The business was started on Spring Street in Watertown and moved shortly afterwards to the Naples spaghetti company building on Dexter Avenue (presently the location of Plaza Travel and Women's World). In 1946 they built their own manufacturing plant at 85 School Street (now owned and occupied by the United Electric Controls Company).

During the 1940s and 1950s, Eastern Coat employed between one hundred and 250 persons, the majority of whom were Armenian and came from similar backgrounds to John's and Peter's. The atmosphere was homey and ethnic and the Armenian language was the prevalent one in the factory, where Christmas and holiday parties reflected Armenian customs and culture.

In the late 1950s John retired from the business and the manufacturing operation was phased out. Peter, however, continued to operate a retail store. The business was moved to its current location at 76 Coolidge Hill Road, Watertown (formerly the location of M.S. Kondazian & Sons, also a clothing manufacturer). Peter eventually bought the Kondazian building and sold the one on School Street to United Electric Controls.

Peter was an active member of both the Armenian and Watertown communities. He was a trustee of the St. James Armenian Church and served as assistant treasurer of the parish building committee. He was a director of the Union Market National Bank, and a corporator of the Watertown Savings Bank.

200

Peter had three sons, Peter, John, and Paul. Upon Peter's death in 1968, his two sons John and Paul took over the management of Eastern Coat.

Community involvement having always played an important part in the Eastern Coat tradition, John and Paul are both active in Watertown civic affairs. John was the first president of the Watertown Chamber of Commerce and is a past president of the Watertown Rotary Club. He is a trustee of the Watertown Savings Bank and the Waltham Hospital, and a director of the Watertown Boys' Club. Paul is the founder and first president of the Watertown Jaycees.

Through personal service, good quality at fair prices, and by advertising (primarily on the Bruins hockey games), they have built a small retail business into one of the area's largest and best known retail clothiers.

Econo-Car of Newton-Watertown
602 Pleasant Street

A fast-growing auto rental system in New England, Econo-Car has strong ties to the Watertown area. Leonard Albert, after a career as an electronics engineer, became the Econo-Car rental licensee for the Newton-Watertown area in 1969 with headquarters located at 602 Pleasant Street in Watertown. It is the first free-standing building designed specifically for auto rental in the Econo-Car system. Together with his wife, Corinne, he operates a large fleet of new, clean, and well-serviced autos and vans. Econo-Car of Newton-Watertown offers free pickup and delivery for customers in their area.

Evans and Faulkner, Incorporated
376 Arsenal Street

The firm of Evans and Faulkner, Incorporated, Commercial Printers and Lithographers, was founded in Watertown, Massachusetts, in 1962 by Robert W. Evans and Robert G. Faulkner, both natives of Watertown. The company, which moved to its present location at 376 Arsenal Street in 1968, was recently acquired by Thomas J. and Marylouise Pallotta McDermott, lifelong residents of Watertown. The continuous growth and expansion of the firm has been achieved through emphasis on providing high quality printing services and by maintaining a diversity of customers in the town of Watertown and the surrounding communities.

The McDermotts have for many years been active in the Watertown community. Tom McDermott has been a selectman in Watertown for eight years, and is presently serving as Chairman of the Board of Selectmen. His wife Marylouise has been a member of the Watertown School Committee for ten years, having served as chairman of that board. The McDermotts are the parents of two sons, John Pallotta McDermott, sixteen years of age and actively involved in the firm after school hours, and Thomas J. McDermott, Jr. (Peppi) who is seven years old.

Everywoman's Sport Center
120 Elm Street

Everywoman's Sport Center, Inc., a sports education and training center for women of all ages and abilities, opened in Watertown on October 1, 1979, at 120 Elm Street. Founded and directed by Debra Glassman, it is the first center for women in the Boston area to provide sports instruction, activities, and physical conditioning programs within a sports physiology framework. The programs are created to focus on all women's needs and unique capacities for physical activity, many of which have been too long neglected. The center emphasizes the importance of women understanding their own physiology as a basis for the development of their general physical capacity and skills in sports.

Everywoman's Sports Center offers a great deal of variety and flexibility in its programs. There are physical conditioning programs that offer an integrated approach to fitness through initial testing, on-going evaluation and education in weight control, nutrition and the development of cardiovascular endurance, muscular strength and flexibility; instruction in many sports activities, i.e., running, bicycling, basketball and self-defense; academic courses, such as Women's Sports Physiology; and special programs, including lectures, films, and trips.

Other unique aspects of the Center's programs are: regularly scheduled drop-in sports activities, i.e., volleyball and basketball; drop-in conditioning for use of the weight room and a running club. Of special note is the physical fitness evaluation laboratory where women can learn about their physical condition and potential and develop a plan that meets their needs and measures their progress toward achieving them.

Foxie's Deli
59 Mt. Auburn Street

Foxie's Deli is owned by Farhad Sanatian, who bought the business in 1972 from its former owner, Steve Jolki. Sanatian says that he believes that at one time the delicatessen belonged to a group of three in the Boston area, all called Foxie's, although the Watertown Foxie's is autonomous. The Newton Foxie is still in existence on Austin Street in Newtonville.

Foxie's serves the general public from its convenient location near Watertown Square on Mt. Auburn Street, and is patronized by customers of all ages and types, especially business people who come for Foxie's well-known grilled Reuben sandwich (corned beef, sauerkraut, and Swiss cheese on dark rye). Foxie's also features club sandwiches, salads, and the usual Jewish delicatessen specialties. Foxie's has ten employees.

Freedom Federal Savings
75 Main Street

The Worcester-based Freedom Federal Savings has been part of the Watertown scene since December 31, 1974, when Northeast Federal Savings of Watertown merged with the Worcester institution known then as First Federal Savings. At the time of the merger Northeast Federal had branches in Cambridge, Newton and Marlboro. In June 1975 First Federal of Worcester changed its name to Freedom Federal to avoid confusion with Boston area institutions also known as First Federal Savings.

Northeast Federal stemmed from the Watertown Cooperative Bank which was founded under a state charter in 1888. In 1953 the Watertown institution changed to a federal charter and became the Watertown Federal Savings and Loan Association. The change to Northeast Federal Savings and Loan Association was made in 1967 when the Watertown Federal Savings and the Cambridge Federal Savings and Loan Association merged.

Freedom Federal Savings as of December 1979 had assets of more than $750 million making it the largest federal savings and loan association in New England. In October 1979 Freedom Federal opened its second branch in Newton, located in Marshall's Shopping Center, Needham Street. This gives the Worcester-based association six full-service offices plus five supermarket banking facilities in the Greater Boston Area.

Gaston Andrey Associates, Incorporated
20 Watertown Street

Gaston Andrey Associates sells and services Saab automobiles. Felix Bosshard, the owner, founded the agency in 1958. The business started as a Gulf station with one employee, and Bosshard expanded in 1972, acquiring the restaurant next door and connecting the two buildings by transforming the restaurant into a showroom. On the site is a stone marker reading, "In the House Standing on This Lot PAUL REVERE made the Colonial Notes ordered by the Provincial Congress, 1775."

Gaston Andrey employs seventeen persons at its Watertown agency, and another seventeen in each of its branch operations in Brookline (5 Waldo Street) and in Framingham (1800 Worcester Road).

General Scanning Incorporated
500 Arsenal Street

Founded by Jean I. Montagu and Pierre J. Brosens in 1968, General Scanning manufactures high-speed electromechanical actuators for use in optical image processing, computer peripherals, and diagnostic medical instruments. It serves a world-wide market, with exports accounting for approximately 25 percent of its sales.

The company is a member of the Massachusetts High Technology Council, and it has found Watertown a propitious location to stay in touch with the progress at major research centers. The location at Arsenal Street is a new 35,000-square foot facility, employing 170 persons.

Glenda's Kitchen
45 Lexington Street at Main Street

Glenda Melendez and Marie McDonough started Glenda's Kitchen in February of 1979 as a new business, and since then it has been growing steadily. The restaurant specializes in Spanish cuisine and also does buffet catering. The bill of fare includes American and Italian dishes and features paella and other Spanish specialties at its daily luncheon specials. Among its regular customers are the Board of Trustees of the Waltham-Lexington Pre-School and a group from the First Congregational Church of Wellesley. The restaurant is open from 11:00 A.M. to 9:30 P.M. daily Monday through Saturday and on Sunday from 12:00 noon to 8:00 P.M.

Haartz-Mason, Incorporated
270 Pleasant Street

Haartz-Mason, Incorporated was incorporated in July 1926 as the Haartz-Mason Rubber Manufacturing Company by John C. Haartz, Sr., and Jesse H. Mason. The company began manufacturing rubber-coated products in November 1926 in a building still used at the present address. Automotive top material was produced for the first six months. Subsequently other items such as raincoat fabrics, materials for sporting goods and the shoe trade were added to the product line.

In February 1930 the company name became Haartz-Mason-Grower Company when James Grower joined the Management. In April 1946 the present corporate name was adopted. The company employs 115 persons.

Diversified products helped the company survive the 1930s depression and then adapt to wartime requirements. The company was the second in the country approved by the Bureau of Naval Aeronautics to supply coated fabrics for life rafts. Similar fabrics were used in life vests, pontoons, and other military applications.

Specialization in coated fabrics since World War II resulted in many products some of which are: electrically conductive shielding tapes for high voltage power cables, inflated protective buildings for Distant Early Warning line radar units, carburetor diaphragms used in gasoline engines, the air-retaining bladder in space suits, and seals in liquid-filled capacitors for television sets.

Through the years the favorable business climate in Watertown encouraged the company to expand the plant to accommodate new machinery for higher quality and increasing sales. During the 1970s a growing percentage of business has been due to sales to foreign customers. Today Haartz-Mason's advanced technology in rubber-coated fabrics has led to their use in many diverse products which enhance our everyday lives.

Hudson Travel Service, Incorporated
235 Main Street

Hudson Tours was first located in the 1930s on Hudson Street in Boston's Chinatown. When Tom Jabaily left military service he took over the business and moved it to Watertown in 1952. The first travel agency in Watertown, it was first located at 640 Mt. Auburn Street in the Coolidge Square area. The second location was at 38 Mt. Auburn Street, at the corner of Baptist Walk. Some of the clients served at that time were Sasaki-Walker, the Hood Rubber Company, Educational Services (now known as Educational Development Center), and Lewis-Shepard Company. The third location was at 7 Main Street (in somewhat larger premises) where the company continued to serve its various commercial accounts and a number of prominent Watertown citizens. The fourth and present location is at 235 Main Street, the site of the former Whitney estate. Hudson Travel was the first tenant in Whitney Plaza and the rest of the units were built around it in 1965.

Thomas J. Jabaily, the owner of Hudson Travel Service, is a former president of Watertown Rotary, past president of the Watertown Chamber of Commerce, member of the Crosscup Pishon Post of the American Legion, charter member of the Nicholas G. Beram Veterans Organization, charter member of the Arab-American Benevolent Association (which hopes to build a home for the elderly shortly), a member of the Masons and the Shriners. He has served as past president of the New England Chapter of the American Society of Travel Agents (ASTA) and is currently serving as ASTA director of area #1 which includes the New England and Connecticut Chapters.

Hudson's services include air, rail, steamship, bus, hotel, and car reservations, travel insurance and travelers' checks. Hudson Travel is an American Express representative. Their new Sabre computer speeds all aspects of travel and makes for an efficient operation.

Hudson Travel's employees have visited many parts of the world and hope to visit even more. Some of the places visited include Africa, New Zealand, Australia, Europe, Hong Kong, Tokyo, Taiwan, Hawaii, Bermuda, the Caribbean, and the Holy Land.

Hyperion Industries Corporation
134 Coolidge Avenue

Hyperion Industries Corporation is a manufacturer of custom and standard power supplies. Titan Transformer Company, a division of Hyperion Industries, manufactures custom transformers. Hyperion Industries Corporation opened for business in November 1957. The initial plans leading to its formation, however, began roughly six months earlier. At this time Melvin Friedman, an engineer in charge of systems design at Raytheon, and L.L. Schley, a manufacturing representative in the Boston area, began forming plans for the founding of a company, which six months later led to the opening of Hyperion.

When the company started in November 1957 there was one employee. In the meantime Friedman continued working for Raytheon, operating the new company by telephone from his desk. In addition to this he worked another fifty hours per week at Hyperion at night and on weekends. In April of 1958 Friedman left Raytheon and joined Hyperion full time.

In its first fiscal year ending June 30, 1958, Hyperion had sales of $31,000 and showed an operating loss of $4,000. The initial losses resulted from a volume of business which was not sufficient to support the overhead and the starting-up costs. The company continued to prosper, however, and today Hyperion Industries employs 150 people and in 1979 had sales of $4,000,000.

Inspired Images
50 Church Street

Inspired Images was started in 1973 by Irene Downes and Joe Briand in their home on the corner of Church and Summer Streets, where it will, they hope, remain for some time. They find the location excellent, near the Massachusetts Turnpike, and close enough to Boston for a reference point, as many of their clients come from a distance. It is also a beautifully sunny corner for their daylight studio.

The studio was started with the intention of being primarily for portrait photography but soon Downes and Briand recognized a real need for good show-business promotional photography. The "better mousetrap" theory is being proved again, as the Watertown studio is starting to attract many former New York clients.

Inspired Images' portrait and wedding work comes from all over eastern Massachusetts, and comprises about half their business at this point. The variety of their commissions ranges from book and album covers to the elephant they were supposed to have photographed in the Hyatt Regency Grand Ballroom on New Year's Eve. (Unfortunately, while being transported from New York City, the elephant lost some skin off its back under a low overpass on Storrow Drive and couldn't appear that evening.)

Irene sometimes thinks of writing her memoirs. She plans to call it "Melanie and the Rabbi," because a few years ago, she and Joe took portraits of Rabbi Earl Grollman and promotional photographs for Melanie, an exotic dancer, on the same day.

Instrumentation Laboratory Incorporated
9 Galen Street

Instrumentation Laboratory Incorporated (IL) is a leading manufacturer of biomedical and analytical instruments. IL instruments are found in laboratories throughout the world.

In clinical laboratories, IL products are used primarily to run tests on body fluids. The results give doctors vital information for the diagnosis and treatment of the seriously ill. In government and industrial laboratories, IL instruments are used to detect potentially harmful metals for pollution studies and for quality control in manufacturing.

IL was founded in 1959 by President Thomas A. Rosse. The company's first product was a blood gas analyzer—used to measure oxygen, carbon dioxide, and acidity in blood. The reliability of the instrument helped establish the company's reputation in medical and scientific circles.

Today IL designs and manufactures over sixty instruments and the necessary supplies to operate them. The company's philosophy has remained the same through the years: to produce reliable, easy to operate instruments that incorporate the latest technology.

Since IL instruments are frequently called upon in life-saving situations, accuracy and speed of analysis are key ingredients. Many of IL's instruments replace time-consuming, manual techniques. In an age of rising health care costs, IL tries to keep costs per test as low as possible. A number of IL's instruments are designed to yield readings from small samples, to accommodate work with infants, the elderly and animals, where larger samples are difficult to obtain.

In its early years IL found a home in Watertown Square and, as the company grew, slowly expanded to take over the entire historic red-brick building that was once the home of Lewandos. In 1968 corporate headquarters was established in Lexington, and the Watertown facility was purchased in 1973 and maintained for manufacturing. The manufacturing facility, prominent in Watertown Square, symbolizes the company's tie with the community. The majority of the 359 employees are residents of Watertown.

Each year, IL provides a scholarship to a qualified Watertown high school student, as well as supporting The Watertown Boys' Club. IL has been honored in past years as Massachusetts Employer of the Year for its commitment to hiring the handicapped.

Ionics, Inc.
65 Grove Street

Founded in 1948, Ionics manufactures desalting equipment for use in water, food and chemical processing, and instruments for monitoring water pollution. It employs 350 persons.

The Joy of Movement Center
23 Main Street

The Joy of Movement came to Watertown in September 1975 to the former location of Sasaki Associates, Inc. (before that the home of the Masonic Temple). It offers instruction in sixty-five different kinds of dance and movement, including ballet, jazz, modern, tap, musical comedy, social dancing, disco, a variety of exercise classes, "jazzercise," dance aerobics, exercise for health and fitness, "feeling good," and yoga. Classes are offered at every level from fundamental to advanced, and are held at the First Parish Church as well as at the studio at 23 Main Street. Hours are Monday through Thursday from 4:00 P.M. to 10:00 P.M., Saturday from 10:00 A.M. to 2:00 P.M., and Sunday from 2:00 P.M. to 6:00 P.M.

K & L Sound Service Company
75 North Beacon Street

The owner of K & L Sound, Lewis S. Freedman, founded the company in May 1971. Located at 245 North Beacon Street, it was the only discount audio store in New England. The store moved in June of 1972 to 264 North Beacon Street, and in January 1974 to its present address.

K & L started as a one-man business and now has forty-five employees. They diversified from being simply a hi-fi store to a professional audio business serving many of the large discotheques in New England.

K & L does the sound reinforcement work (dance music for the cheerleaders) annually at Shaefer Stadium. They also deal with all the major rock 'n roll acts in New England.

In 1976 Audio Forum (owned by K & L) moved out of the second floor at 75 North Beacon and became a store in its own right, now located at 68 Watertown Street. The second floor is now used as office space for the professional department. K & L also owns a third store at 810 Providence Highway, Norwood, Massachusetts, 02062.

Kay's Fruit
594 Mt. Auburn Street

Kay's Fruit was founded in 1947 by Mrs. Azadouhi Kaloustian. At the present time her son, Kirk, is the proprietor.

On September 22, 1979, the *Real Paper* selected the store as the "Best Fruit Store in Boston." What makes this store so special is that it does a volume business in high quality merchandise at low prices.

The store regularly stocks olives, cheeses, cracked wheat (bulgur), rice, lentils, marinated mushrooms, Lebanese bread, oriental specialties, organic fruit, Italian fruit and vegetables in season, and fruits from overseas.

Kays is now about twenty times larger than it was in 1947, however, they manage with only four employees since it is primarily a self-service operation.

Lanno's Restaurant
86 Main Street

The Watertown Sea Grill was established in 1936 by the Fantasia family of Watertown and was purchased by Joseph Lanno in 1952. The name was changed to Lanno's and the restaurant has been operated since 1965 by Joseph Lanno, Jr. Lanno's has been expanded five times, growing from the original capacity of sixty seats to its present capacity of over two hundred. In its various expansions the restaurant has taken over four adjacent stores and has converted the property behind it on Cross Street into a parking lot with valet parking service available. The kitchen has been expanded to twice its original size and banquet facilities for up to ninety persons have recently been added.

Lanno's offers both Italian and American cuisine and serves luncheon and dinner to as many as four thousand diners a week. Their reputation for fine food and good service brings loyal customers from all over the Greater Boston area. Seventy-two employees work at Lanno's, some of whom boast many years of service. Anthony Scioli, a Watertown resident, has worked for Lanno's for forty-one years, starting out as a dishwasher, and is now head chef. Peg Caulfield has been a waitress at Lanno's for over thirty-five years. Lanno's is open daily from 11:30 A.M. to 11:00 P.M. on Monday through Thurs-

day, 11:30 A.M. to 11:30 P.M. on Friday, 11:30 A.M. to midnight on Saturday, and 3:00 P.M. to 9:00 P.M. on Sunday.

Le Bocage
72 Bigelow Avenue

Started in March 1978 by Enzo and Vera Danesi, Le Bocage is a French restaurant with menus that change daily. The restaurant is the successor to Mary Brown's former operation at the Bigelow Avenue location. The restaurant serves dinner daily Monday through Thursday from 6:00 P.M. to 11:00 P.M. and on Friday and Saturday from 5:30 P.M. to 11:00 P.M. Veal dishes are a specialty at Le Bocage and creme brulé is a popular dessert.

Donald J. MacDonald & Son Funeral Home
270 Main Street

The Donald J. MacDonald family has served the town of Watertown since 1935 and with the 350th anniversary of the town will mark its 45th year of service to families in Watertown and surrounding communities. One of the first in Watertown, the Donald J. MacDonald Funeral Home opened in 1935 at 176 Main Street under the direction of Donald J. MacDonald. In 1940 the funeral home was re-located at 135 Mt. Auburn Street where it continued to meet the needs of families for nine years until larger accommodations were required.

In 1948 a duplex house at 270 Main Street was purchased and thoroughly remodelled, and featured two chapels, adjacent rooms, and a smoking room. In 1961 as Watertown grew and needs increased, another renovation was completed with the addition of another large chapel, an enlarged smoking room, and a selection room. In 1968 Donald J. MacDonald, Jr., joined his father's business and together they continue to offer funeral service to the town as the Donald J. MacDonald and Son Funeral Home. Parking facilities were enlarged in 1978.

Of historic interest to townspeople is the 1879 "bird's eye" map of Watertown which hangs in the center chapel at the funeral home; it was given to the MacDonalds by the late Lenore G. McEnery Cooper (Mrs. James H.) of Quirk Street, Watertown. The map shows old structures long since demolished and the acres of farmland that once comprised Watertown. Of particular interest are the Fitchburg Railroad station, the paper mills and other manufacturing units, several hotels, banks, churches, and public buildings. The map also has two inserts—sketches of the Leonard Whitney residence and the Hollingsworth & Whitney Paper Mills.

The Donald MacDonald family continues to be active in community affairs. Donald Jr., is the current chairman of the trustees of the Watertown Free Public Library, as was his father in the mid-1930s, and both Donald and his wife Kelley are members of numerous other civic, fraternal, and church organizations.

Massis Bakery
569 Mt. Auburn Street

Founded in 1977 by the owner, Kevork Ourphalian, Massis Bakery carries many varieties of nuts, and features Armenian pastries: lahmejunes, Syrian bread, and baklava. It it open from Monday through Saturday from 7:00 A.M. to 7:00 P.M. and from 10:00 A.M. to 1:00 P.M. on Sunday.

May's Fashion Shop
30-32 Mt. Auburn Street

Established in 1947 by Mae Cohen, May's Fashion Shop is the fashion center of Watertown, furnishing everything for milady to wear. May's attracts customers from all over the Watertown area and from Newton, Arlington, and Belmont. Visitors from Canada often drop in when they come to visit friends or relatives in Watertown, and many of May's customers come from the Perkins School, for both faculty and students know that May's gives them special service and attention. Louise Felloni, the only employee, has worked at May's since 1953. The shop is open from 9:00 A.M. to 5:00 P.M. Monday through Wednesday, 9:00 A.M. to 5:30 P.M. on Thursday, 9:00 A.M. to 5:30 P.M. on Friday, and 9:00 A.M. to 5:00 P.M. on Saturday.

The Meat Spot
28 Mt. Auburn Street

The Meat Spot was founded in 1948 by Nello Cerqua and his son Henry on the site of the original Star Market store. (In the old days the Mugars had done the actual meat-cutting in the basement of the store.) In 1950 the store was acquired by "Rupe" Baker. In those days the store was famous for its chickens raised at Cedar Haven Farms in Milford, Massachusetts, but in 1970 due to the lack of local slaughtering facilities, the shop was no longer able to carry them.

Baker had formerly operated a Farmland Store in Davis Square, Somerville. Rupe's sons Rupert Jr., now 35, Ronnie, 30, Robin, 28, Jimmy, 26, Pat, 22, and Ricky, 16, have all taken their places behind the counter, with Mary, Rupe's wife, and their daughter, Bonnie, 14, pitching in during the busiest times such as Thanksgiving and Christmas. Rupe's son Rupert Jr., is a sergeant in the uniformed division of the Newton Police Department. Rupe hopes that one of his sons will take over his business when he retires.

Rupe was president of the old Retail Board of Trade in Watertown Square twenty years ago and played a key role in establishing the municipal parking area in Watertown Square and in the relocation of the Registry of Motor Vehicles to Watertown from Waltham. Recently the Meat Spot was used by September Productions for a location shot for a commercial explaining the advantages of IRA-Keogh plans. Special lighting was installed and four actors took seven hours and thirty "takes" to achieve the desired effect for a thirty-second commercial for the Community Savings Banks of upstate New York.

Mount Auburn Cemetery
580 Mount Auburn Street, Cambridge

Founded in 1831, Mount Auburn Cemetery was the first rural garden cemetery in the United States, and probably in the world. Although the mailing address is in Cambridge, all of the buildings, other than the gatehouse, and the largest portion by far of these historic burying grounds are in Watertown.

Here lie the graves of many of the greatest figures of American history, people whose remains in

207

Mount Auburn give it a dignity and tradition unique among American cemeteries: Longfellow, Lowell, Bowditch, Bradford, Homer, Hale and Frankfurter, to name but a few of America's greats. But Mount Auburn is not merely a memorial to great names; it is the respected resting place of over 68,000 mortals from all walks of life.

Here visitors will also find a notable collection of rare trees, both foreign and native, together with uncounted varieties of evergreen and flowering shrubs to enhance the landscape throughout the year. The grounds encompass an area of over 170 acres forming a rural retreat to be perpetually preserved in the center of a growing metropolitan region. Ten miles of paved roads and more miles of paths make every section of the grounds accessible to visitors.

Non-sectarian since its inception, Mount Auburn is a non-profit corporation governed by civic-minded trustees. A substantial trust fund assures owners of proper care of the grounds for all time.

Munhall Fuel Company, Incorporated
25 Summer Street

Founded by George Munhall about fifty years ago in Belmont, Munhall Fuel moved to Main Street, Watertown in 1945. The business started as a gas station and also furnished ice to local residents. The transition into fuel oil was a natural progression as homes converted to oil heat after World War II. The business grew because of Munhall's personalized service and eventually moved to its present location on Summer Street. George Munhall was actively engaged in town affairs, serving as member and chairman of the Finance Committee and also as a member of the School Committee.

After Munhall's death the business was acquired by Robert Manzelli, a longtime friend of the Munhall family, in 1972. The business is now operated by Bob Manzelli and his wife Barbara. Bob Manzelli has been a selectman and state representative and is now purchasing agent of the town. Munhall is one of Watertown's largest independent oil dealers and serves its needs for personalized service in the maintenance and servicing of heating and cooling systems. The company is also expanding into alternative energy sources such as solar heating and wood-burning stoves.

The New England Fuel Institute
20 Summer Street

The New England Fuel Institute (NEFI), an association of over 1,100 independent wholesale and retail heating oil and oil heating equipment distributors, is a nonprofit corporation. Incorporated in 1943, its predecessor organization was known as the Oil Heat Institute of New England.

Since its inception nearly two decades ago, the New England Fuel Institute has been dedicated in its service on behalf of the New England independent heating oil industry. Over this period of time, the Institute has fulfilled its objectives for its members many times over, while serving as a catalyst to important industry actions and activities at the legislative, educational, informational, and industry relation levels. Its efforts are of benefit to the oil heating businessman as well as the consumer, and it has become effective in protecting consumer as well as industry interests. Because of this, the Institute is now recognized as one of the most effective trade organizations of its size and scope in the United States. Its many areas of operation include education, fuel competition, group insurance plans, conventions, expositions, legislation and research.

Besides its technical education activities, the Institute also conducts a continuous ongoing program for increasing the skills of oil heating management and middle echelon executive personnel. The association frequently conducts one and two-day seminars in the management, proprietary and operational areas.

The Institute has excelled in providing general association activities and benefits to its membership, including regular news bulletins, group insurance, publication of the nation's only regional oil heating monthly trade magazine, "Yankee Oilman," group meetings, annual conventions, expositions, as well as representation in Washington.

Nearly a decade ago, NEFI established a private, vocational school in Cambridge, Massachusetts, known as the New England Fuel Institute Technical Training Center. This school, which has recently been moved to Watertown and tripled in size, is fully licensed as a private, vocational school by the Massachusetts Department of Education. The curriculum of the Technical Training Center includes a 160-hour, four-week course for individuals interested in basic, comprehensive training as oil heat installation and maintenance technicians.

Pequog Pottery
134 Main Street

Jamie Oates started his Pequog Pottery in 1976 in a one hundred-year-old building behind his father's law office where he makes functional and decorative pottery by hand. All his pieces can be identified by his distinctive sun symbol which he brought from India. Jamie's pottery objects are usually one of a kind and are often designed to the individual customer's specifications. They can be purchased at the Massachusetts Audubon Society in Lincoln, the Quincy Market, and at the artist's studio in Watertown.

Perkins School for the Blind
175 North Beacon Street

Perkins School for the Blind, a private school for blind and visually impaired children, was chartered in 1829 by the General Court of Massachusetts. In 1912 it moved from Boston, where it was originally located, to its present thirty-eight-acre campus in Watertown. Perkins' director is Charles C. Woodcock who came to the school in 1977. Mr. Woodcock formerly headed the Oregon State School for the Blind and the Iowa Braille and Sight Saving School.

Even though most of the student body comes from New England, Perkins has enrolled students from all parts of the country and a few from overseas. Helen Keller attended there at one time. During the 1970s the school began to enroll an increasing number of multi-impaired blind and deaf-blind students because of special education legislation and changes in the causes of blindness in children.

Also located on the Perkins campus is the Regional Library for the Blind and Physically Handicapped; the Howe Press, which manufactures the well known Perkins Brailler and other equipment for the blind and the New England Regional Center for Services for Deaf-Blind Children. Perkins has 485 employees.

Special proclamations recognizing Perkins upon the 150th anniversary of its founding were issued in March 1979 by Governor Edward King of Massachusetts and by the Watertown Board of Selectmen. The Perkins tower overlooking the Charles River is a familiar Watertown landmark. Its chimes which are heard during the Christmas sea-

son and other times are played by students of the school.

Porter Construction Company, Inc.
84 Arsenal Street

The Porter Construction Company was founded in 1925 under the name of William H. Porter Company by three brothers, William H. Porter, R. Leigh Porter, Stanley D. Porter and a cousin T. Eugene Ellis, all having immigrated from a small village just outside Yarmouth, Nova Scotia. The company started in a rented building on Spring Street, Watertown, but soon moved its office to the basement of 131 Spruce Street, and after a short time moved again to 84 Arsenal Street where it has been ever since.

The company was incorporated in 1931. Stanley D. Porter, a Watertown resident, became its President and Chief Executive Officer, until succeeded by Robert U. Porter, his son, also a resident of Watertown. Vice-President and Construction Manager is Frederick R. Ellis, formerly of Watertown, and son of T. Eugene Ellis.

Since its founding, the company has emphasized quality work, and with few exceptions involved itself in only the private sector of construction. Some of the projects completed in Watertown over the years are: a block of stores built in 1926, and replaced later by the Freedom Federal Office Building on Main Street; Freedom Federal Bank; Coolidge Bank Building; Watertown Savings Bank, East, Mall, King's and Waltham branches; the West Watertown Bay Bank Branch; several projects for Haartz-Mason, Lewis-Shepherd, and Underwood Company; the East Watertown Fire Station; Coombs Motors; Bacon Lab; Masonic Temple, and Mt. Auburn Tennis Center. Now under construction is the Armenian Cultural and Educational Center on Nichols Avenue.

The company has served all of New England with projects such as a hospital in Portland, Maine, in 1942, and over twenty years of extensive renovations, additions and alterations at the Waltham Hospital. It has completed new buildings for Harvard University, Andover-Newton Theological School, Babson College and Gordon College. It built a two and one-half million dollar temple for Temple Israel in Boston, the Needham Methodist Church, and additions to the Wellesley Congregational Church. Industrial and commercial work includes Star Markets in Franklin, Sudbury, Natick, Watertown, Cambridge, and factories from Newburyport to Dedham. The company has worked from Maine to Cape Cod, and from Burlington, Vermont, to Rhode Island.

Quirk Tire Company, Incorporated
275 Arsenal Street

The Quirk Tire Company owns its own building where it markets tires both wholesale and retail to individual customers, local gas stations, and dealers in the Greater Boston area. It deals primarily in Michelin and General Tires. Quirk sells truck tires to customers throughout Maine, New Hampshire, Rhode Island, and Connecticut, and has a shop for the recapping of truck tires. The company has from twenty to twenty-five employees depending on the season. Founded by Edward S. Quirk in 1928, the business is now run by his son Edward, Junior.

Rand's Pharmacy, Incorporated
632 Mt. Auburn Street

Rand's Pharmacy was established by Claude Rand in Watertown in 1926 in a location across the street from the present store. Rand had been trained as a pharmacist in England and was well-known for being able to speak five languages. In 1946 the business was purchased by George Srabian and Anthony Giuggio; Giuggio was a member of the Massachusetts State Board of Registration in Pharmacy. In 1979 the business changed ownership again, this time being purchased by Peter Feldman and Thomas Cantillon.

Rand's Pharmacy serves customers in the Watertown, Cambridge and Belmont areas, and carries a full line of health and beauty aids as well as greeting cards, tobacco, hospital supplies and rentals. The Veterans' Administration Hospital in Bedford is one of its longtime customers. The store also features a luncheonette. It is open from 8:00 A.M. to 7:00 P.M. Monday through Friday, 8:00 P.M. on Saturday, and 8:00 A.M. to 1:00 P.M. on Sunday.

Roberts Wallpaper and Supply Company
14 Mt. Auburn Street

Founded in 1952 by Robert Shafer and Robert Goldman, Roberts Wallpaper and Supply Company offers general decorating advice and supplies and hardware at discount prices to customers in Watertown and surrounding communities. The store is located just off Watertown Square, and is open from 8:30 A.M. to 6:00 P.M. Monday through Thursday, 8:30 A.M. to 8:30 P.M. on Friday, and from 8:30 A.M. to 6:00 P.M. on Saturday.

Royal Furniture Company, Inc.
70 Main Street

The Royal Furniture Company traces its origin back to 1895 when it was known as the Royal Tea Company, operated by Hyman Hootstein, who sold tea and coffee door to door by horse and wagon and covered much of metropolitan Boston concentrating mainly in Brighton, Newtonville, Waltham, Belmont, Cambridge, Somerville, Woburn, and Watertown. In response to customer requests, furniture was soon added to the merchandise offered and a store was opened in Boston under the present name. This store moved to Somerville shortly afterwards.

The store at 70 Main Street, Watertown Square, was opened in 1939 under the management of Joseph H. Bernstein, Hootstein's son-in-law. The company operates two other stores in Somerville and Woburn and is presently owned by Bernard Hootstein (a son of Hyman Hootstein), and Stanley Bennett and Maurice Epstein (manager of the Watertown store), grandsons of the founder. The company is proud to be serving the fourth generation of many of its original customers.

A. Russo and Sons, Incorporated
249 Lexington Street

A. Russo is a wholesale fruit and produce company. Town Garden, its retail outlet, was established in 1972 at 389 Main Street. The business was founded by Antonio Russo in 1925 to service retailers throughout the entire Greater Boston area. There are now twenty employees and the business is operated by Olgo A. Russo. Town Garden is known for its fine fruits and vegetables at competitive prices. It is open from 8:30 A.M. to 6:00 P.M. on Monday through Thursday, 7:30 A.M. to 6:00 P.M. on Friday and Saturday, and 7:30 A.M. to 2:00 P.M. on Sunday.

Sasaki Associates, Incorporated
64 Pleasant Street

Sasaki Associates, Inc. (SA), a pioneer in multidisciplinary planning and design, offers comprehensive professional services in planning, architecture, landscape architecture, civil engineering, and environmental science.

From its office at 64 Pleasant Street, its staff of over 100 professionals serves a broad spectrum of national and international clients.

The firm was started in 1952 by Hideo Sasaki and was called Sasaki and Associates (1953-1958), Sasaki, Walker Associates, Inc. (1958-1964), Sasaki, Dawson, DeMay Associates, Inc. (1964-1974), and Sasaki Associates, Inc. (1974 to present). It has occupied offices on Galen Street, Mt. Auburn Street, and Main Street before acquiring the Chase Mill complex overlooking the Watertown Dam on the Charles River. This renovated space now serves as SA's main office, where 166 persons are employed.

Among the projects the firm has completed are the design of the Plaza in Copley Square, the Boston Waterfront Park, and the site Planning for the University of Massachusetts campus in Boston.

Shawmut Community Bank, N.A.
25 Church Street

In 1832, Andrew Jackson vetoed the act to extend the charter of the Second National Bank of the United States. The veto of this act led to an increase in the number of state-chartered banks. On March 25, 1833, ten new state banks were chartered in Massachusetts, one of them being the Framingham Bank which would become the Shawmut Community Bank.

Under the new charter, the bank elected its first president, Joshua Adams, and raised $100,000 in capital. The bank also decided to print its own currency, as many state chartered banks did at the time, in denominations of one, two, three, five and ten dollars. The bank operated under a state charter until 1863 and the advent of a national banking system.

Under the guidance of President Abraham Lincoln, a bill was passed in 1864 to establish a uniform banking system in the United States. The bank joined the system which eventually evolved into the Federal Reserve System.

In 1929, The Newton National Bank was established with the main office located at 334 Center Street, Newton. The first Watertown Branch was located at 116 Main Street until it moved to its present location at 25 Church Street in 1975. In 1972, the Newton National Bank, Framingham National Bank, and the Waltham Citizens Bank merged to form the Community National Bank. Soon after, in 1974, the name was changed to the Shawmut Community Bank.

The Shawmut Community Bank has been servicing Watertown's banking needs for twenty-five years while actively participating in community affairs. In the years to come, the Shawmut Community Bank will continue to service Watertown's banking needs and to play an active role in the community.

Special Agent Consultants, Incorporated
67 Pleasant Street

Special Agent Consultants, Inc., was founded in 1969 by Leonard M. Frisoli, who remains as its president. Special Agent Consultants is a security consultant and investigative business composed of former special agents of the FBI whose services total over one hundred years of service in the Federal Bureau of Investigation. The business was originally located at 148 State Street, Boston, and in 1971 moved to 215 California Street, Newton, and in March 1977 to its present location at 67 Pleasant Street, Watertown. Special Agent Consultants lists among its clients many of the more prominent law firms and several corporations in the Massachusetts area as well as being security representatives for The National Football League; the National Hockey League; Suffolk Downs Racetrack; Rockingham Park Racetrack, Salem, New Hampshire, and Hinsdale Raceway, Hinsdale, New Hampshire.

Leonard Frisoli has been a resident of Watertown for the past twenty-five years and has served on the Watertown Redevelopment Authority, having been its chairman since 1977.

Special Agent Systems, Incorporated
67 Pleasant Street

Special Agent Systems, Incorporated was founded by its President, Leonard M. Frisoli, in January 1971. The company was originally located at 215 California Street, Newton, in March 1977, the building where it is presently located at 67 Pleasant Street, Watertown, was purchased by Leonard Frisoli. Special Agent Systems share its occupancy with Special Agent Consultants. Special Agent Systems is a burglar and fire alarm business which sells and installs, services, and monitors alarm systems with a 24-hour central station operation. Special Agent Systems presently services over five hundred customers, among which are the Watertown Public School System; several other school systems in the Greater Boston area; the New England Telephone Company; Massachusetts Lottery, supermarket chains, and city, state and federal buildings.

Star Market
24 Mt. Auburn Street

As John Mugar tells it, his Uncle Charlie came to America from Kharput, Armenia, in 1904 and opened a small restaurant in Boston. The family name was DerMugardichian, and the five brothers were Charles, Martin, Sarkis, Arthur and Gregory. John's father, Martin, joined Charlie, and they enlarged "Mugar's Cafe," a white-tablecloth restaurant on Massachusetts Avenue at the corner of Washington Street in the South End. In 1906 they brought Stephen's father, Sarkis, and the other two brothers from Armenia to work in the restaurant. Everyone in the family lived in the upper floors of the five-story building. In 1916 Stephen's father left the restaurant, where he had been working seven days a week as chef, and bought the Star Market in Watertown Square for about eight hundred dollars. The family moved to a house on Palfrey Hill in Watertown. A hard-working and industrious boy, Stephen contributed to the family business by raising chickens at the house on Bartlett Street, for as John says, "Watertown was out in the country in those days." John would help Stephen by collecting the eggs for sale in the store.

When Sarkis died as a result of an auto accident in 1922, Stephen was working as an office boy in

The Star Market, ready for Christmas, 1921.

Boston. Because he had a mother and three sisters to support, he took over the management of his father's store. His cousin John says, "The moment he took over the store things began to happen." His mother had always put a high priority on neatness and cleanliness, and it was second nature for Stephen to keep the store clean. The moment the sawdust on the floor became a little dirty it had to be swept up and fresh sawdust put down.

John joined Stephen in the Watertown operation when he graduated from high school in 1931. "When I started working full-time in 1931 we would get to work at seven in the morning. Meanwhile Stephen had gotten up at four-thirty or five to go to the Boston produce market. The A&P manager didn't come until eight, and sometimes later. I would get at the windows and clean them, put the awnings down, and get the produce stands out front, so by the time the competition arrived at their store, we were all ready for business—lights on, ready for action. Stephen always had the customer in mind and that's why we packaged that saying, 'Take extra good care of the customer and the customer will take care of you!' "

The Star Market expanded to Newtonville in 1932, and in 1937 to Wellesley. Star, in cooperation with DuPont, developed the first cellophane packaging for meat, an idea John had had when he was in the Navy during World War II. The Mugars pioneered the first self-service meat and produce departments. Early in the Watertown store days, Stephen developed a system of making up orders for customers and making deliveries as much as four times a day. "If a customer wanted thread, or a newspaper or Bokar coffee (from the A&P) we would go to the stores and get these for the customer and put it in her order," says John in his reminiscences. "In other words, it was a sign of doing more for the customer." Star was among the first grocery stores to develop conveyor systems, and in 1949 they worked with the Union Paper Bag Company to develop a new larger and stronger grocery bag. Working again with DuPont engineers, they developed the knitted bag in which oranges and onions are marketed.

John went to Tufts and when he returned to work with Stephen he initiated the first employee training program, involving Northeastern and Cornell University faculty members as teachers and giving employees time off to go to school. They initiated profit sharing for employees of grocery stores. They were among the first to paint their store interiors in bright colors instead of the traditional white. Their second Newtonville store (opened in 1948) was their first supermarket, and there they introduced the radar range in 1948, serving hot meals in the store's luncheonette. They introduced the first touch system for cash registers so that the checkers did not have to look at their keyboards. In 1963 the Newtonville store made history when the Star Market built the first store to use air rights over the Massachusetts Turnpike extension. They introduced unit pricing for grocery products in Massachusetts, which became the first state in the nation to enact legislation mandating unit pricing.

In 1964 Star Market merged with the Jewel Companies of Chicago. Although Star has grown from thirty-three stores to sixty-one, the market originally at 28 and now a few feet up the street at 24 Mt. Auburn Street is still serving the Watertown Square community. Recently Star Market has pioneered "No Name" products, and the marking of food products to indicate nutritional values so that the customers can make their decisions based on reliable information. Throughout its history the company's policy has been based on Stephen's conviction that everything should be done to "take extra good care of the customer, and the customer will take care of you."

Store 24
164 Main Street

The Store 24, Incorporated was founded as Quick Shop Foods by Robert Gordon and two associates in 1967. The 24-hour concept was developed in 1972 when Bob was approached by one of his managers who wanted to keep his store open twenty-four hours rather than from 8 a.m. to midnight. Bob agreed to experiment with this idea, which worked. The first store to try this was the Worcester store, then the store in Watertown, the first store still existing in the chain. The increases in sales well offset the additional expense of staying open twenty-four hours. With this change in the hours of the primary seven stores the name was changed to Store 24 and grew into a chain of thirty-three convenience food stores.

Store 24 is a store which services the neighborhood in Watertown seven days a week with items and needs for the whole family, from bread and milk to medicines and diapers for the baby. Their employees do their best to serve the Watertown neighborhood and all neighborhoods where their stores are located.

Town Diner
627 Mt. Auburn Street

Louis Contos came to America from the Greek Island of Lesbos in 1912. In those days the Boston Fish Pier was a busy place, bustling with activity as fishing boats came and went. He and his brother realized that there was a need for a restaurant to serve the business people on the pier, and so they founded the No Name Restaurant, specializing in fresh fish and seafoods. When Louis' son George got out of the army in 1945, he and his father purchased the Town Diner. In 1946 they had done so well that they decided to enlarge the diner and went to a local construction company for help. The head of the construction company became interested in diner design, and the result was a large, roomy unit built on the site, but retaining the appearance of a factory-made dining car. The expanded diner wraps around the original one (now the kitchen) and illustrates mid-forties style by utilizing porcelain enamel, stainless steel, formica and glass block. The menu features homemade muffins, bagels, pastries, fresh seafood in the tradition of the No Name (including broiled Boston schrod and fried Ipswich clams) as well as daily specials. The diner is open from 5:30 A.M. to 8:00 P.M. on weekdays, and from 5:30 A.M. to 4:00 P.M. on Saturday. It is closed on Sundays.

Town Hall Pharmacy
145 Main Street

Founded in May 1957 by Edward M. Fantasia, the Town Hall Pharmacy is located across Main Street from Watertown's Town Hall. The pharmacy carries greeting cards, cosmetics, and candy, and specializes in filling prescriptions and in supplying customers with medical and surgical needs. The friendly and helpful atmosphere has attracted customers from all over the western suburbs, and young employees often go on to become registered pharmacists themselves, serving as interns in the store while attending school. There are six employees, and the Town Hall Pharmacy is open from 8:00 A.M. to 9:00 P.M. seven days a week.

Union Market Station
17 Nichols Avenue

Owned by Robert T. Leonard and Robert J. Caporricco, who started the restaurant in November 1975, the Union Market Station is located across the street from the location of the old Union Market Stockyards. On the walls are blowups of pictures of Watertown in the late nineteenth and early twentieth centuries. The restaurant is furnished with cozy booths and butcher-block tables and attracts a varied clientele. Union Market is open for luncheon from 11:00 A.M. to 1:00 P.M. from Monday through Saturday and on Sunday from 1:00 P.M. to 9:00 P.M. and features mainly American cooking—prime ribs a specialty, and fish of all kinds.

United Electric Controls Company
85 School Street

United Electric Controls Company was founded in 1931 to manufacture accurate, dependable temperature and pressure controls to satisfy special and unique industrial requirements. The prevailing philosophy of the company remains today: offering a problem-solving capability which fills the gap left by standard controls that were either under-or over-designed for many industrial applications. This willingness to study a customer's problem and work closely with him to design a control exactly suited to his particular needs is the keynote of UE's success.

With this philosophy United Electric has grown to a multimillion dollar firm. UE controls are manufactured today in Watertown and in Mississauga (Ontario), Canada, with branch offices located in key cities in the United States. European headquarters are in Munich, Germany. United Electric owns United Sensor and Control Corporation, a subsidiary that manufactures probes for measuring flow, velocity, pressure, temperature and direction of fluids, gases and liquids.

The company was incorporated in July 1931, in South Boston, Massachusetts, and on January 2, 1948, with twenty employees, moved to 85 School Street, Watertown, occupying one half of the lower floor of that building. Quite quickly the company grew to the point that it needed the entire building, and eventually purchased the property. Shortly thereafter it expanded into an additional building on Arlington Street and another on Elm Street. In 1977, it was apparent that additional space was necessary to meet the needs of the expanding business and steps were taken to search for either land or a larger building.

In January 1978, the Company purchased 6.606 acres of land situated at the corner of Dexter Avenue and Cypress Street from the United States Postal Service. Plans were made to construct a new manufacturing building of approximately 100,000 square feet to meet the need of the company's increasing volume of sales. In January 1979 the Town of Watertown approved the issuance of Industrial Revenue Bonds to make available capital funds to cover the cost of the new building. It is expected that full occupancy of the new building will take place in July 1980.

Since the company moved to Watertown in 1948 the number of employees has increased to 460, of which a large percentage are residents of Watertown. United Electric Controls Company is now one of the larger companies in Watertown.

214

United Parcel Service, Incorporated
31 Arlington Street

United Parcel Service, Inc. was founded in Seattle, Washington, in 1907 by James Casey. It extended its service to southern California in the early 1920s and in 1930 it opened a branch in New York City.

At first United Parcel serviced only retail stores as a package delivery service, but in 1953 it began to serve also private industry and the general public. In 1956 it opened a facility in Massachusetts and in 1975 became a national organization serving all states.

In 1957 a facility was built in Watertown, was expanded in 1965, and now employs about five hundred people. There are thirteen other locations in Massachusetts with Watertown being the state headquarters. Watertown was chosen as a major site because of its proximity to Boston and major highways such as the Massachusetts Turnpike.

U.S. Army Materials and Mechanics Research Center
Arsenal Street

The Watertown Arsenal began operations in 1816, and was considered the second oldest Arsenal in the country. Occupying 119 acres on a bluff overlooking the Charles River, it was originally established as a depot for the cleaning, repair and issue of small arms and ordnance supplies. Early manufacturing activities included the making of guns and implements for mechanical maneuvers.

By 1830 the purpose of the Arsenal had been expanded to include the manufacture of field, siege and seacoast guns and carriages. From 1835 until the Civil War the Arsenal primarily produced carriages for 24, 32, and 42 pounder guns, and seacoast carriages for 8 and 10 inch guns. A research arm called the Watertown Arsenal Laboratories, established in 1835, continues today as the Army Materials and Mechanics Research Center (AMMRC).

After the Civil War the famed Emery Testing Machine was installed, to settle the raging controversy over the suitability of steel for making cannon. Tests using the ETM resulted in the adoption of steel for armament throughout the world.

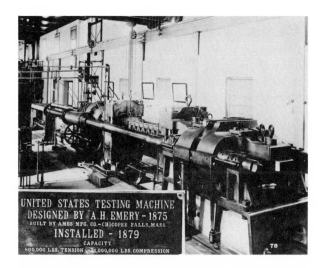

The Emery Testing Machine, a landmark testing unit, now in the Smithsonian.

Views published in Gleason's Pictorial Drawing-Room Companion show the Arsenal grounds in the post-Civil War period as a popular promenade, with families strolling among whitewashed brick buildings on park-like grounds and others enjoying boating on the nearby Charles. During this period the Rodman Casting Process and the classic Rodman seacoast gun, which fired a 350 pound shell more than four miles, were created at the Arsenal. Both were named for the Arsenal's Commander, Col. Thomas J. Rodman.

During the Civil War 100 of the Arsenal's 800 member work force were women, hard at work molding 3,000 tons of iron per year into shot and shell for the preservation of the Union. The Arsenal continued to pioneer in military uses of steel in shells, guns and gun carriages. A highlight of the period just after 1900 was the construction of the Arsenal's administration building, modeled after Philadelphia's Independence Hall.

At the height of activity during World War I the Arsenal employed over five thousand persons. Principal products were antiaircraft carriages, howitzer carriages, forgings for guns and howitzers, high explosive shells and trench mortar tubes. Arsenal scientists and engineers also did extensive work in developing light armor for tanks and body armor.

Between the world wars the Arsenal made many contributions to progress in metallurgy, including the use of radiography and later spectroscopy for steel foundry control, centrifugal casting of gun tubes, all-welded gun carriages and molybdenum high speed tool steel. During World War II the Arsenal and its Laboratories employed ten thousand workers in three eight-hour shifts. Guns and gun carriages continued to be the main production items, but experts from the Arsenal were assigned to assist private industries in gearing up for war production. During the Korean conflict the Arsenal was called upon to develop new and sophisticated weapons. One result was the famous 75 mm Skysweeper, a radar-controlled antiaircraft gun.

In May 1960 the Army's first nuclear reactor was installed at AMMRC, to research the molecular and atomic structures of materials. A decade later the reactor was shut down when newer and more powerful reactors became available at nearby locations. In the early 1960s the Arsenal employed 2,000 people, including the fifth generation of Watertown residents to work for the Army at this site. In 1962 the 127 year-old Watertown Arsenal Laboratories were made a separate entity and renamed the Army Materials Research Agency (now the Army Materials and Mechanics Research Center).

The closing of Watertown Arsenal was announced in April, 1964, with 12 buildings on 35 acres being retained for the new Research Agency. The remaining 55 acres were purchased by Watertown from the General Services Administration in August 1968. Research emphasis has shifted at the Army Materials and Mechanics Research Center. It now holds charters as the Army's lead laboratory for materials, solid mechanics and materials testing technology, employing six hundred persons. Many of the materials developed at AMMRC find their way into space technology, aeronautics, industry and the home.

Unitrode Corporation
580 Pleasant Street

Unitrode manufactures semiconductors which are key components in computers, industrial controls, instrumentation, consumer products, defense and aerospace systems. The company's products are known world wide for their high quality and performance. The company was founded in 1960 in Waltham by George Berman (Chairman of the Board and President) and Malcolm Hecht, Jr., and

moved to Watertown in 1964. Its main plant is on Pleasant Street where it nows employs about six hundred persons. In addition, Unitrode has five other plants in Massachusetts, two in California, and one each in Maine, Mexico and Ireland. World wide, Unitrode employs about two thousand persons. Sales in the twelve-month period ending January 1980 exceeded $80,000,000.

Watertown Animal Hospital
404 Main Street

The hospital offers complete veterinary services twenty-four hours a day to Watertown and surrounding communities. Certified by the American Animal Hospital Association in August 1978, Watertown Animal Hospital exceeded standards set by the organization for all services from surgery and radiology to housekeeping.

Watertown Animal Hospital is the only animal hospital in Watertown and the first (as far as is known) in over twenty years, servicing strictly small animals; dogs, cats, birds, laboratory animals, and reptiles. It offers routine care including vaccinations, laboratory services (including blood and urine tests), fecal and heartworm tests, radiology, anesthesia, surgery, and dental care. Emergency service is offered twenty-four hours a day. Dr. Cusick has a special interest in ophthalmology.

Dr. Cusick, the veterinarian, and his family have been residents of Watertown for the past four years. He graduated from Ohio State University in 1967 with a bachelor's degree in Animal Science and earned his DVM from the same school in 1973. He practiced with a seven-man group for two years in New Jersey and then moved to Watertown.

Watertown Center for the Arts
Coolidge School, 319 Arlington Street

The Watertown Center for the Arts is a community arts council which serves to provide people in and around Watertown with a means for artistic expression. The WCA was incorporated as a non-profit agency in 1976 and since that time has become firmly rooted in Watertown's cultural community. The organization sponsors its own events, programs, and exhibits, and acts as an information resource and artists' referral service. Some of the

WCA's programs include a Young Artists Festival, the Watertown Chorale, the Highlighters (a community theater group), programs for the elderly, and concert series. One of the WCA's major goals is to establish a permanent community arts center, and to this end the WCA is seeking space in the Watertown Arsenal complex. Fees for membership begin at $2.50.

Watertown Health Center
85 Main Street

On June 14, 1977, the Watertown Health Center, under the guidance of the director, Judith Kubzansky, officially opened its doors at 85 Main Street in Watertown under the licensure of St. Elizabeth's Hospital.

The Center's goal from the beginning was to offer a program of comprehensive health services under one roof with the involvement and participation of the community. This, and the goal of providing ambulatory care have been successfully achieved. In line with this, continuity of care (seeing the same physician each time) is considered of primary importance. Health center nurses reinforce the personalized approach to patient care by making every effort to know each patient personally, as do the interpreter, lab technician, secretary and other staff members.

Waiting time is kept to a minimum consistent with good health care. Drop-ins and minor emergencies are seen without interruption of those patients with appointments. Excellent follow-up care, e.g., reporting of lab and X ray results, reminders of future appointments, etc. is consistently provided.

The Center, operating under this philosophy, has grown from seeing ninety persons the first month to one thousand during the month of April 1979. Since June of 1977, there have been 15,570 visits to the Center. This surge in growth indicates that the Watertown Health Center has indeed fulfilled a vital need in the health delivery system for Watertown and surrounding communities.

The Health Center offers the following weekly services: daily adult medicine including two evening sessions, pediatrics, obstetrics, gynecology, podiatry, mental health, nutrition, and evening alcoholism education and counseling series.

Watertown Plumbing and Heating Supply
563 Mount Auburn Street

Watertown Plumbing and Heating Supply Company, Inc. was founded on August 1, 1947, by James C. Tragakis, the president of the company.

Located at 563 Mt. Auburn Street, Watertown Plumbing caters to Boston's west suburban territory. An extensive inventory of plumbing and heating supplies, pipe valves, tools, and accessories is maintained. Among its customers are general contractors, factories, apartment buildings, plumbing and heating contractors, schools, hospitals, and retail trade.

A supply company which grew out of a service tradition, Watertown Supply is considered a specialty house by the trade. All ten employees of this small business are oriented to customer service. Stocking or locating hard-to-find repair parts is not a sideline but the main "stock-in-trade." Two vehicles provide delivery on very short notice. Jim Tragakis and his son Bill are both active in the day-to-day operation of the business.

Watertown Savings Bank
60 Main Street

The Watertown Savings Bank, Watertown's oldest bank, was founded by Nathaniel Whiting, Joshua Coolidge and Charles J. Barry on April 18, 1870, and opened for business on November 10th that year. On that first day, ten accounts were opened totaling $924. Growth since then has been steady and sometimes dramatic, requiring no less than six moves of its main office prior to occupying in 1929 the present building which was completely modernized and greatly expanded during 1975. Development of five conveniently located branch offices and of new services has also been part of the bank's growth.

As a Mutual Savings Bank, depositors are the only shareholders and are such solely through their deposits. Depositors' money is put to productive use by investments primarily in the community and particularly in loans secured by real estate. The Watertown Savings Bank is committed to contributing toward the well-being of the community on the Charles at the crossroads, Watertown.

217

Western Electric Company
705 Mt. Auburn Street

Western Electric's New England Service Center was founded in 1931, when the company had outgrown its original New England facility in South Boston. Western Electric spent $3,141,000 to build the service center in 1931 and in 1959 added a new wing to the building at a cost of $3,307,000.

The Western Electric Company facility on Mt. Auburn Street.

Like its thirty-nine counterparts across the nation, the New England Service Center is essentially a supply and repair center serving the five-state New England Region. The center works closely with the Southborough Distribution Center; together both centers provide the New England Telephone Company with over 16,000 items essential to the installation and maintenance of telecommunications throughout New Hampshire, Vermont, Maine, Massachusetts, and Rhode Island. In addition to reconditioning telephones for home use, the service center reconditions equipment for the telephone company's central offices, teletype machines for use in state police stations, and PBX and data-sets for business telephones. Each month the New England Service Center and the Southborough Distribution Center together ship an average of $18 million worth of new and reconditioned equipment to customers throughout New England. A total of 812 people are currently employed at the New England Service Center.

Western Electric has long maintained a deep commitment to supporting charitable and community organizations. The New England Service Center has sponsored, for over twenty years, a Junior Achievement Company in Watertown, helping juniors and seniors at Watertown High School develop a sense of business through their own experience. The service center also helps support the Watertown Boy's Club, the Jaycees, the United Fund, the United States Bond Drive, the Red Cross Blood Drive, and several local Watertown organizations.

Westvaco Corporation, Container Division
70 Grove Street

Westvaco Corporation manufactures corrugated shipping containers and sells them to companies all over Maine, New Hampshire, Vermont, and also in Massachusetts east of Springfield and the Providence, Rhode Island, area. Prior to 1953 the Watertown box plant was formerly the Hinde & Dauch Paper Company which began in Sandusky, Ohio, in 1888 as a two-man partnership for making butcher paper from straw. The founders of the Company, James J. Hinde and Jacob J. Dauch, soon branched out to include the manufacture of corrugated materials and subsequently introduced the industry's first corrugated box for shipment of canned goods, chicks and also the first insulated box and display boxes. Thus from a modest beginning in 1888 Hinde & Dauch (now Westvaco) has grown to become a leader of the industry, producing more than six billion square feet of corrugated products each year in factories throughout the country.

Westvaco is a billion-dollar corporation having fifteen different divisions in major marketing areas, manufacturing a variety of paper, wood and chemical industrial and consumer products. The Watertown plant is part of the Container Division where since 1946 corrugated products have been made and shipped to customers in all the New England States.

The plant is managed by a four-man team composed of the General Manager, E.J. Kiddie, and three functional managers: Administrative Manager Paul J. Dolan; Sales Service Manager Martin Connolly; and Production Superintendent Fred Hamilton. There are eighty-seven employees. Corrugated is an important part both of the packaging industry and of Westvaco's business.

Corrugated boxes are made from paperboard manufactured from the pine and hardwood trees of the South. Much of the raw material comes from Westvaco's own modern high-speed mills which produce two thousand tons of paperboard per day. The company designs and produces corrugated packaging for hundreds of consumer and industrial products, not only to ship items such as food, furniture and large appliances but also products like live lobsters, dynamite, nails, powdered acid, baby chicks, liquids, cheese and even mice. It makes boxes and interior packing to their customers' exact specifications, and also offers modifications such as curtain coating and wax impregnation to make a box moisture proof.

Wilevco, Incorporated
40 Hunt Street

The first automatic batter mixer with viscosity control was built by Putnam P. Flint in 1955 for Gorton's of Gloucester in the manufacture of "Fish Sticks." The success of the mixer was immediate and necessitated the founding of Wilevco, Incorporated in 1961 with Flint as its first president. In 1965 the company was reorganized and shortly moved to larger quarters. Dorothy Ann Flint, wife of the owner, joined the firm "for just a few weeks" back in 1966 and this temporary arrangement has become permanent. In the fall of 1975 Wilevco moved to its present address on Hunt Street and a year later their son Leverett joined the firm. Leverett is now vice-president and has an eye on the office overlooking the Charles.

Wilevco Mixers and Cryolators (for batter chilling) are sold and leased to leading manufacturers of breaded foods throughout the United States, Canada, Scandinavia, Europe and Australia. Evolving from the initial fish stick operation Wilevco equipment now helps produce quality fish portions, fillets, shrimp, scallops, chicken parts and patties, and vegetables such as okra and a well-known brand of onion rings, as well as breaded meat patties and chicken-fried steak.

It is interesting to note that Carlton Stanley, former manager of the Stanley Motor Carriage Company, was making violins in a garage in Newton next to the garage where Flint built the early batter mixers and today Flint's company is in one of the Stanley buildings as a tenant of Bachrach Photographers.

Appendices

Chamber of Commerce
Membership/1980

ADCO
28 Bridge St.
Watertown, MA 02172

Ade Corporation
149 Grove Street
Watertown, MA 02172

Alberts, Inc.
531 Mt. Auburn Street
Watertown, MA 02172

Walter L. Almond, Insurance Agent
52 Horace Road
Belmont, MA 02178

Andrews Decorating Center
89 Trapelo Road
Belmont, MA 02178

Anthony's Flowers
113 Galen Street
Watertown, MA 02172

Antinarelli Realty
159a Mt. Auburn Street
Watertown, MA 02172

Apahouser-Elcom Co.
101 Walnut Street
Watertown, MA 02172

Aquarius Tours and Travel
15 Main Street
Watertown, MA 02172

Aquidneck Optical
119a Galen Street
Watertown, MA 02172

Architectural Woodwork, Inc.
46 Acton Street
Watertown, MA 02172

Arsenal Auto Service
264 No. Beacon Street
Watertown, MA 02172

Artwork by MaryKay
Box 225
Lincoln, MA 02172

Associated Heating Co.
356 Main Street
Watertown, MA 02172

Associated Radio Co.
92 Main Street
Watertown, MA 02172

Atlantic Battery Co., Inc.
80 Elm Street
Watertown, MA 02172

Automotive Warehouse Co., Inc.
6 Dexter Avenue
Watertown, MA 02172

B & D Auto Electric Co., Inc.
46 Arsenal Street
Watertown, MA 02172

Bacon Industries, Inc.
192 Pleasant Street
Watertown, MA 02172

Barclay Chemical Co., Inc.
150 Coolidge Avenue
Watertown, MA 02172

Barker Steel Co., Inc.
42 School Street
P.O. Box 417
Watertown, MA 02172

John W. Barrett Insurance Agcy., Inc.
144 Main Street
Watertown, MA 02172

Barry Wright Corporation
680 Pleasant Street
Watertown, MA 02172

Bay Bank/Middlesex
39 Main Street
Watertown, MA 02172

Beaconwood Motors
71 Rosedale Road
Watertown, MA 02172

Aram Bedrosian Funeral Home
558 Mt. Auburn Street
Watertown, MA 02172

Belmont Mobil Service
82 Concord Avenue
Belmont, MA 02178

Bemis Associates, Inc.
294 Pleasant Street
Watertown, MA 02172

W.C. Bonner Co., Inc.
80 Oakland Street
Watertown, MA 02172

Bon Ton Rug Cleaners
81 Coolidge Hill Road
Watertown, MA 02172

Boston Coupling Co., Inc.
16 Bridge Street
Watertown, MA 02172

Boston Edison Company
139 Moody Street
Waltham, MA 02154

Boston Gas Company
525 Pleasant Street
Watertown, MA 02172

Robert D. Bree, DDS
489 Mt. Auburn Street
Watertown, MA 02172

Buckley & Scott Whetton, Inc.
150 West St.
Needham, MA 02192

Callan's
159 Mt. Auburn Street
Watertown, MA 02172

Cambridge Analytical Associates, Inc.
222 Arsenal Street
Watertown, MA 02172

Campanelli Properties
1 Campanelli Drive
Braintree, MA 02184

Campbell Hardware, Inc.
36 Pleasant Street
Watertown, MA 02172

Canterbury Clothing, Inc.
203 Arlington Street
Watertown, MA 02172

Robert J. Cappadona Ins. Agcy.
155 Middlesex Turnpike
Burlington, MA 01803

Carlson Television Co.
161 Galen Street
Watertown, MA 02172

Cass the Florist
531 Mt. Auburn Street
Watertown, MA 02172

Century 21 West Realty
413 Mt. Auburn Street
Watertown, MA 02172

Chair Care Corp.
60 Chestnut Street
Watertown, MA 02172

Chamberlain Studio of Photography
26 Mt. Auburn Street
Watertown, MA 02172

Charles Contracting Co., Inc.
75 Rosedale Road
Watertown, MA 02172

Chase & Sons
15 Franklin Street
Watertown, MA 02172

Irwin Cherniak, CPA
245 Main Street
Watertown, MA 02172

Nannette C. Citron, PhD.
34 Kimball Road
Watertown, MA 02172

City Suburban Realty Co.
147 Mt. Auburn Street
Watertown, MA 02172

Clark's Laundromat
410 Main Street
Watertown, MA 02172

Clover Oil Co.
P.O. Box 150
Watertown, MA 02172

Condon & Glossa Ins. Agency
8 Riverside Street
Watertown, MA 02172

Conti Jewelers
501 Common Street
Belmont, MA 02178

A.J. Conti Realtors
486 Common Street
Belmont, MA 02178

Coolidge Bank & Trust Company
65 Main Street
Watertown, MA 02172

Appendices

Coombs Motor Co.
66 Galen Street
Watertown, MA 02172

Cosmetics Plus, Inc.
49 Main Street
Watertown, MA 02172

Creative Catering Services
35 Galen Street
Watertown, MA 02172

Credit Bureau Central of Mass.
15 Howard Street
Framingham, MA 01701

Mr. Alan E. Cremer
8 Elaine Avenue
Maynard, MA 01754

Robert A. Dallas Ins. Agcy.
68 Watertown Street
Watertown, MA 02172

Damco, Inc.
5 Bridge Street
Watertown, MA 02172

H.D. Danis Painting Co.
39 Bradford Road
Watertown, MA 02172

Deignan Construction Co., Inc.
272 School Street
Watertown, MA 02172

Delleville Oil Co.
69 Elm Street
Watertown, MA 02172

Direct Tire Sales
126 Galen Street
Watertown, MA 02172

Doble Engineering Co.
85 Walnut Street
Watertown, MA 02172

Edward Donle, DMD
305 Lexington Street
Watertown, MA 02172

DuBois Corporation
600 Pleasant Street
Watertown, MA 02172

Duffy Associates
541 Pleasant Street
Watertown, MA 02172

Dunbrack Tool & Die Co.
50 Hunt Street
Watertown, MA 02172

Dunkin Donuts
49 Mt. Auburn Street
Watertown, MA 02172

Eastern Coat Mfg. Co.
76 Coolidge Hill Road
P.O. Box 209
Watertown, MA 02172

Eckert/Park Associates
117 Stoneleigh Road
Watertown, MA 02172

Econo-Car of Watertown
602 Pleasant Street
Watertown, MA 02172

Ed's Sunoco Station
600 Main Street
Watertown, MA 02172

Evans & Faulkner, Inc.
376 Arsenal Street
Watertown, MA 02172

Everywoman's Sport Center
120 Elm Street
Watertown, MA 02172

Fallon-Williams Mechanical Contractors
32 Calvin Road
Watertown, MA 02172

Family Fare Restaurant
47 Main Street
Watertown, MA 02172

Philip D. Fantasia, Jr., Dentist
293 Mt. Auburn Street
Watertown, MA 02172

Farina Cycle and Garden Equipment, Inc.
61 Galen Street
Watertown, MA 02172

Jerome Farnsworth, CPA
300 Arlington Street
Watertown, MA 02172

Field Premium, Inc.
24 Bridge Street
Watertown, MA 02172

First Service Insurance Agcy., Inc.
75 Main Street
Watertown, MA 02172

Fisher Associates, Inc.
80 School Street
Watertown, MA 02172

Foreign Auto Import, Inc.
149 Arsenal Street
Watertown, MA 02172

Foxie's Deli
59 Mt. Auburn Street
Watertown, MA 02172

Freedom Federal Savings and Loan Assoc.
75 Main Street
Watertown, MA 02172

Peter Fuller Oldsmobile, Inc.
43 No. Beacon Street
Watertown, MA 02172

Frank P. Gauvin
c/o State Mutual Life Assurance Co. of America
85 Main Street
Watertown, MA 02172

General Scanning, Inc.
500 Arsenal Street
Watertown, MA 02172

Alix Ginsburg, Tupperware Rep.
44 Gilbert Road
Belmont, MA 02178

Goodyear Tire & Rubber Co., The
21 No. Beacon Street
Watertown, MA 02172

Gordon's Watertown Family Liquor Store
40 Mt. Auburn Street
Watertown, MA 02172

Gray's Laundry Centre
25 Church Street
Watertown, MA 02172

S.B. Green & Co., Inc.
314 Arsenal Street
Watertown, MA 02172

Malcolm R. Greene, Optometrist
89 Mt. Auburn Street
Watertown, MA 02172

George Grillo Oriental Rugs
106 Main Street
Watertown, MA 02172

Haartz-Mason, Inc.
270 Pleasant Street
Watertown, MA 02172

Hawes Electric Construction, Inc.
11 Merchants Row
Watertown, MA 02172

John E. Heffernan, Insurance
82 Charles River Road
Watertown, MA 02172

Henry's Florist, Inc.
113 Mt. Auburn Street
Watertown, MA 02172

Richard L. Hickey, General Contractor
10 Winsor Avenue
Watertown, MA 02172

E.H. Hinds, Inc.
19 Coolidge Hill Road
Watertown, MA 02172

Home Locators
123 Mt. Auburn Street
Watertown, MA 02172

Hope, Inc.
128 Arlington Street
Watertown, MA 02172

Hudson Travel Service
235 Main Street
Watertown, MA 02172

Inspired Images
50 Church Street
Watertown, MA 02172

Instrumentation Laboratory Inc.
9 Galen Street
Watertown, MA 02172

Insulfab Plastics, Inc.
69 Grove Street
Watertown, MA 02172

Intervelop, Inc.
160 No. Beacon Street
Brighton, MA 02135

Ionics, Inc.
65 Grove Street
Watertown, MA 02172

Ivanhoe Sports Center
315 Main Street
Watertown, MA 02172

Ives Safety Tire Co., Inc.
51 Watertown Street
Watertown, MA 02172

J.W. Home Improvement
159 Mystic Street
Arlington, MA 02174

Mr. Robert Jamgochian, Insurance
405 Mt. Auburn Street
Watertown, MA 02172

The Joy of Movement Center
23 Main Street
Watertown, MA 02172

Mr. Robert Aram Kaloosdian, Attorney
43 Mt. Auburn Street
Watertown, MA 02172

Kelly Health Care
11A Main Street
Watertown, MA 02172

Kev's Travel Service, Inc.
One Washington Mall
Boston, MA 02108

Kharidia Associates
358 Lake Street
Belmont, MA 02178

Kodaly Musical Training Inst.
23 Main Street
Watertown, MA 02172

Richard A. Landers
32 Whites Ave.
Watertown, MA 02172

Lanno's
86 Main Street
Watertown, MA 02172

Le Bocage Restaurant
72 Bigelow Avenue
Watertown, MA 02172

Lefkowith Furniture
55 Main Street
Watertown, MA 02172

Leon of Italy
84 Leonard Street
Belmont, MA 02178

Lifeline Systems, Inc.
51 Spring Street
Watertown, MA 02172

Linco Tool & Machine Co.
264 Arlington Street
Watertown, MA 02172

Pat Loheed, Landscape Architect
17 Main Street
Watertown, MA 02172

Lord and Lady Formal Wear
161 Mt. Auburn Street
Watertown, MA 02172

Loughran, Corbett, and McDermott,
  Attys., Inc.
42 Spring Street
P.O. Box 228
Watertown, MA 02172

Rick Lubin & Sons
71 Arsenal Street
Watertown, MA 02172

Lubin's Rink & Bowling Supply
521 Mt. Auburn St.
Watertown, MA 02172

H.R. McBride, Realtor
24 Church Street
Watertown, MA 02172

McCue's Taxi Service
7 Main Street
Watertown, MA 02172

Donald J. MacDonald and Son Funeral Home
270 Main Street
Watertown, MA 02172

Joseph A. MacDonald Funeral Services Inc.
6 Riverside Street
Watertown, MA 02172

Brian McGuire Co.
106 Wilson Drive
Framingham, MA 01701

MacLeod & Moynihan
110 Arlington Street
Watertown, MA 02172

The McNamara Construction Co., Inc.
55 Irving Ave.
Watertown, MA 02172

McNeil Management & Services
420 Providence Highway
P.O. Box 407
Westwood, MA 02090

Mailco, Inc.
59 Rosedale Road
Watertown, MA 02172

Manzelli Oil Co.
284 Orchard Street
Watertown, MA 02172

A.F. Marcantonio and Son
16 Marcia Road
Watertown, MA 02172

Mason & Frey Landscape Architects
243 Trapelo Road
Belmont, MA 02178

Mass. Gas & Electric Light Supply Co.
604 Pleasant Street
Watertown, MA 02172

Mass. Prosthetics Inc.
25 Main Street
Watertown, MA 02172

Massa Boutique
13 Main Street
Watertown, MA 02172

The Mattress Man
660 Arsenal Street
Watertown, MA 02172

Medi-Tech, Inc.
150 Coolidge Ave.
Watertown, MA 02172

Mr. James I. Mello
10 Nyack Street
Watertown, MA 02172

Metco Tile Distributor, Inc.
291 Arsenal Street
Watertown, MA 02172

Metropolitan Civic Ballet Center, Inc.
23 Main Street
Watertown, MA 02172

Microcomputer Laboratories
50 Hunt Street
Watertown, MA 02172

Midas Muffler Shops
76 Arsenal Street
Watertown, MA 02172

Charles N. Miller Co.
10 Bridge Street
P.O. Box 240
Watertown, MA 02172

Mr. G's Deli
6 Bigelow Avenue
Watertown, MA 02172

Monaco Mechanical Co.
92 California Street
Watertown, MA 02172

Monoson Microsystems
51 Main Street
Watertown, MA 02172

Morse Body Mfg. Co., Inc.
69 Howard Street
Watertown, MA 02172

Mount Auburn Cemetery
580 Mt. Auburn Street
Cambridge, MA 02138

Mt. Auburn Press
102a School Street
Watertown, MA 02172

Napoli Pizza Palace
9 Main Street
Watertown, MA 02172

Carmine E. Nardone Jr. Funeral Home
373 Main Street
Watertown, MA 02172

National Car Radio Sales and Service, Inc.
65 North Beacon Street
Watertown, MA 02172

Natoli Realty Co.
451 Common Street
Belmont, MA 02178

W. J. Nealon Commercial Realty Co.
68a Watertown Street
Watertown, MA 02172

New England Fuel Institute
20 Summer Street
Watertown, MA 02172

New England Telephone
1660 Soldiers Field Road Ext.
Brighton, MA 02135

The News-Tribune
18 Pine Street
Waltham, MA 02154

Newton Floorcraft Linoleum Tile & Carpet Co.
130 Galen Street
Watertown, MA 02172

Norton Protective Clothing Company
76 Stanley Avenue
Watertown, MA 02172

Oakley Country Club
410 Belmont Street
Watertown, MA 02172

James M. Oates, Attorney
134 Main Street
Watertown, MA 02172

Odell Company
60 Acton Street
Watertown, MA 02172

Palfrey Street School
119 Palfrey Street
Watertown, MA 02172

Roy C. Papalia, Attorney
42 Spring Street
Watertown, MA 02172

Pat's Diner
13 No. Beacon Street
Watertown, MA 02172

Paul's Tap Inc.
394 Main Street
Watertown, MA 02172

Peabody Trading Company
2A Mt. Auburn Street
Watertown, MA 02172

Peerless Pressed Metal Corp.
191 Arlington Street
Watertown, MA 02172

Perkins School for the Blind
175 No. Beacon Street
Watertown, MA 02172

Phillips Properties, Inc.
50 Hunt Street
Watertown, MA 02172

Phillips Street Auto Body, Inc.
262 No. Beacon Street
Watertown, MA 02172

Porter Construction Co., Inc.
84 Arsenal Street
Watertown, MA 02172

Postal Finance Co.
P.O. Box 441
Burlington, MA 01803

Potter & McArthur
50 Hunt Street
Watertown, MA 02172

The Protestant Guild for the Blind, Inc.
456 Belmont Street
Watertown, MA 02172

Quincy Market Cold Storage & Warehouse Company
555 Pleasant Street
Watertown, MA 02172

Ramada Inn of Boston
1234 Soldiers Field Road
Brighton, MA 02135

Rand Typography, Inc.
30 California Street
Watertown, MA 02172

Randy's Car Wash
49 School Street
Watertown, MA 02172

J.M. Reardon Funeral Home
231 Belmont Street
Belmont, MA 02178

Redden Lumber Co.
138 Waltham Street
Watertown, MA 02172

Regal Floor Care
408 Trapelo Road
Belmont, MA 02178

ReproPrint
11 Main Street
Watertown, MA 02172

Reynolds Industries, Inc.
33 Mt. Auburn Street
Watertown, MA 02172

Rich Construction Co., Inc.
15 Speedway Ave.
Brighton, MA 02135

Richard's Parker Drug
137 Mt. Auburn Street
Watertown, MA 02172

Edward A. Robertson
77 Shattuck Road
Watertown, MA 02172

Rockwell Funeral Service
195 Mt. Auburn Street
Watertown, MA 02172

Rolm of New England
80 Coolidge Hill Road
Watertown, MA 02172

Royal Furniture Co., Inc.
70 Main Street
Watertown, MA 02172

Ruland Mfg. Co., Inc.
384 Pleasant Street
Watertown, MA 02172

SCA Services, Inc.
60 State Street
Boston, MA 02109

St. James Armenian Apostolic Church
465 Auburn Street
Watertown, MA 02172

St. Stephen's Armenian Apostolic Church of Greater Boston
38 Elton Avenue
Watertown, MA 02172

Sales Aids, Inc.
208 Calvary Street
Waltham, MA 02154

Salo, Inc.
43 Parker Street
Watertown, MA 02172

The Sandwich Hut Restaurant
123 Galen Street
Watertown, MA 02172

Sasaki Associates, Inc.
64 Pleasant Street
Watertown, MA 02172

Edward Scribner Co.
161 Galen Street
Watertown, MA 02172

Edward G. Seferian Attorney
419 Mt. Auburn Street
Watertown, MA 02172

Seminara AMC
694 Mt. Auburn Street
Watertown, MA 02172

Sequemat, Inc
76 School Street
Watertown, MA 02172

Serg's Auto Service Center
257 Sycamore Street
Belmont, MA 02178

Shawmut Community Bank NA
25 Church Street
Watertown, MA 02172

Snow White Cleansers, Inc.
152 Galen Street
Watertown, MA 02172

Spark-Mart, Inc.
405 Main Street
Watertown, MA 02172

Sparkill Floor Covering
83 Spring Street
Watertown, MA 02172

A.T. Specht Co., Inc.
10 Munroe Avenue
Watertown, MA 02172

Special Agent Consultants, Inc.
67 Pleasant Street
Watertown, MA 02172

The Store 24, Inc.
164 Main Street
Watertown, MA 02172

Stormtite Aluminum Products Mfg. Corp.
170 Belmont Street
Watertown, MA 02172

Suburban Appliance Service Center
60 Arsenal Street
Watertown, MA 02172

Tilcon-Warren, Inc.
48 Coolidge Avenue
Watertown, MA 02172

Tony's Auto Body
50 Prentiss Street
Watertown, MA 02172

Town Hall Pharmacy
148 Main Street
Watertown, MA 02172

Transport Refrigeration Service, Inc.
370 Pleasant Street
Watertown, MA 02172

Travel by Betty Doherty, Inc.
639 Mt. Auburn Street
Watertown, MA 02172

Union Market Station
17 Nichols Avenue
Watertown, MA 02172

United Financial Planning Corp.
2122 Commonwealth Avenue
Newton, MA 02166

United Parcel Service, Inc.
15 Arlington Street
Watertown, MA 02172

U.S. Army Materials & Mechanics Research Center
Watertown Arsenal
Watertown, MA 02172

Unitrode Corporation
580 Pleasant Street
Watertown, MA 02172

Urell, Inc.
86 Coolidge Avenue
Watertown, MA 02172

V.I.P. Auto Body
136r Arlington Street
Watertown, MA 02172

Vahey's Package Store
392 Main Street
Watertown, MA 02172

Val's Cleaning Service
40 Phillips Circle
Waltham, MA 02154

The Waltham Hospital
Hope Avenue
Waltham, MA 02154

Watertown, Town of
Free Public Library
Sigrid Reddy, Director
123 Main Street
Watertown, MA 02172

Watertown, Town of
High School
Manson Hall, Principal
George Yankowski, Guidance Counselor
51 Columbia Street
Watertown, MA 02172

Watertown, Town of
Town Treasurer
Philip Pane
Administration Building
Watertown, MA 02172

Watertown Animal Hospital
404 Main Street
Watertown, MA 02172

Watertown Center for the Arts
21 Irving Street
Watertown, MA 02172

Watertown Florist
455 Main Street
Watertown, MA 02172

Watertown Health Center
85 Main Street
Watertown, MA 02172

Watertown Mall Merchants Assoc., Inc.
550 Arsenal St.
Watertown, MA 02172

Watertown Plumbing & Heating Supply Co.
563 Mt. Auburn Street
Watertown, MA 02172

Watertown Press, Inc.
55 Mt. Auburn Street
Watertown, MA 02172

Watertown Savings Bank
60 Main Street
Watertown, MA 02172

The Watertown Shopper
10 Dale Street
Waltham, MA 02172

Watertown Stationers & Printers
19 Mt. Auburn Street
Watertown, MA 02172

Watertown Sun
19 Flett Road
Belmont, MA 02178

Watertown Wire Products Co., Inc.
385 Pleasant Street
Watertown, MA 02172

Welcome Wagon Internat'l
340 Lexington Street
Watertown, MA 02172

West End Chevrolet, Inc.
110 South Street
Waltham, MA 02154

Western Electric Company, Inc.
705 Mt. Auburn Street
Watertown, MA 02172

Westvaco Corporation
80 Grove Street
Watertown, MA 02172

J. Malcolm Whitney, Insurance Agcy.
443 Mt. Auburn Street
Watertown, MA 02172

Wilevco, Inc.
40 Hunt Street
Watertown, MA 02172

Stephen M. Winnick, Attorney
63 Church St.
Watertown, MA 02172

Woman's World Health Spa
210-216 Dexter Avenue
Watertown, MA 02172

C.N. Wood Co., Inc.
570 Arsenal Street
Watertown, MA 02172

Zani's
68 School Street
Watertown, MA 02172

George T. Zevitas, Attorney
63 Mt. Auburn Street
Watertown, MA 02172

Civic and Social Associations*

American Legion Post 99 and Women's Auxiliary
  215 Mt. Auburn Street
AMVETS Post 14
  375 Main Street
AMVETS Post 41 and Women's Auxiliary
  215 Grove Street
Ancient Order of Hibernians and Women's Auxiliary
  151 Watertown Street
Boys' Club of Watertown, Inc.
  25 Whites Avenue
Chamber of Commerce
  75 Main Street
Concerned Citizens of Precincts Four and Five
  49 Chester Street
Daughters of the American Revolution
  115 Worcester Street
East Watertown Betterment Association
  160 Arlington Street
Ecumenical Life Center
  120 Lexington Street
Emblem Club
  Elks Hall, 268 Arlington Street
Friends of the Watertown Free Public Library
  123 Main Street
Italian-American Social Club
  104 Arlington Street
Italian-Americans Veterans Post 30 and Women's Auxiliary
  104 Arlington Street
Jolly Elders
  St. John's Methodist Church, 80 Mt. Auburn Street
Kiwanis Club
  Lanno's Restaurant, 86 Main Street
Knights of Columbus Council No. 155
  111 Watertown Street
League of Women Voters
  207 Lexington Street
Lions Club
  Perkins School, 175 No. Beacon Street
Order of Elks
  Elks Hall, 268 Arlington Street
Pequossette Aerie of Eagles
  44 Mt. Auburn Street
Pequossette Club (Senior Citizens)
  Watertown Senior High School, 51 Columbia Road
Pequossette Chapter of the Order of the Eastern Star
  Masonic Hall, 32 Church Street
Pequossette Lodge A.F. and A.M.
  Masonic Hall, 32 Church Street
Rotary Club
  Lanno's Restaurant, 86 Main Street
Sacred Heart Seniors
  Sacred Heart Church Hall, 780 Mt. Auburn Street
Senior Citizens
  Woodland Towers, 55 Waverly Avenue
Senior Neighbors
  Eagles Hall, 44 Mt. Auburn Street
Sons of Italy and Women's Auxiliary
  520 Pleasant Street
Veterans of Foreign Wars
  Burnham-Manning Post 1105, 295 Arsenal Street
Victory Lodge A.F. and A.M.
  Masonic Hall, 32 Church Street

Compiled from information supplied by the organizations.

Watertown Art Association
  Phillips Congregational Church, 111 Mt. Auburn Street
Watertown Boosters
  P.O. Box 160
Watertown Center for the Arts
  21 Irving Street
Watertown Garden Club
  First Baptist Church of Watertown, 134 Mt. Auburn Street
Watertown Grange
  Church of the Good Shepherd, 19 Russell Avenue
Watertown Historical Society
  Fowle House, 26 Marshall Street
Watertown Jaycees
  Zani's, 68 School Street
Watertown Woman's Club
  St. John's Methodist Church, 80 Mt. Auburn Street

Churches in Watertown

Apostolic
St. Stephens Armenian Apostolic Church of Greater Boston
  Elton Avenue
St. James Armenian Apostolic Church
  465 Mt. Auburn Street

Baptist
Belmont Street Baptist Church
  Templeton Parkway
First Baptist Church of Watertown
  134 Mt. Auburn Street

Eastern Orthodox
Greek Orthodox Church, Taxiarchae
  Bigelow Avenue

Episcopal
Church of the Good Shepherd, Episcopal
  19 Russell Avenue

Methodist
St. John's Methodist Church
  80 Mt. Auburn Street

Nondenominational
Community Church of Watertown
  Main and Gilbert Streets
Mt. Auburn Gospel Center
  226 Mt. Auburn Street
Watertown Evangelical Church
  182 Arlington Street

Roman Catholic
Sacred Heart Church
  Mt. Auburn Street
  (Rectory: 770 Mt. Auburn Street)
St. Patrick's Church
  Main Street
  (Rectory: 25 Chestnut Street)
St. Theresa's Church
  Mt. Auburn Street
  (Rectory: 248 School Street)

Unitarian-Universalist
First Parish Church of Watertown
  35 Church Street

United Church of Christ - Congregational
Armenian Memorial Congregational Church
  32 Bigelow Avenue
Phillips Congregational Church
  111 Mt. Auburn Street

Bibliography

PUBLIC RECORDS

Massachusetts, Provincial Congress, *The Journals of each Provincial Congress of Massachusetts in 1774 and 1775 and of the Committee of Safety . . .* under the supervision of William Lincoln. Boston: Dutton and Wentworth, 1838.

Shurtleff, N. B. ed. *Records of the Governor and Company of the Massachusetts Bay in New England.* 6 vols. Boston: William White, 1853.

Sullivan, J. J. comp. "Documents relating to Town Lands along the Charles River in Watertown." [1895] Manuscript in Watertown Free Public Library Collection.

Sullivan, J. J. *Report on Town Lands along Charles River.* Watertown, Mass.: Fred G. Barker, 1895.

Watertown. *Annual Reports,* 1868-1978.

Watertown. *Fishery Records,* 1st Book, 1799-1826.

Watertown. "A Grant of the Great Dividens lotted out by Free Men to all Townsmen then inhabit . . . June 25, 1636." [1644] Manuscript in Watertown Free Public Library Collection.

Watertown. [Original Documents of] "The Proprieters of the Common and Individual land in Watertown." [1644-1742] Manuscript in Watertown Free Public Library Collection.

Watertown. *Record of the West Precinct of Watertown, Massachusetts, 1720 to 1737-38.* Waltham: Board of Aldermen, 1913.

Watertown. *Records,* vols. 1-8, 1634-1829.

Watertown. *Records comprising East Congregational and Precinct Affairs, 1697-1737* and ["The Bailey Book"] *Record Book of the Pastors, 1686-1819.* Boston, 1906.

Watertown. Assessors. *Statistics of Industry in Watertown,* 1845.

Watertown. Election Commission. *List of Persons Seventeen Years of Age and Upwards as of January . . .* 1971-1979.

Watertown. Listing Board. *List of Persons Twenty Years of Age and Upwards as of January 1 . . .* 1939, 1941-1970.

Watertown. School Committee. *Reports.* 1849-1978.

Watertown. School Department. *Charrette 1970.* [Official Report August 1970, edited by Joan Tuttle.]

Watertown. Street Widening Committees. "Reports, Records and Proceedings": v.1 Galen, North Beacon and Arsenal Streets, 1902-1908. v.2 North Beacon and School Streets, 1910-1914. v.3 Mt. Auburn Street, 1896-1898. Manuscript in Watertown Free Public Library Collection.

Watertown. Watertown Arsenal Alternative Use Committee. *The Evolution of a Plan; the Final Report . . .* for the [U.S.] Economic Development Administration, Office of Technical Assistance . . . 1975.

UNPUBLISHED MATERIALS

Benton, Mrs. Everett C. "Scrapbook of Cushing Gardens." [1947] In Belmont Public Library, Belmont Room.

Burke, Charles T. "A Topographical History of Watertown." 1975. Typescript in Watertown Free Public Library Collection.

Burke, Charles T. "Watertown Free Public Library" 2d ed. 1977. Typescript in Watertown Free Public Library Collection.

Burke, Charles T. "Watertown in the Eighteenth Century." 1977. Typescript in Watertown Free Public Library Collection.

Burke, Charles T. "Watertown in the Revolution, 1770-1781." 1973. Typescript in Watertown Free Public Library Collection.

Burke, Mary. "My Girlhood in Mount Auburn." [1945] Typescript in Watertown Free Public Library Collection.

Curran, Joseph Leo, ed. "Harriet Goodhue Hosmer: Collected Sources." 1974. 7 vols. Watertown Free Public Library Collection.

"History of the Watertown Free Public Library, Watertown, Mass." 1953. Typescript in Watertown Free Public Library Collection.

Hodges, Maud D. "One Hundred Years of Watertown High School." 1957. Typescript in Watertown Free Public Library Collection.

Kreider, Alan. "The Transfer of the Locus of Political Power in Watertown, Mass. 1660-1739." 1965. Typescript in Watertown Free Public Library Collection.

McCourt, Edward G. "The Metropolitanization of Watertown, Mass. 1890-1918." 1970. Typescript in Watertown Free Public Library Collection.

Rand, Edward Augustus. "Watertown Historical Society Scrapbooks." [1900?] 5 vols. Watertown Free Public Library Collection.

Ripley, Margaret E. "Early Churches of Watertown." 1975. Typescript in Watertown Free Public Library Collection.

Watertown, Mass. Free Public Library. "Letter From John Masters at Watertown in New England to Lady Barrington and others in England, 14 March 1630/1." Reproduction, Original in Collection of the British Museum Eg2645 p22274.

Watertown, Mass. Free Public Library. Local History Files.

Young Men's Assembly, Watertown, Mass. "Scrapbook." [1895-1898] Watertown Free Public Library Collection.

NEWSPAPERS

Boston Gazette and Country Journal, 1776, 1777, 1781.

The Chronicler of Societies and Business in Watertown. 1911-1918.

Mt. Auburn Memorial 1859-1860.

Pequossette 1873-1881.

Watertown Enterprise 1879-1903.

Watertown Press 1870-1875.

Watertown Press 1955-1980.

Watertown Sun 1921-1980.

Watertown Tribune 1903.

Watertown Tribune Enterprise 1903-1947.

MAPS

Bailey, O. H. and Co. *Map of Watertown, Massachusetts* [Birdseye Map], 1898.

Beers, J. B. and Co. *Map of the Town of Watertown, Middlesex County, Mass. from actual surveys.* 1874.

Bond, Henry. *A Map of the Original Allotments of Land and the Ancient Topography of Watertown (Proper).* Boston: Little, 1855.

Boston, Archives of the Commonwealth. *Fac-simile of Map of New England, made in 1633,* reprinted in 1846 by William B. Fowle. Maps and Plans, Third Series, v.59:6, No. 14a.

Boston, Archives of the Commonwealth. *Map of New England in 1677,* From William Hubbard's "Present State of New England"; a Fac-simile Reprint by William B. Fowle in 1846. Maps and Plans, Third Series, v.59:6 No. 104.

Boston, Archives of the Commonwealth. "Plan of a Tract Called Nonsuch in Watertown." September 26, 1687. Maps and Plans, Third Series, v.3:1, No. 140.

Boston, Archives of the Commonwealth. "Plan of Watertown, Showing Streets and Residences." 1720. Maps and Plans, Third Series, v.5:32 No. 321.

Eaton, S. Dwight and Whiting, Ellridge. *Map of Watertown, Mass. Surveyed by Order of the Town.* 1850.

Hales, John G. *Plan of Watertown from Survey Made in June 1830.*

Massachusetts. Metropolitan Park Commission. *Plan of Charles River from the Waltham Line to Boston Harbor,* prepared . . . [by] a Joint Board consisting of the Metropolitan Park Commission and the State Board of Health. Boston, 1894.

Plan of Watertown, the Colored Portion Showing the Part Proposed to be Taken From It for the Town of Belmont. [1859?]

Roby, I. *Water Privilege at Watertown Bridge.* 1829.

Watertown, Mass. Engineering Dept. *Maps of Watertown, Mass.* 1925, 1931, 1945, 1953, 1962, 1973, 1977.

Watertown Historical Society. *Homestalls, Dwellings and Other Buildings of Old Watertown, illustrated and described.* 1899.

Watertown, Mass. Engineering Dept. *Zoning Map of Watertown,* 1931, 1933, 1976.

BOOKS, PERIODICALS AND PAMPHLETS

Anthony, Katharine. *First Lady of the Revolution, the Life of Mercy Otis Warren.* Garden City, New York: Doubleday and Co., 1958.

Baldwin, Frances B. *From Pequossette Plantation to the Town of Belmont, Mass., 1630-1953.* Belmont, Mass.: Belmont Citizen, 1953.

The Bank on the Colonial Highway. Watertown, Mass.: Watertown Savings Bank, 1929.

Barber, John Warner. *Historical Collections . . .* Worcester: Warren Lazell, 1848.

Bartlett, J. Gardner. *Simon Stone Genealogy, Ancestry and Descendants of Deacon Simon Stone of Watertown, Mass., 1320-1926.* Boston: Stone Family Association, 1926.

Betts, Richard. *The Streets of Belmont and How They Were Named, Including a Chronological History of the Development of the Town.* Belmont, Mass.: The Historical Society, 1974.

Bond, Henry. *Genealogies of the Families and Descendants of the Early Settlers of Watertown, Massachusetts.* 2nd ed. Boston: New England Historic-Genealogical Society, 1860.

[Bright] *A Glimpse at Watertown* by a "native." Boston: 1851.

Brown, Frank Chouteau. "Architecture, 1620-1750." *House and Garden* 75 (1939): 35-50.

Brown, Frank Chouteau. [Browne House] "Watertown, Massachusetts." *Pencil Points* May 1937 pp. 323-338.

Burke, Charles T. *Puritans at Bay, The War Against King Philip and The Squaw Sachems.* New York: Exposition Press, 1967.

Burke, Charles T. *Watertown, Town on the Charles.* Watertown, Mass.: 350th Anniversary Celebration Committee, 1980.

The Cambridge of 1776 . . . with which is incorporated the Diary of Dorothy Dudley. Edited for the Ladies Centennial Committee by A. G. Cambridge, Mass., 1876.

Carr, Cornelia ed. *Harriet Hosmer, Letters and Memories.* New York: Moffat, Yard and Co., 1912.

Child, Lydia Maria. *Letters,* with a Biographical Introduction by John G. Whittier. Boston: Houghton Mifflin and Co., 1882.

Coolidge, Emma Downing. *Descendants of John and Mary Coolidge of Watertown, Mass. 1630.* Boston: Wright and Potter, 1930.

Crosby, Irving B. *Boston Through the Ages, the Geological Story of Greater Boston.* Boston: Marshall Jones Co., 1928.

Curtis, Benjamin R. ed. *A Memoir of Benjamin Robbins Curtis L.L.D., With Some of His Professional and Miscellaneous Writings.* 2 vols. Boston: Little, Brown and Co., 1879.

Cutter, G. W. *The Geology of Watertown, Mass.* Boston: Geo. H. Ellis Co., 1915.

Dictionary of American Biography. New York: Charles Scribner's Sons, 1964.

Dobbs, Judy D. *A History of the Watertown Arsenal, Watertown, Massachusetts, 1816-1967.* Watertown, Mass: Army Materials and Mechanics Research Center, 1977.

Drake, Samuel Adams. *History of Middlesex County, Massachusetts . . .* 2 vols. Boston: Estes and Lauriat, 1879.

Drake, Samuel G. *Biography and History of the Indians of North America . . .* 4th Ed. Boston: J. Drake, 1835.

Elliott, Clark A. *Historical Sketch of the Eighth Meeting House.* Watertown, Mass.: The First Parish of Watertown, [1976]

[Elliott, Harmon] *The Story of a Father and Son or "Unscrewing the Inscrutable."* 3d ed., 1941.

Fields, Annie. "Celia Thaxter." In *Authors and Friends.* 5th ed. Boston: Houghton Mifflin and Co., 1896.

Fish, Anna Gardner. *Perkins Institution and its Deaf-Blind Pupils, 1837-1933.* Perkins Publications no. 11. Watertown, Mass.: Perkins Institution and Massachusetts School for the Blind, 1934.

Fiske, John. *The Beginnings of New England,* Boston: Houghton Mifflin and Co., 1902.

Foote, Henry Wilder. "Mr. George Phillips, First Minister of Watertown." *Massachusetts Historical Society Proceedings* 63 (1930): 193-227.

Forbes, Esther. *Paul Revere and the World He Lived In.* Boston: Houghton Mifflin Co., 1942.

Francis, Convers. *An Historical Sketch of Watertown in Massachusetts From the First Settlement of the Town to the Close of its Second Century.* Cambridge, Mass.: E. W. Metcalf and Co., 1830.

Graves, Gertrude Montague. *Reminiscences of the Family of Captain John Fowle of Watertown, Massachusetts With Genealogical Notes of Some of his Ancestors, Descendents and Family Connections.* Boston: David Clapp and Son, 1891.

Hamilton, Charles. *The Signature of America, a Fresh Look at Famous Handwriting.* New York: Harper and Row, 1979.

Harris, W. T. *Epitaphs from the Old Burying Ground in Watertown.* Boston, 1869.

Heaton, James P. "A Study in Industrial Evolution. VIII, Watertown." *Current Affairs* April 17 and 24, 1922.

Horsford, Eben Norton. *The Discovery of the Ancient City of Norumbega.* Boston: Houghton Mifflin and Co., 1890.

Horsford, E. N. *Watertown: the Site of the Ancient City of Norumbega.* Watertown Historical Society, 1890.

Hurd, D. Hamilton comp. *History of Middlesex County Massachusetts, with Biographical Sketches of many of its Pioneers and Prominent Men.* Philadelphia: J. W. Lewis and Co., 1890.

Ingraham, W. H. *Address of W. H. Ingraham and Oration by J. H. Lovering at the Centennial Celebration, White's Hill Grove.* Watertown, Mass. 1876.

Johnson, Edward. *Wonder-Working Providence 1628-1651.* Edited by J. Franklin Jameson. New York: Charles Scribner's Sons, 1910.

League of Women Voters of Watertown. *This is Watertown, a Study of Town Government.* Watertown, Mass., 1979.

Locke, Henry Dyer. *An Ancient Parish, an Historical Summary of the First Parish, Watertown, Massachusetts.* Tercentenary Committee of the Parish, 1930.

McFarland, J. Horace. "Furnishing the Streets in Suburban Communities," *Suburban Life* (February 1911), 94-95.

Middleton, Elinore Huse comp. *History of St. John's Methodist Episcopal Church in Watertown, 1836-1936.*

Moody, Robert E. *The Saltonstall Papers, 1607-1815.* Collections of the Massachusetts Historical Society vol. 80. Boston: Massachusetts Historical Society, 1972.

Nelson, Charles A. *Waltham, Past and Present; and its Industries.* Cambridge, 1879.

Norcross, James E. *A Memorial History of the First Baptist Church, Watertown, Mass., 1830-1930.* Cambridge, Mass.: Hampshire Press.

Oakley Country Club. *Notes on Seventy-five Happy Years at the Oakley Country Club* . . . Watertown, Mass., 1973.

Pinkney, Helen R. *Christopher Gore, Federalist of Massachusetts, 1758-1827.* Waltham, Mass.: Gore Place Society, 1969.

[Pratt, Frederick B. and Others] *Charles Pratt, an Interpretation 1830-1930.* Brooklyn, N.Y.: Privately Printed, 1930.

Robbins, Ellen. "Reminiscences of a Flower Painter." *New England Magazine* 14 (1896) 440-451, 532-545.

Robinson, George Frederick. *Great Little Watertown, a Tercentenary History.* Watertown Historical Society, 1930.

Robinson, George Frederick. *John Hunt (Gentleman) and some of his Descendents.* Watertown Historical Society, 1935.

Robinson, George Frederick, and Hall, Albert Harrison comp. *Watertown Soldiers in the Colonial Wars and the American Revolution.* Watertown, Mass.: The Historical Society of Watertown, 1939.

Saint Patrick's Parish, Watertown, Mass. *One Hundredth Anniversary, 1847-1947.* Boston: Alhambra Press, 1947.

Seton, Anya. *The Winthrop Woman.* Boston: Houghton Mifflin Co., 1958.

Sontheimer, Elizabeth comp. *Watertown Demographic and Economic Profile.* Watertown, Mass. Chamber of Commerce [1980].

Stone, Orra Laville. *History of Massachusetts Industries; Their Inception, Growth and Success.* Boston: S. J. Clarke Publishing Co., 1930.

Strock Jr., Daniel. *Pictorial History of King Philip's War.* Hartford: Case, Tiffany and Co., 1852.

Thaxter, Celia. *Letters.* Edited by her friends A. F. and R. L. Boston: Houghton Mifflin and Co., 1852.

Two Hundred and Fiftieth Anniversary of the First Parish of Watertown, Mass. Boston: Geo. H. Ellis, 1881.

Tyler, Mary Hunt (Palmer). *Grandmother Tyler's Book; the Recollections of Mary Palmer Tyler (Mrs. Royal Tyler) 1775-1866.* Edited by Frederick Tupper and Helen Tyler Brown. New York: G. P. Putnam's Sons, 1925.

Vaughan, Mosetta I. *The Meeting Houses of the First Congregational Society of Watertown, Mass.* Historical Society of Watertown, 1942.

Vaughan, Mosetta I. *Sketch of the Life and Work of Convers Francis D. D.* Watertown Historical Society, 1944.

Vernon, Hope Jillson. *The Poems of Maria Lowell, with Unpublished Letters and a Biography.* Providence: Brown University Press, 1936.

Warren-Adams Letters, 1743-1777. Collections of the Massachusetts Historical Society vol. 72. Boston: Massachusetts Historical Society, 1917.

Waterman, Charles F. *Fishing in America.* New York: Holt, Rinehart and Winston, c1975.

Watertown, Mass. Committee on the 325th Anniversary. *Watertown, The Mother Town, 1630-1955: 325 Years.* Watertown, Mass.: Eaton Press, 1955.

Watertown Mass. *Directories* [Business and Residential] 1869-1942.

Watertown's Military History [by] A Committee representing the Sons of the American Revolution and the Isaac B. Patten Post 81 G.A.R. Boston: 1907.

Weiss, John. *Discourse Occasioned by the Death of Convers Francis D.D.* Cambridge, Mass.: Privately Printed, 1863.

Weiss, John. *Life and Correspondence of Theodore Parker.* 2 vols. New York, 1864.

Whitney, Solon F. *Historical Sketches of Watertown, Massachusetts.* Watertown, Mass. 1893.

Whitney, W. H. *A Watertown Farm in Eight Generations, a Memorial to the Whitney Family.* Cambridge, Mass. 1898.

Winthrop, John. *Journal. "History of New England", 1630-1649.* Edited by James Kendall Hosmer. 2 vols. New York: Charles Scribner's Sons, 1908.

Woodbury, George. *The Story of a Stanley Steamer.* New York: W. W. Norton and Co., 1950.

Woodman, Walter C. *The Stanley Steamer.* Watertown, Mass., 1972.

Young, Alexander. *Chronicles of the First Planters of the Colony of Massachusetts Bay 1623 to 1636.* Boston: Charles C. Little and James Brown, 1846.

Young Men's Assembly, Watertown, Mass. *Ideal Watertown.* Watertown, Mass.: Watertown Enterprise, 1898.

Illustrations and Credits

The Watertown Free Public Library has been blessed over the years by townspeople, organizations, and librarians who have donated, collected, and organized a comprehensive photographic file on all aspects of Watertown history. The majority of the illustrative materials appearing in this book are part of that collection and are indicated by the abbreviation WFPL.

We are very grateful to those individuals who lent us additional photographs to illustrate ethnic and organizational history; to Jeremy Cole and Christine Harris, CETA photographers working at the library who copied old photographs and slides to make much of this material available; and to Paul L. Watson who developed and printed several photographs and did the drawing of Watertown Square in 1935.

All illustrations are listed in the order in which they appear in the book. The abbreviated title of each is followed by the photographer's or delineator's name where such information is known, the source, and the page number on which the illustration appears.

231

Index

242

PLAN OF
WATERTOWN VILLAGE.

WATERTOWN originally including parts of Waltham and Newton was incorporated a town 1630. At present it contains six and a half square miles. The Latitude of Town Hall is 42° 22'. Longitude west from Greenwich 71° 11' 27". Population 1850 7582.

REFERENCE.

SCALE — 1000 FEET THE INCH

CATHOLIC CHURCH.   METHODIST CHURCH.   TOWN HALL